DAWN LANGMAN undertoo[k] training in Australia, followed by seven years of performing and teaching at secondary and tertiary levels. Her quest for an integrated approach that includes the spiritual dimension led her to train with Maisie Jones at the London School of Speech Formation in the method developed by Rudolf and Marie Steiner. She then taught for ten years at Emerson College in Sussex. Following this, Dawn trained in Michael Chekhov's acting technique with Ted Pugh and Fern Sloan of the Actors Ensemble in New York. Returning to Australia, she founded the School of the Living Word, where for eight years she continued to research the integration of Speech Formation with Chekhov's technique. She currently teaches this methodology at the Drama Centre, Flinders University, South Australia.

In the same series:

The Art of Acting, Body – Soul – Spirit – Word, A Practical and Spiritual Guide

The Integrated Actor, Body – Soul – Spirit – Word, A Practical and Spiritual Guide (forthcoming 2015)

THE ART OF SPEECH

Body – Soul – Spirit – Word

Speech Formation in Relation to the English Language – A Practical and Spiritual Guide

DAWN LANGMAN

Artwork by Raphaela Mazzone

TEMPLE LODGE

First published in Great Britain in 2014 by Temple Lodge Publishing,
Hillside House, The Square
Forest Row, RH18 5ES

E-mail: office@templelodge.com

www.templelodge.com

A catalogue record for this book is available from the British Library

ISBN 978 1 906999 65 0

Cover by Morgan Creative
Typeset by DP Photosetting, Neath, West Glamorgan
Printed and bound by 4edge Limited, Essex, UK

I thank the students who worked with me throughout the years. Together we engaged in the research on which these books are based.

I thank William, whose generosity throughout the years has made my work possible and Patricia for her faithful friendship and support.

Thanks to the following friends and colleagues whose encouragement and feedback have given me invaluable assistance in various development stages of the text: Annika Andersdottir, Michael Burton, Louise Coigley, Lindsay Dearlove, Sibylle Eichstadt, Judith Pownall Gerstein, Dr Jane Gilmer, Sarah Kane, Katerina Vlachou.

And for the tireless enthusiasm and efforts of my copyeditor Clare Strahan without whose collaboration the books would never have reached completion. Thanks also to Raphaela, for her patience and willingness to experiment, for the talent and hard work that enabled her to fulfil my vision for the illustrations.

And last, I thank all the poets and especially Shakespeare, whose words provide a template for the English language. His inspiration is consistently invoked in the three books of this series. It is to find the way to speak his words we need this path and it is by speaking them we learn.

We would that words become shooting stars, like gods,
that they would rise up from the dead page
into living forms of light and dark
into fountains of colour.
O, if we could only love his words enough,
be large enough to speak them.

                                      Dawn Langman

For Darling Maisie
and all the pioneers of Speech Formation.

For My word you bring to birth in the world
in My own breath which I breathe in you
and through the sacrifice of your own being
by which I pour Myself into the chalice
your self must die always to form
I give thanks.

Contents

Table of Illustrations

Acknowledgements

The Art of Speech is my contribution to the deeper understanding of that work which will always be far greater than any one individual can grasp. For almost a century the impulse Rudolf Steiner gave for a renewal of the Art of Speech has been taken up by successive generations. It was first developed through the untiring work of Steiner's wife, Marie von Sivers. She took responsibility for training the first Speech artists in the German language in Dornach, Switzerland. The work has subsequently spread to other countries and other languages. I trained in English in the school founded by Maisie Jones and it is within that stream that I continue to evolve my understanding and practice of the work.

I honour the pioneering teachers who have worked so hard to establish and remain true to this impulse for the future. A handful of women have, in my awareness, significantly pioneered the development of Speech Formation in the English-speaking world. Each, drawing from the source, has carved a different channel for its waters.

Christy Barnes was an inspiring pioneer of the work in America. Virginia Brett worked for many years in Dornach, eventually carrying the impulse to Hawaii and America.

Australian Alice Crowther trained in Dornach in both Speech Formation and Eurythmy. Chekhov invited her to introduce this work to actors who had come to train with him at Dartington Hall in England. When that training was curtailed by the outbreak of World War Two, she returned to Australia and founded 'The Studio', inspiring many.

Mechthild Harkness trained in Speech Formation and Eurythmy and worked in Europe, England and America. She married the Australian actor, Alan Harkness who had trained with Chekhov at Dartington, but their plans to bring their joint work to Australia were cut short by a tragic accident. She came alone and founded the Harkness Studio in Sydney, developing a four year training in Speech Formation and Drama.

Maisie Jones founded the London School of Speech Formation (now known as Artemis School of the Living Word), a four year training to which students still come from many countries.

Sophia Walsh, from New Zealand, travelled for many years between Dornach in Switzerland and the United States, bringing Speech Formation to America and inspiring many English-speaking students who trained in Dornach.

I thank Ulrike Brockman whose teaching at Emerson College first revealed this work to me. I thank the other teachers whose different understandings of the work have enriched my own, especially Mechthild and Sophia with whom I have been privileged to work.

I thank the colleagues who have inspired me; Annika Andersdottir, Christopher Garvey, Berenice Kavanagh, Geoff Norris.

I thank the students who worked with me throughout the years. Together we engaged in the research on which these books are based.

And last, I thank all the poets and especially Shakespeare, whose words provide a template for the English language. His inspiration is consistently invoked in the three books of this series. It is to find the way to speak his words we need this path and it is by speaking them we learn.

> We would that words become shooting stars, like gods,
> that they would rise up from the dead page
> into living forms of light and dark
> into fountains of colour.
> O, if we could only love his words enough,
> be large enough to speak them.
>
> Dawn Langman

INTRODUCTION

Stars once spoke to us.
It is world destiny they are silent now.
To be aware of that silence
brings pain
to human souls.

But, in the deepening silence,
grows and ripens what we may speak to stars.
To be aware of our speaking
strengthens
human spirits.

Rudolf Steiner[1]

Speak, O human being !
And thou revealest through thee
the coming into being of worlds.
The coming into being of worlds
reveals itself through thee,
O human being,
when thou speakest!

The Mysteries of Ephesus, Rudolf Steiner

The Word at the crossroads

In February of 1938, *Le Théâtre et son Double* (*The Theatre and its Double*) was published in France. This series of essays and manifestos by French actor, director, playwright, poet and philosopher of the theatre, Antonin Artaud, reshaped performance practice in the twentieth century. In April of that same year, at the age of 42, Artaud was moved from the psychiatric hospital to which he'd been admitted on his enforced return from Ireland, into an asylum in Paris. It was not his first time in such an institution. Over the next ten years until his death in 1948, he was transferred from one asylum to another, finally dying in the clinic at Ivry, just outside of Paris.

Artaud wrote, just nine months or so before his death:

> What is a real madman? It is a man who has preferred to go mad in the socially accepted sense, rather than give up a certain higher idea of human honour.

> That is how society has organized the strangulation in lunatic asylums of all those it wants to be rid of or protect itself from, because they have refused to be accomplices in certain supremely dirty acts. Because a madman is also a man to whom society does not want to listen. So it wants to prevent him from telling intolerable truths.[2]

Despite straitjackets and electric shock therapy, Artaud could not be prevented from telling his intolerable truths. Nor has it been so easy to dismiss them since the insanity of World War II, and they have resonated in the theatre culture since.

*   *   *

The insights of Artaud — whose extraordinary sensitivities to the suffering and riddles of our time sentenced him to a life of torment; whose genius lay in diagnosing the disease and articulating the pain of twentieth century humanity and who searched relentlessly for an art of theatre that would lance the boil and free the suffering body of society from its poisons — provided no remedies that healed. Yet his tormented ravings, that still echo through his recorded voice, the anguish of which cannot be erased from the memory of those who hear it, are spun through with threads of gold. Although he could not himself realize his ideas, they have recast the way in which western human beings think about and practise performance art. It is as though he was the sacrificial taster, whose destiny required him to drink the last drop of the cup of pain brewed in the vat of Western consciousness to warn us that the draught was poisoned.

In 1924, in Dornach, Switzerland, at around the same time Artaud was experiencing what would result in his manifesto, Rudolf Steiner delivered 19 lectures on Speech and Drama to an audience of professional actors and interested public. The actors had expressed a burning need for their art to be reconnected with its spiritual source and were searching for a new kind of training. Steiner's indications placed a new *art of speech* at the centre of renewal for the art of acting, and were taken up by many who sought that reconnection. Their contribution has remained largely unacknowledged outside those communities that have concerned themselves with Steiner's work, and until now has made no recognizable impact on Western mainstream practice. Although his life was one of sanity and clear, untiring service to the world, Steiner, too, has been regarded as a madman. He may well remain considered so by those whose criterion for what is real consists solely of what can be verified exclusively by physical, material perception. Yet we have seen in the case of Artaud that madness in itself was not sufficient cause to deny his ideas serious consideration. Although Steiner's brand of 'madness' has been too progressive to resonate with the theatre culture of our time, his indications may well constitute future theatre practice.

*   *   *

Steiner and Artaud both travelled on the road of human suffering, each witnessing the treading of the grapes of wrath and the pouring of the bloody vintage on the fields of World War I. Each man felt deeply how the insanity of western civilization had expressed itself in that monstrous clash of ideologies, technologies and national pride and exposed the desperate need for changes in the individual and society. Each recognized that words as they were, as they had come to mean, had lost their power. Blunted by centuries of lies, empty of content that is not abstraction, words could not be trusted. And even if they could, humans no longer knew how to speak them in a meaningful way. The Word was dead.

As Steiner and Artaud stood together at this point on the road, each witnessed visiting performances from Asia that resonated deeply for them both with the recognition of theatre that expands our consciousness beyond appearances and empty words.

Steiner described, in the third of his *Speech and Drama* lectures, a performance given in London at the British Empire Wembley Exhibition.[3] He saw how it was born out of —

> ... the recognition that there must be art in our speaking, and that the forming of speech has accordingly to be learned, just as much as one has to learn to sing or to play a musical instrument, or to follow any other art. The Greeks were fully alive to this necessity; the whole style of their dramatic art leaves us in no doubt on this point... A true feeling for poetry survived there. Only a few days ago I was vividly reminded of how this feeling for style was still present in the Greeks and showed itself in their dramatic performances. When we were in London, we were taken to a theatre and witnessed the performance, not of a Greek drama, but of an oriental singing drama ... you have an impression of

something quite beautiful when, without being confused or led astray by the countenance, you behold on the stage the gesticulation of the rest of the human being whilst the speaking or singing, which is all that the countenance should be required to contribute, supplies the appropriate inner complement of what gesture is able so grandly to reveal.

Speech as 'formed gesture' — that is the highest of all; since gesture has then been spiritualized, has been taken up into the realm of the spirit. Speech that is not formed gesture is like something that has no ground to stand upon.

In a not dissimilar way Artaud was also addressing the issue of speech and gesture when six years later, in July 1931, he witnessed a performance by a Balinese company at the Colonial Exhibition in Paris. The impressions from this, absorbed osmotically by Artaud's naked sensibilities, reappeared later in his first *Manifesto for a Theatre of Cruelty*.[4]

But this tangible objective theatre language captivates and bewitches our senses by using a truly oriental concept of expression. It runs through our sensibility. Abandoning our Western ideas of speech, it turns words into incantations. It expands the voice. It uses vocal vibrations and qualities, wildly trampling them underfoot. It pile-drives sounds. It aims to assault, to benumb, to bewitch, to arrest our sensibility. It liberates a new lyricism of gestures which, because it is distilled and spatially amplified, ends by surpassing the lyricism of words. Finally it breaks away from language's intellectual subjugation by conveying the sense of a new, deeper intellectualism hidden under these gestures and signs and raised to the dignity of special exorcism.

We can almost see these two great contributors to theatre art stand together as they gaze back into that ancient sensibility where words came forth with primal power, recognizing what they had become in our western intellectual culture. I can imagine Steiner utterly supporting Artaud's further observation:

In Europe . . . actors in a trance no longer know how to cry out, since they do nothing but talk, having forgotten they have a body on stage, they have also lost the use of their throats. Abnormally shrunk, these throats are no longer organs, but monstrous talking abstractions. French actors now only know how to talk.[5]

However, where Artaud concluded that actors must be taught to 'scream' and 'pile drive sounds', Steiner and Artaud had reached a fork in the road.

* * *

I have profound reverence for what Artaud endured to make us aware the cup was poisoned and for those who have had the courage to take seriously what he tried to bring to our attention. Some of the most significant performance practice of the twentieth century has been inspired by experiments with his ideas, including his notion of *Theatre of Cruelty*. It is a way that says 'sometimes we must be cruel to be kind'. If words are dead, then they can no longer penetrate our blunted sensibilities, and we will find other ways to shock the audience awake. We will even abandon words altogether and return to gesture only, images, sound, whatever will get through to a deeper reality. *Physical theatre* is a current term used to describe a theatre that has moved away from words.

The most influential work arising from Artaud's ideas, while taking the physical/ emotional demands on actors to the limit in the quest to expose the vulnerable and depraved extremes behind the civilized veneer, is often surprisingly chaste. Jerzy Grotowski and Eugenio Barba have demonstrated what is possible when Artaud's intuitions are explored with disciplined devotion to the training of an actor's instrument. Peter Brook has long since moved on from an initial deep investigation of Artaud's insights.[*] But he has shown that the fruits of this could be absorbed into an evolving theatre practice grounded in his own artistic vision, deep sanity and spiritual discipline. His *Mahabharata*, for example, had the power to stir an entire theatre-going generation with a new vision of our human and theatrical potential. None of these pioneers would utterly abandon speech, but they have wanted to return to its primal roots.

Experimentation with the human voice and how to release its vast range of expressive possibilities has formed a large part of innovative theatre practice since Artaud's lifetime. Even in theatre which has partially or largely abandoned language as a meaningful tool of communication, performers use their voices to contribute to the landscape of sound and other sensory impressions which can impact an audience.

Nevertheless, there remains a vast abyss between a human voice able to explore and release more primal, pre or non-verbal experience and the capacity to handle language with expressive power. For those of us who want to bridge this gap and find a way to work with texts, including the masterpieces crafted out of words, Steiner invites us to investigate the spiritual reality of speech and human language.

*   *   *

The resurrection of the word Steiner pointed to, lies in an exploration of the consonants and vowels themselves. For him, language was not just an arbitrary, sophisticated set of signals for what were once primal utterances; grunts, cries, murmurs, squeals, groans, moans, shouts and screams, trancelike invocations. Rather, speech is

---

[*] Jerzy Grotowski – Polish founder of Theatre Laboratory, his most well-known writing is *Towards a Poor Theatre*; Eugenio Barba – Italian founder of Odin Theatre in Denmark and author of many books on theatre practice; Peter Brook – English Theatre and film director, based in France since early 1970s, author of *The Empty Space*.

bestowed upon us as the means to express not only the immediacy of our pain or sensory delight but to guide us through their labyrinth. Consonants and vowels are in themselves expressions of precise creative powers in the universe that have created us to consciously participate in their creating, when we speak. Our mouth is shaped so we can express not only our primitive sensations but also their transformation through the understanding and refining of experience made possible by words.[*]

Michael Chekhov suggested that raw experience is transformed into art when it is permeated by the principles of ease, form, beauty and the whole.[†] In such an aesthetic, what is the place of Artaud's scream? While honouring the pain which has produced it, we ask whether the actor could reach another level by seeking not to avoid that pain, but to penetrate beyond its immediate sensation and wrestle with it until it yields up its blessing.

This does not mean that actors should never scream at all. But *how* would they scream? We can ask what is required to speak words wrought from the sensation of a scream such as those Lear utters when he enters with the body of Cordelia in his arms: *Howl! Howl! Howl! Howl! Howl! O you are men of stones. Had I your tongues and voices I'd use them so that heaven's vaults should crack.*[‡] If an actor's raw howl of grief affects an audience with primal power why dilute or blunt that experience with words? At one extreme is Artaud whose boundaries became so blurred that he offered his own naked sensibilities as sacrifice on the altar of the stage. At the other is the actor who manages the sentence structures of our greatest texts in sonorous voice but uses that voice to hide behind, to avoid certain aspects of human experience. I think this must be what Artaud had in mind when he said, 'no more masterpieces!'. But there is a third possibility which indicates a different artistic goal; to transform raw emotion into the fully penetrated word. That will require actors in the future who have so penetrated *speech* and *language* that they can use the spoken word not to dilute or avoid experience but to communicate precisely its entire range.

Born of the same bloody vintage of World War I, was the impulse of Alfred Wolfsohn who explored the boundaries of the human voice. His investigations into the relationship between the range of inner experience we are prepared to open ourselves to and the corresponding range of tone the human voice can scale was developed further by his protégé, the opera singer, Roy Hart.[§] The work of the Roy Hart Theatre

---

[*] See, *The Integrated Actor*, the purpose of the arts.

[†] See, *The Art of Acting*, chapter 5.

[‡] *King Lear*, Act 5.

[§] Roy Hart (1926–1975) founded the Roy Hart Theatre in 1967/8. In 1974, it moved from London to the South of France where it has continued as a centre for research, teaching and performance since his death in a car accident in 1975.

has continued to evolve since the death of its inspirers, and to explore the boundaries of art and therapy. Hart's research into his own extraordinary vocal range of eight octaves, led to his proclaiming the ideal of an 'eight octave human being' and a process of opening to the heights and depths of our experience with the human voice acting as both means of access and a barometer.

The paths of these related yet very different impulses may well cross and fructify each other at some point in the future.

Although Steiner's writings and lectures and the paths of practice developed by his pupils in nearly every area of human work, from medicine to agriculture, education and the arts and sciences, have pointed to a way of healing that need not end in madness, Steiner has been excluded from participation in the wider culture by a wall-of-silence. Perhaps this has been necessary until now so that the work he has inspired could mature to the level that would demonstrate the contribution it could make.[*]

The fork in the road where Steiner and Artaud stood together was marked with a sign:

> The Word is Dead!

The Art of Speech sets out to show Steiner's way to the resurrection of the Word. It is signposted:

> Long Live the Word!

---

[*] See *The Integrated Actor* for an examination of speech in the broader stream of theatre practice for the future.

An autobiographical note

My teacher at the crossroads

While teaching and lecturing in speech and drama at Adelaide Teacher's College, the place where I had originally trained, I read *Movement, Voice and Speech*, the last of a series of books on speech by my mentor and beloved teacher, Musgrave Horner.[6] I saw in it a glimpse of an approach to speech for which I had unconsciously been searching. Having experimented with expressing what I understood were his ideas, I showed Musgrave my attempts. The dear man was bewildered. We did not speak of it again at that time. Then I read Rudolf Steiner's *Speech and Drama* lectures[*] and was inspired by all he had to say about the consonants and vowels. I experimented with my students, integrating his ideas with Rudolf Laban's research into *effort actions* and what I had gleaned from Musgrave's book. In time, I was led to England to study Steiner's work and I found Maisie Jones, who became my guide and teacher on the path of Speech I had been searching for.

It was in my second year at what was then called The London School of Speech Formation that Musgrave came to visit me.[†] Well into his 70s, he made what was to be his last trip 'back home'. After so many years spent as his devoted student and then his colleague, he was intrigued that I had undertaken four more years of training in the art of Speech. In letters, I had tried explaining my excitement and my wonder at the new world opening up to me and how I was encountering every aspect of my work with him transforming into new dimensions of experience. However, I was still a novice at articulating my discoveries. Musgrave always responded with respect for what I had embarked upon, mingled with bewilderment that I had done so.

Now, it had been agreed that he and his wife, Jane, would come for lunch and afterwards, with Maisie's willingness, observe a class. Lunch was a joyous reunion of kindred spirits. He asked many truly interested questions about this new approach to speech and I did my best to express what still felt largely inexpressible. When the moment came to go, he stopped, looked firmly at me and said with great humility, 'I have decided not to come to your class.'

Disappointed, I apologized, thinking I had upset him. This great man responded with honesty and courage, saying, 'I want you to understand. I want you to know that if I were 18, this is where I would begin. But I'm too old now and scared.' He insisted, nevertheless, on being introduced to Maisie and I was privileged to witness the gracious meeting of these two central teachers in my life. One had embodied for me the riches and wisdom of the past. The other held the future.

---

[*] Rudolf Steiner, *Speech and Drama Course*, 1969.

[†] Now the *Artemis School of the Living Word* (see Appendix C).

Musgrave left before the class began. On his return to Australia, in all our years of correspondence, he never ceased to express appreciation for and interest in what I did. I have pondered often on the destiny connecting us; through him, my path with Speech Formation woke to consciousness and through me he glimpsed before his death a new path for speech that reaches far beyond our present time. I cannot but be awed that a man who had authored several books on speech in the English language and been considered in his time a master of his art had recognized enough to say that, given other possibilities, 'this is where I would begin'.*

Movement, Voice and Speech, which played such an important role in the first part of my story, is still an invaluable source of reference concerning the intimate relationship between the life of soul, the movement of the body and the voice.[6] The seed that was planted through his book prepared me to recognize the potential of integrating Chekhov's work with Speech Formation and grew into my need to do so.

The shock of the new

Speech Formation has sometimes been perceived as 'weird' by ears unused to it. This may well be why, until now at least, it has not made a bridge into the wider world of theatre practice. The new always seems weird when it appears. Music, which for our present ear has achieved the measure of respectability, Beethoven's last quartets for example or Stravinsky's *Rite of Spring*, caused discomfort, even riots when first performed. The dictionary traces the Old English word 'weird' to Old Saxon and Old Norse roots, defining it as 'strange or bizarre', 'suggestive of or relating to the supernatural' and 'connected to our experience of fate'. All three relate to Speech Formation.

When I first heard a recital of Speech Formation, I expected that, at the very least, the heavens would open; I was full of abstract thoughts about the spiritual nature of speech and language and mystical ideas of how such things might sound.[†] I was disillusioned, to say the least. With nothing on which to base my response except my past experience of speech as physical phenomena, my soul rejected it, judging it as pretentious and exaggerated.

A year or so after this disappointing first encounter, the heavens did open, after all. I participated in a class taught by the very person whose performance had aroused such antipathy in me, Ulrike Brockman. I shall be forever grateful for her humble and

---

* Prior to coming to Australia, Musgrave had been a teacher and examiner at The Guildhall in London and the London Academy of Music and Dramatic Art. In Australia he became the Chairman of the Speech and Drama Authority, Australian Music Examinations Board.

† See 'An autobiographical note' in *The Art of Acting*, Appendix C. This event took place at Emerson College where the author went in 1973 to study Rudolf Steiner's work.

inspiring teaching that began a process that would create new pathways of perception, not only in my ears, but in my whole instrument.

As my ears began to 'hear', I recognized that at least part of my problem had been the lack not only of an organ that could speak what speech was to evolve to in the future, but one that could perceive it. I came to understand that *only by the doing of it* could such new organs evolve out of the old. Over the next years, as I graduated and began to teach, my organs of perception became more finely tuned. My experience of language and speech in the surrounding culture, which once had been my measure, changed. Qualities increasingly acceptable in an era dominated by mass media, which with Musgrave's training I had found merely challenging, now became unbearable.

Speech that sounds robotic, actors that can only shout or scream or otherwise cannot be heard above a whisper, unclear articulation or speaking so quickly that what is said is rendered unintelligible; these unfortunate realities are not considered weird. They have become acceptable and sound normal to our ears. Is *this* not weird?

A note on imitation

Every aspect of this new approach to speech requires re-perceiving, rethinking all we know about 'speech'. The activity Speech Formation asks of us lies outside our everyday experience of talking. Because of this, it was largely through *imitation* that Marie Steiner communicated to the first generation of students what otherwise would have remained beyond anyone's ability even to imagine, let alone to implement.

Could anyone learn to play the violin, for instance, without first hearing how it sounds and imitating what to do in order to achieve what they hear? Certain aspects of the Speech technique are difficult, perhaps impossible, to grasp without an initial demonstration. If these aspects are *not* communicated, there is a danger that speech will never move beyond subjective self-expression which, though it is a valid part of the creative life, can obscure other levels of the Self requiring to evolve and be expressed: levels only accessed by an activity of spirit that draws upon a future part of our humanity. Each successive generation who has taken up this work increasingly requires a process that goes beyond that first imitative level and appeals to their conscious understanding.

In my first years of teaching Speech Formation, I discovered that the mainstream acting processes in which I had first trained and which were brilliant for exploring the landscape of the soul, could not access the realms of spirit where Speech Formation has its source. When I met Michael Chekhov's work, I found the missing portion of the map. I sensed that the psycho-physical[*] process he articulated was the key that granted actors access to dimensions of the spirit in their work.

---

[*] See, *The Art of Acting.*

I am forever grateful to the guides who led me to Chekhov's acting methodology: a bridge between our ordinary selves and the awesome demands Speech Formation makes of us. Its gently nourishing process bestows, at every moment, the possibility of engaging with full consciousness in what we research and attempt. Chekhov's techniques provide a bridge between the student's starting point and what Chekhov called the 'great cosmic gesture' found in Steiner's work.[*] Within his methodology, a student is led step-by-step from the familiar self which is their home towards the glimpsing of the greater Self; the one encompassing the cosmos, stars and planets.

Over the years I have found using Chekhov's methodology to teach Speech Formation has resulted in it sounding increasingly acceptable to ears unused to it. Now as I am privileged to bring this holistic methodology to mainstream acting students in the Drama Centre at South Australia's Flinders University, I see how it has rendered what was once perceived as weird, completely natural; not in the sense that it is how we naturally talk but in the sense that when, through the Chekhov work, we engage the spiritual dimension of ourselves in such a way that it permeates and organizes our instrument, then Speech Formation is the natural way to speak.

Perhaps it is time for the 'weird', in this context, to become acceptable.

---

[*] See, *The Art of Acting*, 'Michael Chekhov – a brief introduction'.

THE CONTEXT

Scope of the book

The Art of Speech is not a manual for *how* Speech Formation should be taught. A book cannot replace a living teacher. It provides, rather, a meditative path to accompany an English training. Nevertheless, I have found it impossible to explore the esoteric depths of Speech Formation without anchoring these thoughts to specific exercises and approaches. In addition, it provides a long-needed text in English for those who may not undertake a training but wish to understand the impulse Rudolf and Marie Steiner gave for a new approach to speech and language. While knowledge of Steiner's work is not essential, it is assumed readers are open to an approach that is grounded in its fundamentals.

The supersensible dimensions of Speech Formation distinguish it from other speech techniques, yet these are not so easy to articulate. To my knowledge, this is the first book written for the English language in which the principles that underlie the practice of this Art of Speech have been investigated and expressed in a systematic way.[*] However, the living process of this work can in no way unfold in a pre-determined sequence. Rather, the aspects I have striven to illumine in each chapter might shine or ray in to the centre at any time or place within the journey.[†]

Spoken and written English

The huge gap between the written letter and the spoken sound is a challenge faced by everyone who learns the English language. Dr Johnson, who created one of the first truly comprehensive English dictionaries, tried to bring order to the verbal chaos which had arisen by the eighteenth century by fixing spelling. However, the consciousness contained in words cannot be fixed. It continues to evolve in what is spoken, resulting in an ever-widening gap between the spoken and written word. Each vowel, for example, when spoken, has been turned into a range of diphthongs which array themselves around the pure placement. The same spelling may well be pronounced in several different ways, eg: *cough, rough, though, thought*. In general, we are exploring spoken sounds, not letters. To write about the sounds of the English language, then, presents a challenge.

Variations in the symbols abound, even within the International Phonetic Alphabet (IPA) first created at the end of the nineteenth century. In order to be as clear as possible about which consonant or vowel is meant here, we will use the following table of phonetic symbols and representative words for the most commonly occurring sounds in Standard Received English (SRE), for example: (/uː/ sh<u>oe</u>).

---

[*] For details regarding books by colleagues in preparation at the time of publication, see Appendix B.

[†] This will mostly be determined by a teacher's intuition when responding to a student's individual needs.

International Phonetic Alphabet (IPA)

Phonetic symbols for the consonants (SRE)

/ŋ/   = ng   (so<u>ng</u>)

/ʍ/   = wh   (<u>wh</u>en)

/θ/   = th   (<u>th</u>ing)

/ð/   = th   (<u>th</u>e)

/ʃ/   = sh   (<u>s</u>ugar)

/ʒ/   = sh   (plea<u>s</u>ure)

/tʃ/ = ch   (<u>ch</u>ild)

/dʒ/ = j   (<u>j</u>udge)

/ɬ/   = ll   (wa<u>ll</u>)

/j/   = y   (<u>y</u>ear)

All other symbols for the consonants remain as per the usual alphabet, eg: p, l, k, d, s.

Phonetic symbols for the vowels

Simple or Pure vowels

/ɪ/	(s<u>i</u>p)	/ɔ/	(d<u>o</u>t)
/iː/	(m<u>e</u>)	/ɔː/	(<u>awe</u> or f<u>all</u>)[*]
/e/	(m<u>e</u>n)	/ʊ/	(t<u>oo</u>k)
/æ/	(m<u>a</u>n)	/uː/	(sh<u>oe</u>)
/ʌ/	(c<u>u</u>p)	/ə/	(<u>a</u>way)[†]
/ɑː/	(st<u>a</u>r)	/ɛ/	(h<u>ea</u>rd)[‡]

---

[*] This English short vowel has the same pure placement as its longer form /ɔː/ as when it appears in the English word 'awe' or 'fall'. This is the same placement as appears in the German long vowel (as in <u>oh</u>ne). Otherwise, our nearest equivalent to this placement in a longer vowel tends to turn into the diphthong /ɔə/ as in d<u>oo</u>r.

[†] Known as the neutral vowel.

[‡] This is the nearest in the English language to the German vowel oe/ö as in sch<u>oe</u>n/sch<u>ö</u>n or the French vowel as in c<u>oeu</u>r.

Diphthongs

/eɪ/ (d<u>a</u>te)	/eə/ (d<u>a</u>re)[*]
/oʊ/ (n<u>o</u>)	/ɔə/ (d<u>oo</u>r)
/aɪ/ (l<u>i</u>fe)	/ʊə/ (t<u>ou</u>r)
/aʊ/ (<u>ou</u>t)	/ju/ (imb<u>ue</u> or f<u>ew</u>)[†]
/ɔɪ/ (j<u>oy</u>)	/uɪ/ (s<u>wee</u>t)
/ɪə/ (<u>ea</u>r)	

Including /uɪ/ (s<u>wee</u>t) in this context is a controversial choice. The English combination would normally be regarded as the consonant /w/ followed by a vowel /iː/ (m<u>e</u>). The /w/ is designated as a 'glide'. This means that it comes into being in that mysterious interface where vowel 'glides into' or becomes a consonant. I have chosen to place it as a diphthong when it occurs in combination with the /iː/ (m<u>e</u>), not to insist upon this designation but to prepare for a detailed consideration of these sounds in relation to an observation Steiner makes.[‡]

Speech Formation (*Sprachgestaltung*) was pioneered in the German language which contains some vowels not heard or spoken in their pure form in SRE. Where this is the case, I have found it useful to draw attention to these German vowels and their nearest equivalents in English. Over the years this has enabled me to build a clear framework within which to explore the placements, which I call micro-gestures, and the corresponding inner life they reveal. I imagine they can be experienced by anyone, regardless of their mother tongue, and recognized when they occur in any language.

The sounds of which words are made give us keys to the vast treasure house of experience all languages contain. The evolving consciousness of any people lies buried in the changes to their language. These changes invite us to explore such questions as: why do English speakers rarely roll the 'r'? Why, except when 'r' begins a word, do we still spell it but no longer speak it? How might we understand the phenomenon that a people departs from the pure placements of the vowels into an almost infinite range of diphthongs which they write down in an equally infinite range of spellings? I hope to open an investigative path by which the questions that arise within the English language in particular, may be explored.

---

[*] This is the nearest in the English to the German vowel ä as in mädchen.

[†] These last two are the nearest approximations in the English language to the German vowel ue/ü [phonetic symbol =/y/] as in m<u>ue</u>de/ m<u>ü</u>de.

[‡] See Meditative exploration of the micro-gestures of the vowels, chapter 1.

Steiner's Speech exercises

The voice and Speech exercises found in mainstream textbooks seem, at first sight, not significantly different from printed texts of English renderings of Rudolf Steiner's Speech exercises. In each, we find similar sequences of 'nonsense' syllables that serve as useful drills for the development of certain skills. Given our human longing to make meaning, we may be frustrated trying to make sense of them, but this lack of conceptual content ensures the exercises serve as a clear archetype. What is won through working with the archetype can then be applied to different kinds of content in varying contexts of meaning. What distinguishes Steiner's exercises is the unique methodology with which we work. As we shall see, we are embarking on a journey that will lead us into an entirely new relationship to the sounds of language. It is difficult to enter such a new relationship while we are still attached to the familiar meanings we assign to words.

We largely have no sense of the relationship between the symbols we refer to as 'letters' and the sounds we speak. Likewise the sounds that words are made of and the 'meaning' we attribute to those words have little connection to each other in our common use of language. Perhaps the one exception lies in our concept of *onomato-poeia* which retains an echo of an older consciousness that recognized *experience* and *the sounds of language* are directly linked. Words that demonstrate this quality are made up of sounds that imitate audible experience – such as *sizzle, splash, crash, screech* and *tinkle.*

Steiner invites us to consider that there is such a relationship between the sounds of human speech and all categories of our experience. Our ability to sense this connection has largely been obscured by the conceptual meaning assigned to words – what we generally refer to as the *content* of a text. By regularly working with his exercises, sounds begin to yield up or reveal their intrinsic content. This newly acquired *experience* of consonants and vowels will fuse with what hitherto we understood to be the *meaning* of a word and deeper levels of that meaning will arise.

Steiner created the Speech exercises from his perception of each sound's specific qualities and gesture. Because this comes from a particular place and action in the mouth, the sound itself can teach our instrument to speak, if we invite it to. In order for our speech instrument to unfold its full potential, each exercise needs to be explored until, yielding up its wisdom, it works back with formative power on our speech organs.

The path of Speech Formation is a methodology for research, more so than a definitive body of content. The Speech exercises and artistic texts which formed the basis of the original training in the German language presuppose a background and a relevance that can no longer be assumed. Sound sequences given by Steiner in German needed transformation into English and to achieve this required understanding and mastery of the archetypal functions that the sounds embody and the knowledge that the English language is a vessel for a different consciousness which needed to unfold in a different people. Such was the achievement of the founders of the different streams of Speech Formation in the English language to whom we remain indebted.

The original Speech exercises were given by Rudolf Steiner in German. Significant models and suggestions for the English language were made by Maisie Jones, Mechthild Harkness and Sophia Walsh.[7] The exact authorship of some English versions is difficult to trace, passed on through a primarily oral tradition and lost within the unrecorded history of those early years and I welcome any further information anyone might have. In the meantime, any inaccuracies or ambiguities are unintentional.

The Speech exercises of Rudolf Steiner presented here are primarily those modelled for the English language by Maisie Jones. Those by other artists will be acknowledged with the initials of their author, for example: Mechthild Harkness (MH) and Dawn Langman (DL).

Esoteric foundations

This book makes explicit the sacred, ancient and modern mysteries implicit in the oral tradition handed down from Marie Steiner's work. The early decades were coloured by reluctance to speak about these things more openly, lest this wisdom be reduced to abstract thoughts that paralyse creative energy. I am convinced that now, nearly a century since the first seeds were planted, those who wish to meet Speech Formation are thirsting to understand the mysteries that permeate every detail of this new technique. Without that understanding, they are forced to imitate forms and activities they cannot fill and permeate with their own *creative individuality*.[*] In expressing these esoteric aspects of the work I have been guided by these lines from the meditation Steiner called the *Foundation Stone*.[8]

> Practice Spirit Vision
> In quietness of soul
> Where the eternal aims of Gods
> World Beings Light
> On thine own I bestow
> For thy free willing.

---

[*] See *The Art of Acting.*

Terms of reference

THE FOURFOLD HUMAN BEING

Steiner viewed the constitution of the human being from various perspectives. His description of the *threefold constitution* of the human being: *body, soul* and *spirit*, provided key terms of reference regarding our explorations of Chekhov's techniques in *The Art of Acting*. In our investigation of Speech, we expand these terms of reference by introducing Steiner's concept of the *fourfold constitution* of the human being.

From this perspective the human being is regarded as an *I* (or *Ego*) who, in order to evolve on earth, inhabits three 'sheaths' or bodies; these sheaths Steiner called the *physical, etheric* and *astral bodies*. Just as he used the terms *body, soul* and *spirit* precisely, so does he use these new terms equally precisely. Here follows Steiner's own description, from *Theosophy*:

> Just as one ascribes to the human body the three forms of existence, mineral, plant and animal, so one must ascribe to it a fourth – the distinctively human form. Through his mineral existence [physical body] man is related to everything visible; through his plant-like existence [etheric body] to all beings that grow and propagate their species; through his animal existence [astral body] to all those that perceive their surroundings and by means of external impressions have inner experiences; through his human form of existence he constitutes, even in regard to his body alone, a kingdom by himself.

Just as *The Art of Acting* considers Steiner's use of *body, soul* and *spirit* in terms an actor might find meaningful, we now consider this expanded terminology in relation to Speech. We shall use the opening words of the Gospel of St John as a lens through which to look at these aspects of ourselves. They express, in the profoundest way, the mystery at the heart of Speech Formation. The Greeks named it *Logos*. With this word, they named the thinking that creates and is not separate from the word with which it names itself.

> In the beginning was the Word
> And the Word was with God
> And the Word was God
> All things were made by Him
> And without Him was not anything made that was made.
> In Him was Life
> And the Life was the Light of men
> And the Light shines in the darkness
> But the darkness has not comprehended it...
> And the Word became flesh and dwelt among us full of grace and truth.

Let us imagine a Being of Love that wills to manifest Itself in such a way that It could know It is the One Self in all. To do this, It creates a vessel that could bear such consciousness; a consciousness which *knows that it is conscious of itself being conscious.*

Physical body

> All things were made by Him.

And so this Being weaves for Itself, first, a garment we call the physical body; condensing the ineffable wisdom of Itself into the laws of physical space and time, the chemistry of matter, the mineral kingdom.

Etheric body

> In Him was Life.

Love practises, next creating forms through which the infinite, ever-living stream of life can flow. The kingdom of plants unfolds.

It learns to be without desire, relinquishing those forms to death, when It moves on. Yet not before It plants the seed through which this life can manifest again and again in rhythmic cycles: mysteries of birth and reproduction, death, further birth. Drawing from the world-ether, the life which is in all things, It weaves into the physical, mineral body It has built, a portion of that life which belongs to each specific form alone. This we call an etheric body. Not able yet to recognize Itself, It offers life to serve the consciousness that is to come.

Astral body

> And the Life was the Light of men.
> And the Light shines in the darkness.
> But the darkness has not comprehended it.

Experimenting further; how to imbue those living forms with consciousness; to weave out of Its own all-sensing Self, organs and functions, fibres and cells that mediate sensation. Each little portion of the all-sensing wisdom of the stars and planets, condenses its aspect of the whole, making itself an expert in its speciality. Each aspect of the Self, configured in the form of one specific animal, has woven out of universal astral substance, an astral body that can bear one aspect of the universal soul. The light is now within. We see it in their eyes. The eyes of animals reveal the birth of inwardness. Self that knows, but does not yet know It knows.

Self-conscious self — the I AM or Ego

And the Word became flesh and dwelt among us.

This is my body, one garment, woven out of three, fitting for my Presence. Now, at last, I can become a human being. I stand, I speak, I think. I AM. I can know myself as Love and I can know I know.

THE LEVELS OF SPIRITUAL COGNITION IN RELATION TO SPEECH

To develop such a relationship to the sounds of language, we approach them with the faculties of spiritual cognition described by Steiner as appropriate for healthy modern consciousness. In *The Art of Acting* these were identified as *thinking* based on clear observation, *imagination*, *inspiration* and *intuition*. To do so means we become spiritual scientists in our practice of the Art of Speech.

Thinking based on clear observation

A basic textbook informs us of the anatomy and physiology of speech organs, the physics of sound waves and so on. This information is to be respected; it results from many hours of patient observation of phenomena, penetrated with clear thinking. We owe to it many advances that have taken place in remedial Speech, in the understanding of pathology in speech and language and the technology of sound and communication which has revolutionized our modern world. Is it necessary to look further? Only if I want relationship, only if I sense and want to know a *being*.

Take the sound /b/. Rational consciousness identifies it as a consonant; a voiced, bilabial plosive. This means that it is formed by the closure of the lips, which stop the breath until the resulting pressure forces them open. The released breath vibrates the vocal folds/chords or larynx, creating what the ears receive as sound. This sound, reinforced within the resonating chambers in the head and throat, emerges as a /b/.

The sound /p/ is also produced by release of the breath from the stoppage caused by closure of the lips. However, in this case the breath does not vibrate the vocal chords, transforming into voice. Instead, while retaining its quality as breath, it is sharply released, or aspirated. Therefore /p/ is described as a voiceless, aspirated, bilabial plosive.

Knowing that a sound is a *voiced* or *unvoiced bilabial plosive* can be helpful if I cannot form the sound correctly. But accurate though this description is, the artist in me is completely uninspired. For although such terminology has its place and we shall learn to further value what it teaches us, on its own it does not invite us to the rich feast that language offers when we begin to know the beings of the sounds.

How might we describe /b/ if we behold it with our hearts? How might we listen to it, speak it, taste it, perhaps express in movement the effect it has on us, the way we then perceive it? How might our experience of /b/ transform at each successive level of cognition?

Imagination

My imagination starts creating pictures: when I speak /b/ I sense I am forming something warm and solid, firm yet smooth, blunt perhaps, or slow and curved, with a gesture that encloses, holds, surrounds. Yet we have learned in *The Art of Acting* that gesture can arise only from intention to communicate. If there is intention to communicate, there is 'someone', then, who so intends, a being who would speak through me.

Inspiration

My heart begins to sense not 'just' a sound /b/ but *presence*; a 'someone' who is warm, embracing, reliable and thoughtful: someone with firm boundaries, comfortable with their inwardness, who likes to go deep down inside their soul. Such a being has profound substance and is slow to arouse but, once aroused, is capable of bashing down barriers that stand between. This presence has specific qualities, quite different from those that emanate from /t/ or /f/ for instance, should I also open myself to these in an imaginative way.

Current philological theory favours the view that the names we give to our experience are arbitrary. We have begun, however, to feel our way into a /b/. Perhaps now we begin to sense that there is genius at work. A mind which matches sounds to our experience is giving birth to words: baby, beauty, bower, belly, embrace, abundance, bitch, batter, abuse, bumble, bee, bud, build.

We allow our hearts to open further. We sense this genius is infinitely larger and more powerful than any single human being. Might it be that in the greater universe exists a Presence, experiencing itself through our experience and forming us to speak its name? For when human beings utter /b/, we name an aspect of experience no other sound can name.

Intuition

Through practice I train my instrument until this presence can express itself through me. I must learn how to apply my will to serve the will of 'b'. In the quest to serve that being's will more faithfully, I come to understand it at a deeper level. This level of knowledge or cognition, which can only result from the work to understand what a being/sound requires of me in order to express itself, is what Steiner means by *intuition*.

In general, *The Art of Speech* moves between the levels of clear perception, thinking and *imagination* with some excursions into *inspiration,* while Book 3, *The Integrated Actor,* invites the reader to venture more deeply into the levels of *inspiration* and *intuition.*

THE PRACTICE

Chapter 1

Our Divine Teachers

Provided our vision is free and unclouded
we shall be able to recognise in the sounds of speech our divine teachers...[9]

Imagine that any mind ever *thought* a red geranium!
As if the redness of a red geranium could be anything but a sensual experience
and as if sensual experience could take place before there were any senses.
We know that even God could not imagine the redness of a red geranium
nor the smell of mignonette
when geraniums were not and mignonette neither.
And even when they were, even God would have to have a nose
to smell at the mignonette.
You can't imagine the Holy Ghost sniffing at cherry-pie heliotrope.
Or the Most High, during the coal age, cudgelling his mighty brains
even if he had any brains: straining his mighty mind
to think, among the moss and mud of lizards and mastodons
to think out, in the abstract, when all was twilit green and muddy:
'Now there shall be tum-tiddly-um, and tum-tiddly-um,
hey-presto! scarlet geranium!'
We know it couldn't be done.
But imagine, among the mud and the mastodons
God sighing and yearning with tremendous creative yearning, in that dark green mess
oh, for some other beauty, some other beauty
that blossomed at last, red geranium, and mignonette.

Red Geranium and Godly Mignonette, D.H. Lawrence

A most rare vision — sounds as beings

Dissecting a corpse gives us facts about anatomy. This way of knowing is a product of the analytical thinking achieved in the last centuries that is possible because we have detached ourselves from the *being-ness* of which we are a part. This detachment lets us view the outside world as separate: an object we can manipulate for whatever purpose suits us. Consequently, we experience ourselves as *free* in relation to the object of our observation — but the price we pay for that freedom is an ever increasing sense of alienation from the world.

This alienation may increase to agonizing levels until, out of that very freedom, we begin the long journey to reverse the process; for nothing can satisfy us now except that we find ourselves again in relationship. I cannot have relationship unless I recognize the other as a *being*, not a *thing*. Yet I need to find a way to take along with me into this relationship, the clarity of independent thinking I have won at such a cost.

It is only when we behold another with our heart, that we can sense its being. Research increasingly acknowledges the need for such a multi-levelled knowing.* Yet it is necessary to overcome the habit, practised over centuries, of invalidating what our hearts contribute to the wholeness of our knowing. Our rational minds may still dismiss what our hearts tell us as 'merely subjective', condemning the other to remain a 'thing'.

Martin Buber was one of many pioneers to champion heart-knowing.[10] He characterized the different forms of *I–It* and *I–Thou* consciousness. When we behold the other as *thou*, we recognize that it has 'selfness'. We then perceive form and behaviour as expressions of that self. Steiner suggests we have twelve senses and it is our *sense of the I* or *Ego* with which we sense the selfness or being of another.† What could sense self – but self? It can only be our self that senses the being or selfness of the other.

Vowels and the etheric

Steiner has made two fundamental observations relating to the difference between consonants and vowels:

- When we speak the consonants, we imitate activity and qualities of form we perceive around us in the world.
- Vowels express our inner life of soul.

Let us first explore his observations concerning vowels. It's fairly common to respond to the experience of beauty, of a sunset for example, by exclaiming ah! /ɑ:/ (st<u>ar</u>). This vowel may well express emotions such as wonder, awe and gratitude. Closer observation may reveal how such beauty quickens an increased sense of life in us. A contrasting mood of sorrow or despair might equally cause our souls to sigh in ah! /ɑ:/, but now we sense that life is draining from us.

---

*Since the 1960s, for example, the term 'emotional intelligence' has been used to indicate the need to include the dimension of emotion in the range of ways we understand and process our experience. Although researchers differ as to how they assess its validity, the debate exists at all because for a growing number the attempt to validate experience exclusively in terms of 'intellect' has proved increasingly inadequate in dealing with the problems facing individuals, society and the earth.

† See *The Art of Acting*, chapter 3, The 12 senses.

Such first-hand observation helps us to make sense of Steiner's indications in the first of his *Speech and Drama* lectures where he describes how the impulse to speak arises in the astral body. Because the astral and etheric bodies are interwoven, when the speech impulse interacts with the etheric it is expressed in vowels. It is indeed as though vowels come from that deep place where organic processes and soul interface. A broader examination of the role performed by exclamations bears this out.

Think of the three great 'Oh!'s exclaimed by Lady Macbeth in her sleepwalking scene. They arise from some deep place beyond her conscious awareness or control. As those great vowels pour forth from a depth of anguish we can hardly bear to contemplate, we sense also that they bear her ebbing life away upon their wings of sound.[*]

Consonants and the creative spirit

When the impulse that arises in our soul needs to express what appear to be *objective* aspects of the outer world, then our soul opens to that part of us that shares in the divine creative spirit; who can dive into the cauldron of the elements and imitate the creator. The I AM in us is conscious that the varied behaviour and activities of different consonants not only depict diverse aspects of creation but have the power to create — and the I AM is the creator.

It is difficult to form a consonant without being awake and active in our will, although we can speak a vowel in a dreamy state or even as we drift off to sleep. In fact those states make the overall quality of speech, vocalic.[†] Think, as well, how someone under the influence of alcohol slurs their consonants, making them more like vowels.

But we cannot speak /t/, for example, unless we are active. The impulse to speak may indeed first arise within the astral body but we can only do justice to the consonants if we are fully present and in command of the elemental material at our disposal — co-creators with the conscious creative spirit of the universe.

Speech-exploration 1 (group/partner work)

Close your eyes and listen to a teacher or partner speak a sequence of vowels followed by a sequence of consonants. Observe how they affect you. Is there a difference? Discuss your experience.

---

[*] See chapter 5 for greater detail regarding the nature of these life forces, which Steiner refers to as etheric. Speech-exploration 15 provides an opportunity to explore the world of exclamations.

[†] Vowel-like.

Speech-exploration 2 (partner work)

One of you is a visitor and the other is a guide. Imagine that you live on a planet where only vowels are spoken.

1. As you move around, the guide describes and explains everything about the planet using only vowels; the visitor responds using only vowels.
2. Change roles.
3. Discuss.

Speech-exploration 3 (partner work)

One of you is a visitor and the other is a guide. Imagine that you live on a planet where only consonants are spoken.

1. As you move around, the guide describes and explains everything about the planet using only consonants, the visitor responds using only consonants.
2. Change roles.
3. Discuss.

Speech-exploration 4 (partner work)

Collect a variety of things that provide different sensations of touch: rough, smooth, sharp, blunt, straight, round, soft, hard, shiny, warm, cold, wet, dry, etc.

1. One of you is blindfolded and the other brings to you as many different touch sensations as can be experienced in a ten or fifteen minute period. Don't rush. Take time for each set of sensations to be thoroughly experienced.
2. Change over.
3. Make yourself comfortable on the floor. Someone who can bring the consonants to life will speak a sequence of them to you. Just listen. Allow the different qualities to touch you. Try to differentiate their qualities according to the listed categories and any others that occur to you.
4. Stand and experiment with speaking as many consonants as you can actively recall. Try to recreate as speaker the quality of the sensation it produced in you as listener.

The consonants and the four elements

Steiner connected the consonants with the four elements of earth, water, air and fire. In investigating this suggestion, we make our first conscious effort to experience the consonants at the *imaginative* level of cognition. We will also consider the clear physiological basis for consonants and vowels described in any mainstream textbook. Such descriptions identify the speech organs used in their formation, whether they are voiced or unvoiced, and how we use our breath to form them. Figure 1 illustrates the placements in the mouth where the consonants are formed, so we can experiment with these descriptions and make our own observations.

At the same time, we shall move towards our first perceptions of the sounds when we describe the four elements of earth, water, air and fire and enter into their activity. Such a pathway is suggested by the idea that arose in the Ancient Greek culture. By around fifth century BC,[11] human beings had largely lost the original capacities of supersensible perception they had once possessed and which enabled them to feel that they were integrated with the divine creative forces of the cosmos. As they became less able to perceive these states directly, they tried to understand the nature of the universe by thinking about their observations of the natural processes surrounding them. Empedocles was one philosopher who concluded that nature is composed of these four elements or 'roots' (fire, air, water and earth) and that all natural processes result from their interactions.

Steiner describes how the universe has condensed through progressive planetary stages. Beginning with the stage of warmth or fire, it eventually arrived at the so-called solid state of matter we associate with our present planetary stage of earth.[12] This imagination provides a pathway for artistic exploration of the creative processes at work within the universe and their connection to the consonants. We shall observe and think about the qualities of each element, then investigate their connection to the consonants through sound and movement.

To view the sounds through the perspective of the elements provides an opportunity for the imagination to be active. Artistic possibilities become immediately obvious. However, characterizing consonants in this way should never be dogmatically adhered to; sounds behave in different ways in different contexts. These ideas, explorations and suggestions for practice are a starting point for your own experiments and designed to be accompanied by Chekhov's exercises for the qualities-of-movement.[*]

---

[*] See *The Art of Acting*, chapter 1.

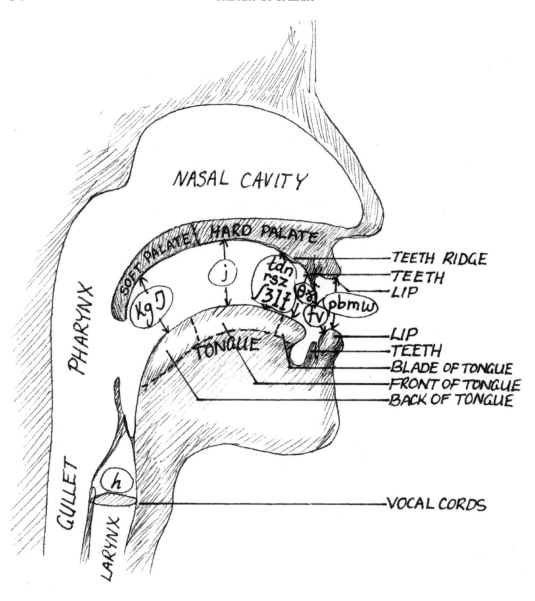

The speech organs in relation to the formation of the consonants

Figure 1

The element of fire

Fire is a state of energy not yet condensed into degrees of matter and comes closest to what we might imagine as the state of origin of things. Heraclitus, another of the pre-Socratic philosophers, regarded it also as the state to which all things return.

A range of consonants behave like fire. Some create a strong sensation of heat or energy. Others onomatopoeically resemble sounds that we associate with fire's activity. All are formed by the intensity with which the breath stream is directed against, and resisted by, the points of contact in the mouth. It is as though one point of contact acts like a flint against which the other point of contact strikes, igniting the stream of breath as though into a spark or sizzle, hiss or flame.

We experience it like this because the breath is not obstructed totally but makes an audible friction while escaping through its narrow stricture. We hear it very clearly still as breath. This creates a sense of energy not yet condensed into material form.

Mainstream terminology calls such consonants *fricatives*. Producing fricatives requires fiery energy from the speaker. The sound, in turn, generates enormous energy and movement. Some fricatives we designate as *unvoiced*, because they do not activate the larynx on their passage through. These seem nearest to the form pure energy takes and furthest from the density of earth.

The relationship between the human voice and matter can be observed in the increasing density of voice which comes about when boys transition into manhood. This maturing of the voice results from the thickening of vocal chords which takes place at this time.

Any ordinary flow of language will require, at some point, the voiceless fricative to take hold of the voice. This it can only do by fusing with the vowel. For a voiceless or 'less-physical' consonant to grasp the 'earthy' voice, it is necessary to be consciously active. Some fiery consonants, on the other hand, are known as *voiced*. They already bear the voice or vowel element within them. In these we sense how fire begins to densify, or penetrate and warm material substance.

Fire-sounds

/f/

A voiceless labiodental fricative. The upper teeth press against the lower lip and partially obstruct the stream of breath. The hard edge of the teeth acts like a flint against which the lower lip can strike. The vocal chords do not vibrate at all, creating a sensation of pure energy.

/v/

A voiced labiodental fricative, formed in the same way as /f/, except that the vocal chords vibrate. This leads to an impression that energy has engaged with or begun to penetrate the earth.

/s/

A voiceless alveolar fricative. The stream of breath is now obstructed when the sides of the tongue press against the upper teeth and support the tip or blade of the tongue to be suspended just beneath the teeth (or alveolar) ridge. This enables the stream of breath to be directed with a razor-sharp precision. Free of the voice, white hot, like steam, we can use it to sense and probe in realms beyond the visible.

/z/

A voiced alveolar fricative. Formed in the same way as /s/ except that we allow the breath to vibrate the vocal chords on its passage through. This causes it to sear into earthly substance, penetrating, warming it. In turn, as it is absorbed by the earthy voice, its razor-edge is blunted.

/ʃ/ (sugar)

A voiceless palato-alveolar fricative. The tongue tip moves slightly back. Sensation of the fiery breath plunging into water, stirring itself into a shower, showers of froth, gradually receding into shallows, fire always lurking just below the breathing, heaving surface.

/ʒ/ (pleasure)

As for /ʃ/, except that as it activates the voice so it is warmed by it.

/θ/ (thing)

A voiceless dental fricative. The tongue tip pokes through the teeth and partially obstructs the breath where it makes contact with the upper teeth. Fire licks towards the air, seeking oxygen. Breath in its own transparency refines itself to be a delicately probing instrument; tip of the tongue through teeth, touching mysteries of edges, sensing them emerging and dissolving.

/ð/ (the)

As for /θ/, except that it is voiced. Warming as it probes beneath the surface, meeting and creating the resistance of the voice.

/h/

A voiceless glottal fricative. The breath is partially obstructed in the region of the glottis which is the gap between the vocal chords. Closest, most intimate, it is breath itself; nothing added, let it in and out. Gasping, panting, heat to warm a living soul, on the way to feeling; breath caught in surprise, in wonder, reaching for a vowel, becoming laughing, weeping.

/ʍ/ (<u>wh</u>en)

A voiceless bilabial glide. Breath channelled through the carefully contracted lips; further on its way to feel itself, sucking in a sudden shock, blowing out a flame.

/w/

A voiced bilabial glide. The term 'glide' describes a sound emerging somewhere between vowel and consonant. We first encountered this when, earlier, we noted the transition from the /uː/ (shoe) into the /w/. Now breath, engaging with the voice, is warmed. Warm soul within stammers at the threshold; wanting to express, come out.

The following explorations invite us to activate the fiery consonants so that they burn the vowels that lie along their path, into transparency. When this occurs, it is as if the earthly substance of the voice is set alight and made to glow.

Speech-exploration 5 — fire

> Vicious vipers whip through thistles.
>
> DL

> Ha! Forceful rush!
> This showers as chaff
> from threshers flail

When this has been achieved, we can carry that activity into the following:

> Scatter, as from an unextinguished hearth,
> Ashes and sparks, my words among mankind!
>
> *Ode to the West Wind*, Shelley

> Fear death? to feel the fog in my throat,
> The mist in my face...
> I was ever a fighter, so — one fight more
> The best and the last!
>
> *Prospice*, Browning

The element of air

These lines by Hopkins describe the transparency we associate with air. It lets light through. We see through air but we cannot see air. We see what blocks the light because its level of vibration is not fine enough to let light through. Yet what can be so fine, so tender can be wild as well.

> Wild air, world mothering air,
> Nestling me everywhere,
> That each eyelash or hair
> Girdles; goes home betwixt
> The fleeciest, frailest-flixed snowflake . . .
> Who, this one work has to do —
> Let all Gods glory through . . .
> I say that we are wound
> With mercy round and round
> As if with air . . .

The Blessed Virgin Mary Compared to the Air We Breath, Hopkins

The rolled 'r' /ɾ/ can be as rumbustious and rough as a hurricane, yet can refine itself to such transparency, be as fragile, breathe as gently as a breeze.

Technically, it is a form of fricative, in that the breath stream is only partially obstructed when we form it. Yet the escaping breath does not arouse the sensations which we generally associate with heat or warmth. It is called (wondrous to consider, by those who made such names!) a *voiced retroflex*. The stream of breath is partially obstructed when the tongue tip or blade is struck towards the centre of the hard palate. In SRE, /ɾ/ is not rolled, but formed by the lips closing softly and passively around it. It is most often silent unless it begins a word. However, when we roll or trill it, /ɾ/, as the Scots still do, there is perhaps no other consonant that can more express the airy quality than 'r'.

To achieve the rolled /ɾ/, the tongue tip first presses against the centre of the hard palate. The stream of breath then blows it off. The muscle asserts itself against that breath and yet again is forced down from the roof. Faster and faster the action is repeated. Air and matter battle for supremacy, causing vibration of the vocal chords, producing /ɾ/. At its most dense, it sounds like a propeller winding up. But these movements can take place with such rapidity and fineness that we cannot see the propeller turn; matter moving at such speed it disappears. Just like the air, we cannot see it. As an engine becomes airborne, so too can the voice stream out in a ribbon of light; so fine it seems like gossamer, at one with air's own nature.

Speech-exploration 6 — air

> radiant rollick
> rolling airily
> restlessly rippling

MH, DL

> rateless ration
> roosted roomily
> reason wretched
> ruined Roland
> royalty roster

These lines, practised while imagining the air and moving in the quality of *flying*, can teach the voice transparency. The sequences of syllables will stream out into space upon the wings of 'r'.

Part of our greater purpose is to bring life into speech and language, which have become devitalized. Another is to expand beyond our everyday experience of ourselves. We do this when we stretch into the greater archetypes we find within our cosmos. Therefore, it matters not that we may rarely roll the 'r' in SRE. We do it now in order to awaken an aspect of ourselves that might otherwise remain asleep.

Exercising with the rolled /r/ first is more likely to arouse sensations connected with the air and airy movement. This encourages the permeation of our voice with its transparency. The achievement of these airy qualities means we shall be able to apply them when we return to the unrolled English 'r' and speak those lines from Hopkins. We can then experiment with the following lines from a sonnet by Wordsworth. These require transparency but the flying quality-of-movement by which we have achieved it must be transformed to outer stillness.

> It is a beauteous evening calm and free
> The holy time is quiet as a nun
> Breathless with adoration . . .

Sonnet, Wordsworth

We have moved from fire to air. Spirit is ready now to condense still further on its journey towards solid form.

The element of water

When I consider the range of watery qualities, I marvel how the liquid element is always moving, seeking other pathways, covering surfaces, dissolving and uniting what had hardened into solid form and separated. At its densest, it can sweep away whole continents or villages and towns within its flood. In stillness it moves still, forming the calm surface of a lake or pool. When it mingles with the air it is light and full of bubbles.

The consonant /l/ is described as voiced, bilateral and lingua-alveolar. This means the tip or blade of the tongue now touches the alveolar ridge. The tongue's sides are lowered, letting breath escape. Technically, then, /l/ too, is a form of fricative.

As we experience the sensation that arises as we form this sound, following where it leads, we discover how /l/ behaves in just the ways that water does. We observe the tongue guiding our voice-filled breath so that it spreads as smoothly over the hard palate as liquid glides and spreads on surfaces. The 'l' invites us into the behaviour of water.

Speech-exploration 7 — water

lulling leader limply/limpid liquid lazily[*]	(smooth surface of lake)
liplessly laughing	(bubbling creek)
loppety lumpety lackety lout	(flood-tide)

By joining the activity of /l/, according to its nature, our whole instrument is invited to participate in these behaviours. This will prepare us to apply these qualities artistically.

The sea is calm tonight, the tide is full.

Dover Beach, Arnold

In coop and in comb the fleece of his foam
Flutes and low to the lake falls home.

Inversnaid, Hopkins

Summers bubble sound of sweet creek water
Dwindles and is silent.

The Bull, Judith Wright

Roll on, thou deep and dark blue ocean, Roll!

The Ocean, Byron

We are ready to condense still further into matter.

The element of earth

The quality we generally associate with earth is solid density, in its varying degrees. Consonants that demonstrate this quality are known as *plosives*. A plosive forms because the speech organs achieve complete obstruction of the breath before releasing

---

[*] DL.

it. The resulting pressure consolidates the sound, endowing it with a solid quality. It is as though when we speak a plosive, our action imitates what takes place when energy condenses into matter. Like earth itself, plosives manifest in a range of densities and textures.

The consonants which seem to have the greatest density are:

/b/ a voiced, bilabial, un-aspirated plosive
/d/ a voiced, alveolar, un-aspirated plosive
/g/ a voiced, un-aspirated, velar plosive[*]

The unaspirated quality of these three means that the breath is absorbed into the sound and is no longer evident as breath. This leads us to perceive the sound as *solid*. It is as though the fire of the creative spirit, expressing itself through breath, has fully inhabited and therefore disappeared into its physical form.

If we form these sounds exactly, but without vibration of the larynx, we turn them into unvoiced, aspirated plosives. Through these we sense a kind of transubstantiation. The sound still has some of the solidity and clarity of form that characterizes earthly substance; at the same time spirit-fire, now audible again as breath, seems somewhat loosened from it. In the case of /p/ and /k/, we sense that spirit-fire departing and releasing from the matter it inhabited. In contrast /t/ awakens an impression of spirit-fire still arriving, still forming its abode here on the earth.

/p/ an unvoiced, bilabial, aspirated, plosive
/t/ an unvoiced, alveolar, aspirated plosive
/k/ an unvoiced, velar, aspirated plosive

Speech-exploration 8 requires us to move flexibly between the contrasts of the voiced and unvoiced bilabials. The speaker alternates, experiencing, first, the potential of the /b/ to teach the voice its quality of gathered density, then the radiating gesture of the /p/ with its potential to explode the voice into the space.

Speech-exploration 8 — earth

> proxy prized
> bather broomstick
> polka pushing
> beady basket
> prudent pertness
> bearskin bristled

---

[*] Velar = formed by the tongue on the soft palate.

We have observed that the element of earth reveals itself in varying degrees of density. Mixed with, or condensing out of, liquid, its substance is viscous, like that of mud or lava. Certain consonants share this malleable quality of density. These are the *nasals.* Plosives are formed by a momentary but complete obstruction of the breath in both mouth and nose. Nasals are also formed when the breath is completely obstructed in the mouth, but allowed to escape through the nose.

The /m/ is called a voiced, bilabial, nasal because, although the breath is totally obstructed in the mouth by closure of both lips, it still can find a passage through the nose.

The /n/ is known as a voiced, alveolar, nasal. Once again the breath stream can pass out through the nose although obstructed in the mouth, this time when the tongue tip or blade is pressed against the alveolar ridge.

Each sound can manifest in either of two ways, depending on its place in a word. Appearing at the end of a syllable or word it reveals a sustained, legato quality, producing a liquid-like sensation, (hu<u>m</u> or i<u>n</u>). At the beginning of a syllable or word, it can reveal a staccato quality, producing a sensation of a firmer, sharper edge, (<u>m</u>ock or <u>kn</u>ock).

Designated as a nasal, /ŋ/ (so<u>ng</u>) has difficulty manifesting in staccato form because the /n/ forms a cushion, softening the firmer edge of /g/. Here, breath is obstructed in the mouth by pressing the back of the tongue into the soft palate. As a result, /ŋ/ tends to embody the viscous quality of earth.

All three nasals bring the gift of musicality into our speaking because of the way in which they utilize the resonance arising in the nasal cavity.[*]

Speech-exploration 9 – earth

> tricked deep dingle
> deep biting narrow copper
> dark too dark

Speech-exploration 9 is structured so that the nasal consonants interact with the other plosives. This allows us to find differing degrees of density and compression in the substance of the voice. It utilizes voiced and unvoiced sounds in all three pairs of plosives. The progression of plosives, relieved by only a few syllables providing flexibility, creates a sense of unrelenting pressure. The quality of commitment this demands of a speaker might be likened to that demanded of a sculptor who uses a

---

[*] See chapter 3 to explore how to take advantage of this gift. See the section on articulation for an investigation of the speech organs themselves in order to penetrate more deeply still into the nuances each sound can waken in us.

gouging instrument to carve into the density of wood or stone. Working with consonants combined with Chekhov's exercises for moulding, floating, flying and radiating ensures that work with the voice is integrated with the body and the soul, according to our psycho-physical principle.[*]

Speech-exploration 10 — moulding

moulding mountains
bigger boulders
digging deeper
gripping granite
carving crags
tying knots

DL

Speech-exploration 10 is intended to be spoken while engaged in full-bodied moulding. It encourages the integration of combined body/voice capacities within our instrument with qualities of earth. When you have achieved the appropriate degree of vocal density, apply it to the following texts. Any text, of course, is likely to contain a range of consonants whose qualities embody all the elements. In this case, our intention is to achieve an overall sensation of earth-density. We learn to imbue each sound, no matter its intrinsic nature, with the density of earth and permeate the whole image with its quality.

He clasps the crag with crooked hands

The Eagle, Tennyson

Then lips cracked open in the stone hard peaks
And rocks begin to suffer and to pray

The Harp and the King, Judith Wright

Our goal is to experience that consonants are not simply a range of vocal noises arising from the different technicalities of their formation. We approach them first as activities with quite precise and differentiated qualities and dynamics (level of *imagination*). Then, proceeding further, we begin to sense how these are expressions of living beings we can recognize and get to know within the spectrum of our soul's experience (level of *inspiration*). These living beings have created the organs of articulation which allow them to express themselves when we speak. When we

---

[*] See *The Art of Acting*, chapter 1, moulding, floating, flying, radiating.

approach the sounds in this way, seeking to unite ourselves with what each being wills to express (level of *intuition*) then the appropriate activities arise within our instrument that enable us to make these sounds. Such an approach requires a fundamental shift in our way of thinking about speech.

Yet, after all, it is these very beings that instruct the baby, who has no conscious knowledge of which parts of the mouth engage in speaking. Between the child who babbles with such joy and vigour and the empty voices of so many adults lies the death of inspiration and imagination. It is my experience that if these can be repaired and healed then, in most cases, our mouths will know what to do.

Combinations

In the macrocosmic universe, the elements of earth, air, water, fire are often to be found in combinations. So too, within the range of consonants we use in English, we might experience how some arise out of a combination of earth and fire: /ts/ (objec<u>ts</u>) and /ks/ (fi<u>x</u>). Some arise out of a fusion:

/ʒ/ (ju<u>dge</u>)

A voiced affricate. This is formed when we explode the earthy plosive /d/ through the aperture created when we speak the fricative /ʒ/ (plea<u>s</u>ure), which is both voiced and fiery.

/tʃ/ (<u>ch</u>ild)

A voiceless affricate. This is formed when we explode the earthy plosive /t/ through the aperture created when we speak the fricative /ʃ/(<u>s</u>ugar), which is both fiery and unvoiced.

We do not form these complex sounds by simple addition of two single consonants. Fiery activity is required to compress the two sounds into one. Each sound penetrates the other until they fuse, creating quite new substance.

How a word means

We are ready to explore the level of meaning a consciousness of sounds contributes to the usual meaning we attribute to a word. Let us take as an example the single word, *world*. *World* takes us on a journey through four consonants. In their order, they reveal the process of transformation through the four elements from fire to earth. It is as though the word contains a 'fossil record', so to speak, of the evolutionary cycles described by Steiner as the process by which our earth came into being. This will be particularly obvious if we roll the 'r'. So that we do not dismiss this as an abstract idea, I suggest we try the following.

Speech-exploration 11

1. Warm-up with Chekhov's qualities-of-movement.
2. When it feels organic, introduce the speaking of the consonants into the movement. Play with them, in any order, eventually arriving at the following sequence:

    radiating /w/
    flying   /r/ (rolled 'r')
    floating   /l/
    moulding   /d/

3. Let each quality live fully before transforming to the next.
4. Condense the time of the sequence until you can transition from one sound to the next, allowing a whole breath for each consonant.
5. Condense the process further until you can make the journey from fire through to earth — /wrld/ — out of one breath.
6. During these stages, make the transition from full-bodied movement to subtle until only the sounds themselves reveal the movement.[*]
7. Speak *world* in such a way that you experience the transformations as you speak. We shall examine the vowel's significance later. For now simply let it slip into place within the journey of the consonants.

Enspiriting the consonants

We have considered how speaking consonants requires a different order of activity than that required for speaking vowels. This is so, even at the level of our everyday communication, quite apart from levels of intensity required by art. While vowels can emerge from our mouth when we are relatively passive, even half asleep, as when we

---

[*] See *The Art of Acting*, Terms of reference, full-bodied movement.

yawn, to speak a /s/ or /f/ or /b/ demands a formative activity only possible when I AM present. It is this we mean, then, when we say that to create a consonant requires activity of spirit. When I achieve this consciously, I have a sense of 'being in the driver's seat' when I speak.

The art of speaking

We are accustomed to regard the expression of the *content* of a text as the goal of our artistic striving. Our investigations invite us to consider that *the act of speaking* in itself could be artistic. To embark upon this path is to begin a healing process of the long accepted split between technique and art.

How might this be?

Let us consider the practical implications for the speaker if we return now to our original description of /b/ as a 'voiced bilabial plosive'.[*] On its own, this way of labelling the attributes of /b/, leaves us with a sense of detachment. From this detached perspective, I might describe my action thus. To say /b/ I close my lips so that, for a moment, I obstruct my breath completely. When I have built up the required pressure, I release it, in such a way that it vibrates my vocal chords as I do so. I relate to my speech instrument as I would to a machine: merely a series of parts which, if they do their job, produce the correct sound /b/.

I need to integrate this level of investigation with the imaginative level my artistic sensibilities demand.

How would I approach that same action with imagination, imbued with artistic feeling and experience, without abandoning accurate observation and clear thinking? I describe that same action in terms of my creative intention or objective, somewhat as follows:

I want to express a sense of form that is dense, enclosing, and embraces substance. My lips enable me to express these qualities in speech. They are so soft, so able to express tenderness, and yet can so firmly press and mould into each other that they block the passage of my breath. This means I can build up its pressure, focusing it through my vocal chords until it is warmed and thickened by my voice. And now, at last, I sense my breath has reached the density of substance that my lips can shape and mould. I release it into space imprinted, carved and sculpted with their gesture.

It is impossible for my mouth to achieve this experience isolated from the rest of me. For this to happen, my mouth must be supported by creative tensions and activity that permeate my psycho-physical organization.[†] Only when the whole of me is active can speech be a creative act.

---

[*] See page 24, Thinking based on clear observation.

[†] See *The Art of Acting*, chapter 1, 'The Psycho-Physical Principle'.

I have described this process with a single sound in such detail in order to provide a model to encourage your investigation into other sounds. First, we make conscious the precise physical processes involved if we would speak a sound. We do this by isolating them from the greater wholeness within which they reside. Then, we engage with those same processes but as creative artists. Teeth, lips, palate, tongue, breath and their interactions become no less precise an instrument but are themselves en-souled. In this way, we restore them to their greater wholeness.

Ensouling the vowels

I remember being taught to speak 'the five vowels' as a child in school. They all felt more-or-less the same and articulating them correctly in an everyday sense was rather like making empty shells. What was once called 'elocution' required that those empty shells be polished to perfection; but they had no inner content. Awkwardness at such an abstract approach, a sense that it was false or dishonest in some way, led to a rejection of this old approach to speech. Without an understanding of the deeper realities of consonants and vowels, this abandonment of elocution has resulted in a trend where 'anything goes' so long as it doesn't require speakers to sound in any way 'unnatural' or depart from their everyday voice and speech patterns.

Our approach consists in the attempt to attune ourselves as total instrument, so that when we speak /ɑː/ (st_ar), for example, we can communicate just that specific aspect of experience which /ɑː/ expresses. To achieve this with each vowel leads to a rich palate of possibilities for the actor who wishes to express the finest nuances within a text. It would then be possible to colour a single word, a whole phrase or passage with the soul mood of /ɑː/ (st_ar) or /uː/ (sh_oe). Actors would then have the means to respond to the objective truth in language itself and to marry this with their artistic intuition.

I wish to stress that such an approach is not about advocating the imposition of any standard of 'correct' pronunciation, such as that referred to as SRE. Instead, we are invited to look at the range of vowels in somewhat the same way that a painter might look at a palate of colours. The painter learns to know the primary colours and the infinite degrees and qualities arising from their interaction. Out of such knowledge comes the capacity to express in colour the infinite nuances of our experience.

In just the same way, we may come to know the 'primary colours' of the vowels. This will open up the possibility to explore the variations that arise within our unconscious speech patterns. We will not judge them as correct or incorrect. Rather, we shall begin to perceive them as a range of nuances which have arrayed themselves around each primal placement. Each regional accent, individual habit or foreign variation will reveal a different set of nuances. When these are penetrated, then a speaker is able, in the same way as a painter, to consciously choose the nuance of expression s/he intends. The alternative is the repetition of unconscious patterns which cannot express anything beyond that self-perpetuating framework.

The octave of the vowels

In much the same way that musicians learn to recognize the true pitch of each tone on their instruments, we can experience the sequence of pure vowels as an octave that encompasses the range of human soul-gestures. That octave then, provides a template. Within the training of our sensibilities that it provides, variations, such as those occurring in the English language, can be noticed and identified. The spectrum of vowels expresses the spectrum of our inner life. Our path is to observe the physical formation of the vowels, then allow what we discern at higher levels of spiritual cognition to arise from those observations. The vowels result from the shaping of the breath stream according to:

- whether the tongue is high or low or towards the front or back of the mouth
- whether the tongue is arched or flat, and in what degree of tension
- whether the lower jaw moves up or down in relation to the tongue's movement
- degrees of tension
- the shape with which the lips frame the above activities; whether they are contracted or expanded, rounded or horizontal.

Figures 2–4 show how the vessel of the mouth can change its shape to channel the stream of breath:

The /ʌ/ (c<u>u</u>p) and /ɑː/ (st<u>a</u>r), are short and long forms arising from the same placement: shaped when the tongue is low and forward in our mouths and the lips stretched and expanded to their greatest width and height.

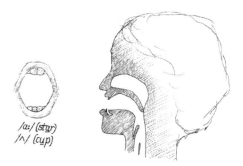

Figure 2 – vowel placement 1

In contrast, the short /ʊ/ (t<u>oo</u>k) and long /uː/ (sh<u>oe</u>) are shaped when the tongue moves up and back, while the lips round themselves into their most contracted form.

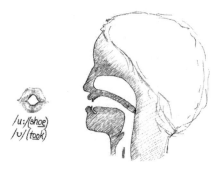

/uː/(sh**oe**)
/ʊ/(t**oo**k)

Figure 3 – vowel placement 2

To shape an /iː/(m**e**), the lips stretch sideways and the tongue moves upwards until its edges press firmly against the sides of the upper teeth.

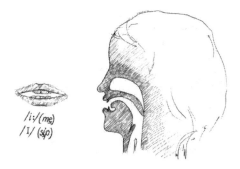

/iː/(m**e**)
/ɪ/ (s**i**p)

Figure 4 – vowel placement 3

If we sound each vowel in order from 1 to 8, we can observe for ourselves the progression of variations which enable us to speak each vowel. As you progress through the vowels in this sequence, become aware of the sensation you are moving from the back to the front of your mouth.

The sequence of eight simple or pure placements

Placement 1	short	/ʌ/ (c**u**p)
	long	/ɑː/ (st**a**r)
Placement 2	short	/æ/ (m**a**n)
Placement 3	short	/e/ (m**e**n)[*]

---

[*] And appears in German in its long form (**e**wig).

Placement 4	short	/ɪ/ (s<u>i</u>p)
	long	/iː/ (m<u>e</u>)
Placement 5	short	/ɔ/ (d<u>o</u>t)
	long	/ɔː/ (<u>awe</u>)
Placement 6		/œ/ (as in German sch<u>ö</u>n)
Placement 7		/y/ (as in German m<u>ü</u>de)
Placement 8	short	/ʊ/ (t<u>oo</u>k)
	long	/uː/ (sh<u>oe</u>)

Placement 6 does not occur in SRE in its pure form. Our nearest equivalent is /ə/ (<u>a</u>way), known in English as the *neutral vowel*. It is an important feature of our language, contributing to its distinctive flow and rhythm. It can replace other vowels if they are unstressed in a word or phrase. So, for example, we do not pronounce the 'a' in *bread <u>a</u>nd butter*, as /æ/ (m<u>a</u>n) but rather /ə/. The English vowels, short /ə/ as in (<u>a</u>way)[*] and long /ɛ/ as in (h<u>ea</u>rd) might be considered our nearest equivalents to the sixth placement.

The English language also contains no simple or pure vowel arising from the seventh placement. The diphthongs /ʊɪ/ (s<u>wee</u>t) or /ju/ (imb<u>ue</u>) might be considered our nearest equivalents to the seventh placement. The first of these /ʊɪ/ (s<u>wee</u>t), is the result of sliding from the short vowel /ʊ/ (t<u>oo</u>k) to /ɪ/ (s<u>i</u>p). The second, of sliding from the /ɪ/ (s<u>i</u>p) to the long vowel /uː/ (sh<u>oe</u>).

Another feature of the English language is the number of diphthongs that have evolved, the most common of which are listed in the IPA. Diphthongs are created by sliding from one vowel to another such as /aɪ/ (l<u>i</u>fe), /au/ (<u>ou</u>t) and /ɔi/ (j<u>oy</u>). In this respect it is important to observe that the long vowel, often designated in the English language by the letter 'o' as in (n<u>o</u>), is not a pure or simple vowel; it is a diphthong /ɔʊ/ created by sliding from /ɔ/ (d<u>o</u>t) to /ʊ/ (t<u>oo</u>k).

The octave of the vowels, precisely identified by the phonetic symbols, embodies the spectrum of our soul's experience. Chekhov's psycho-physical principle explored in *The Art of Acting*, teaches us to consciously penetrate our movement until we experience our bodies and their gestures as bearers of precise sensation.[†] Our mouth is no less capable of gesture than our arms and hands; no less able to use sounds, for example, to radiate, fly, mould or float, expand, contract, caress or

---

[*] See the IPA. [International Phonetic Alphabet.]

[†] See *The Art of Acting*, chapter 1, 'The Psycho-Physical Principle'.

strike. We can train our awareness that the moving jaw and tongue, in interaction with the palate, teeth and lips, are parts of our larger expressive instrument. We are generally unaware that our mouth shares the gesturing potential of the whole body of which it is a part, and that the larynx shares the muscle tensions which reflect our souls' responses to the world and are distributed throughout the larger musculature of the body.[13] If we pay attention to the movement in our mouth that makes each consonant or vowel possible, we recognize it is a gesture; a bearer of precise sensation which embodies and expresses our experience: a *micro-gesture*. As our knowing deepens of what the micro-gestures of our mouth express, our ability to use them consciously transforms consonants and vowels from abstract, arbitrary vocal noises to precise bearers of experience. We now focus on the micro-gestures that produce our vowels.

Speech-exploration 12

1. Consciously place your mouth in the position required by each vowel. Give yourself plenty of time to experience the movements and tensions involved.
2. According to our psycho-physical principles, become aware of the sensation aroused in your soul by those movements and tensions.
3. Now let that sensation permeate your whole body and with your whole body create a form that expresses that sensation. The micro-gesture is now supported by and integrated into the gesture of your whole instrument.
4. Take time to examine the sensation. Can you identify which aspect of your soul life is expressed in that gesture?

The relationship of inner experience to the gestural nature of the vowels can be deepened and broadened through the study of eurythmy. It is important, nonetheless, to make your own discoveries. Following, are some of mine. I present them not as definitive, but to contribute to the investigation.

Meditative exploration of the micro-gestures of the vowels

/ɑː/ (st<u>a</u>r)

My mouth is open with no barriers or boundaries. My jaw drops to its lowest level, my lips relax into that surrender and my tongue falls into the full length of its cradle from back to front. I sense something like the soul state of a child or baby that has not yet learned to fear. Awe, wonder, content, acceptance, are easily evoked. I sense how these emotions can slide into naivety, resignation, sentimental sympathy. I can surrender as much to the dark side of the spectrum as to the light.

/æ/ (m<u>a</u>n)

My jaw moves slightly upwards and the front of my tongue bunches up, moving back to do so. In contrast to the sensation of surrender in /ɑː/ (st<u>a</u>r), my lips tense and, contracting slightly, frame my open mouth with a firm edge. A sensation of alertness!

/e/ (m<u>e</u>n)

Alertness intensifies as the tongue tenses further, flattening its edges that press against the teeth's resistance at the roof of the mouth. To support this action, my jaw moves slightly up and my lips contract further from their previous position, framing the action of the tongue and teeth with an even firmer edge. This gesture has aroused in me a sensation of something like resistance. I awaken further to a sense of separateness which could lean either to aggression or profound attention.

/eə/ (d<u>a</u>re)

This diphthong is our nearest English equivalent to the German pure or simple vowel ä.

   I slide from the tightly formed /e/ (m<u>e</u>n) into the more relaxed sensation of the neutral /ə/ (<u>a</u>way). I have a choice. I can allow the firm edge of /e/ (m<u>e</u>n) to permeate the /ə/ (<u>a</u>way). When I do this, I experience that firmness extend itself into a whole surface with which I meet the world. If I allow the more relaxed /ə/ to work back on the /e/, then I experience a sensation of release, relief, of letting go at last.

/ɪ/ (short as in s<u>i</u>p) and /iː/ (long as in m<u>e</u>)

The gesture in my mouth intensifies still further. The lower jaw rises to its highest position, supporting the edges of the tongue to press firmly against the upper teeth and roof of the mouth. My lips stretch to the left and right into a narrow slit. A sensation of utmost focus and awareness of myself. As a violin string is stretched to the exact pitch of tension which enables it to sound, so too, the string of my own self feels precisely tuned. The gesture arouses sensations of enthusiasm, confidence, a certainty of self that can be present with another without a loss of boundary and so experience an interest which can lead to true compassion. This same gesture can arouse a sense of being over-wakeful, nervous, or tempt me into overweening pride, the arrogance of hubris.

   With this vowel I am firmly established in the middle of my mouth. I am still behind the boundary created by my teeth. A strong sense of myself arises at this centre of the octave.

   Before we move across that boundary towards the front, let us explore the diphthongs which are formed by combinations of the vowels explored thus far.

/eɪ/ (d<u>a</u>te)

I dive into the gesture of this diphthong. It still arouses the same sensations of strong focus and self-awareness which characterize its two component sounds but in the movement between one sound and the other I sense a tiny interval of time in which I can assess my response. This results in a slight sensation of detachment. I am more in control within that sense of separation, less invested, able to consider how to act.

/aɪ/ (l<u>i</u>fe)

This diphthong arises when I move from /ɑː/ (st<u>a</u>r) to /ɪ/ (s<u>i</u>p). If I slide unconsciously from one into the other, my soul wants to dissolve into an infinite horizon and lose herself in sympathy; merge in bliss or someone else's pain. She wants to stroke and to caress. However, if I make this transit consciously, I can permeate the dreamy sensation which accompanies the gesture of the /aː/ with the sensation of extreme self-consciousness arising from the gesture of the /iː/ (m<u>e</u>). To do this means I penetrate what takes place first in time with what will only later be revealed. The capacity to do this reminds me of what Michael Chekhov called the sense of the whole.[*]

It is important to experience both possibilities because this diphthong is so fundamental to an English speaker. It is the personal pronoun, the sacred name which each of us can only utter for ourselves, and designated by the letter 'I'.

Something took place in the consciousness of English-speaking people which caused a transition in the English language from the Saxon 'ich' to the English 'I'. It took several hundred years but, by the time of Shakespeare, the consciousness of self that wanted to unfold within the English language, expressed itself in the diphthong /aɪ/. If we work with gesture and sensation in the way suggested earlier, we can explore these changes.[†]

/ɔ/ (d<u>o</u>t) and /ɔː/ (<u>awe</u>)

As I move from the gesture of /iː/ (m<u>e</u>), behind the teeth, with its clear sensation of a boundary, into the roundness of the lips required to shape the /ɔ/ or /ɔː/, I sense that I move across the threshold of the teeth towards something new. It is as though my lips would stretch right off my face, straining to reach out to surround what lies before me. The gesture in my mouth is one of reaching to embrace and enfold. My tongue moves back and down to settle in my jaw which moves down with it. This gesture attracts into my soul, such emotions as possessiveness, longing, sorrow, tenderness, fulfilment.

---

[*] See *The Art of Acting*, chapter 5.

[†] See chapter 8.

/ɔɪ/ (j<u>oy</u>)

This diphthong arises when I make /ɔ/(d<u>o</u>t) into a launching pad from which to spring into the /ɪ/(s<u>i</u>p). My lips move so quickly from the forward, rounded stretch of /ɔ/ to the back and sideways stretch of /ɪ/. This action is not a simple movement from the one into the other. The second gesture is prepared within the first. The powerful dynamic that results arouses the sensation that I am a tightly coiled spring as it releases or just before it is released. My soul is resonant with exultation and exuberance: j<u>oy</u> at the one extreme, b<u>oi</u>sterous n<u>oi</u>se *at the other. Between, if I AM fully present, I experience a sense of* p<u>oi</u>se, *of finely balanced tensions.*

/œ/ (German ö)

To achieve the micro-gesture for this pure vowel, which does not appear in English, English-speaking people need to place their mouth in the position that they would to speak an /ə/ (d<u>o</u>t) but instead say /e/ (m<u>e</u>n). If we are not accustomed to it, this superimposition of one placement on the other may be uncomfortable. But if we are attentive, it is precisely this uncomfortable sensation that informs us of a delicate, uncertain striving towards something not yet known but dimly sensed. On completion of the journey through our octave we shall appreciate the multi-layered gesture out of which this vowel is born. We may sense how it contains an intimation of the complex, sometimes ambiguous relationship our soul can have towards what is still to be accomplished on its journey. As we do so, we may sense how closely it relates to the English vowels /ə/ (<u>a</u>way) and /ɛ/ (h<u>ea</u>rd).

/ə/ (short as in <u>a</u>way) and /ɛ/ (long as in h<u>ea</u>rd)

The tension in the micro-gesture eases somewhat. I sense I am not so finely tuned as in the /œ/, yet my lips still contract towards the forward, rounded gesture of the /ɔ/ (d<u>o</u>t) or /ɔ/ (<u>awe</u>). The tongue's delicate under-surface comes in contact with the sensitive surface at the bottom of my mouth and the inside surface of the lower teeth and lip. Such a delicate touching of these surfaces awakens in my soul sensations of searching, sensitively feeling the way forward, finding a way into the unknown. No wonder, then, that when I hesitate, experience unc<u>e</u>rtainty *in searching for a word I give expression to it in the exclamation er! I sense vulnerability; how easily I can be* h<u>ur</u>t. *And if I am, the sound seems to* em<u>er</u>ge *from deep down in my guts; a primitive response as though I would* reg<u>ur</u>gitate *what lodged itself so deep inside.*

/y/ (German ü)

We have come to the micro-gesture that corresponds to the seventh in our octave. The correct placement or micro-gesture for this pure vowel is achieved by attempting to say /iː/ (m<u>e</u>) while the mouth is in the position required to speak /uː/ (sh<u>oe</u>). As in the case of /œ/, this results in a superimposition of the shape and structure required to speak the one sound, on the completely different shape and structure required to speak the other. *This time a sensation of unbearable tension is aroused; I sense something in me is refined to the ultimate degree, straining to be puri-fied until the essence is attained.*

/œ/ and /y/ are included in our sequence although their placements are not part of SRE. Yet, the very struggle we English-speakers may encounter with these unfamiliar micro-gestures may well be what wakes us up to the sensations they arouse; as often happens when we cannot take a thing for granted. Without an experience of these sixth and seventh intervals within our octave, our range of soul expression would remain forever lacking in these parts of its spectrum. If we become familiar with these placements, we add these colours to our palate of expression and they provide a framework within which we can explore and understand the English diphthongs which have evolved around them.

Although the pure vowel we identify with the phonetic symbol /y/ and which appears in the German ü (m<u>ü</u>de) does not appear as such in SRE, it is still a feature of the way English is spoken, for example, in Scotland. There, the English /uː/ (sh<u>oe</u>) will be pronounced as /y/, or /duː/ (d<u>o</u>) spoken with a Scottish accent, will be pronounced as /dy/.

The next two diphthongs demonstrate the tendency within the English language to move around the centre of the note, as it were. It is as though the soul, in its need to express ever finer nuances of her experience, feels her way both back and forth around the central placement.

/uɪ/ (sw<u>ee</u>t)

Steiner pointed out to early students of eurythmy that in this combination /ui/ the English-speaker comes closest to the German experience of /y/. This 'diphthong' occurs most commonly in English whenever our spelling of a word includes /w/ followed by an /ɪ/ or /iː/. We remember that /w/ is designated as a glide. It exists just on that edge between our inner and our outer worlds, where the vowel /uː/ and consonant /w/ slide back and forth between each other.

My lips contract and round themselves, straining forward. My tongue arches high at the back of my mouth, sensing keenly that the goal is near but, just before they can achieve the gesture which gives rise to /uː/, my lips pull back to /iː/ and, as they do, they pass through /w/. Somewhere in transition from the /uː/ (sh<u>oe</u>) to /iː/ (m<u>e</u>) I pass through /y/. The sensation generated by this micro-gesture is of utmost delicate refinement.

In these examples, we sense how poets have intuited this 'meaning' of the combi-nation /wiː/:

Not I, Not I, but the <u>wi</u>nd that blows through me.
A fine <u>wi</u>nd is blo<u>wi</u>ng the new direction of time.
If only I let it bear me, carry me.
If only it carry me.
If only I am sensitive, subtle, O a <u>wi</u>nged gift!
If only I yield myself and am carried by that fine, fine <u>wi</u>nd that blows its way through the
    chaos of the world . . .

                          Song of a Man who has Come Through, D.H. Lawrence

How s<u>wee</u>t the moonlight sleeps upon this bank.
Here <u>wi</u>ll <u>we</u> sit and let the sound of music
Creep in our ears. Soft stillness and the night
Become the touches of s<u>wee</u>t harmony.

                                Merchant of Venice, Shakespeare

/juː/ (imb<u>ue</u> or f<u>ew</u>)

The /j/ (<u>y</u>ear) is the other consonant we designate as a glide, existing on that edge between a vowel and consonant. It becomes a part of the English diphthong /juː/ (f<u>ew</u>) when the lips, which are stretched sideways at the teeth to frame the narrow slit of /iː/ (m<u>e</u>), now move towards their most contracted, round and forward place. In following this gesture of our lips from /iː/ to /uː/ (sh<u>oe</u>), we become aware how huge the journey is. If we, then, slide back and forth between this and the previous diphthong we sense how each is the reversal of the other's gesture. Both diphthongs seem to hover back and forth around the seventh placement in the mouth, /y/ (German ü), as though not quite able to commit themselves. Just like the seventh, /juː/ arouses and expresses an uncomfortable tension, as of something unresolved.

We express delivery from extreme discomfort by exclaiming 'phew!' but the exclamation seems to retain a nuance of that near disaster, so narrowly escaped. At one end of the spectrum sensations of repugnance may arise, as when, made aware of certain fumes we want to p<u>u</u>ke or utter 'p<u>ew</u>!' At the other end, sensations of a straining after p<u>u</u>rity and b<u>eau</u>ty that the M<u>u</u>se can ind<u>u</u>ce through certain m<u>u</u>sic. We are aware how the self's striving for a finer sensing of itself, which relates it to the seventh micro-gesture in the octave of the vowels, finds expression in the English diphthong in such phrases as: 'I utterly rep<u>u</u>diate! ref<u>u</u>se absol<u>u</u>tely to coll<u>u</u>de!'

The relationship between the seventh vowel in our octave, these two last diphthongs and this most refined degree of sensing can be experienced in the word: intuit. The final syllables (in-tu-it) require us to move from the one diphthong to the other: in/tjuː‑wɪt/. Within our mouth we sense how we move towards our goal and then away, back towards the feeling of the self that we achieved in /iː/ — thus feeling our way forward to the final step, intuiting what is to come.

/ʊ/ (short as in t<u>oo</u>k) and /uː/ (long as in sh<u>oe</u>)

And now, at last, we reach the goal. *I follow the gesture as my lips strain forward, gathering themselves into the most contracted, tiny rounded opening. The intense driving force, so focused on my lips, forbids any relaxation of intention. Yet I detect a sensation of something that has freed itself from the intensity of what was unresolved in those two last diphthongs.*

The octave is complete. I sense that I am coming and have finally come through. *It is as though what had obstructed me has finally* removed *itself so that my goal is or can, at last, be reached. Anything too* crass, not true, *is sheared away until my soul is able to* pass *through the needle's eye, fit through that tiny aperture formed by my lips. Such a contraction and focusing of self is sustained until the resolution is achieved. The weight of such responsibility is huge, awakening fear and apprehension such as we express in* ooh!

Our journey through the octave of the vowels is complete. Within its compass we have travelled from the primal oneness of the /aː/, through all degrees of separation, arriving in the centre at the conscious experience of self in /iː/. We have experienced how that conscious self then finds its way through a complex interaction of both hesitations and determination. From these arise the stages and degrees by which the self achieves its goal: conscious alignment with the greater Self in /uː/.

And in the diphthong /aʊ/ (<u>ou</u>t*), as I accompany its gesture, I experience the octave. It begins in /ɑː/ with its passage in the mouth open all the way from back to front. It moves through each placement and achieves, at last, the contracted roundness of the lips producing /uː/. I experience in this sound, a sensation of power and fullness, a gesture that embraces all around.*

Each vowel attracts certain feelings and emotions. Yet the vowel itself expresses an archetypal gesture of my soul towards the world, not, in itself, to be identified with a particular emotion. It is as though the gesture, according to its context, acts like a force-field, attracting certain feelings or emotions to its sphere.

This approach allows us to attune our instruments to the infinite expressive possibilities that come about when we can layer each feeling or emotion with the archetypal gesture of each vowel. This layering is most fruitfully explored when we combine Chekhov's 'qualities and sensations' with vowel-work.*

---

* See *The Art of Acting*, chapter 3. See also *The Integrated Actor* to explore the artistic possibilities of this.

Exercises for vowels

Vowels express what lives in our souls. When called upon to speak them in this deeply conscious way, we may feel exposed and wish to hide. If we learn to use the activity of consonants to clothe or house the vowels, these revelations of our inmost soul will not seem so confronting. The opportunities that follow require that we:

- attune ourselves to the fundamental gesture of each vowel
- learn how to let its supporting consonants bear it into space so that its unique soul gesture can permeate each line.

As always, it is the sound and not the spelling which is our guide. In this next exploration, it is the sound /ɑː/ (st<u>a</u>r) that matters.[*]

Speech-exploration 13 — vowel exercises

/ɑː/ (st<u>a</u>r) — stage 1

> the p<u>a</u>rcel m<u>a</u>ster <u>a</u>sks mail
> r<u>a</u>ther m<u>a</u>rshal cr<u>a</u>fty K<u>a</u>rl

Each line becomes a stream into which the ongoing gesture of /ɑː/ can pour. The first syllable *the* can seem unimportant, as though the real content of the line only begins with *parcel*. Yet the stream of the first line needs to be gathered as a whole and launched as a whole by that fiery, voiced 'th'. *The* is then an integral part of the line and not left behind inside the mouth. This teaches us that commitment to project our vowel into space begins with the very first syllable and doesn't 'kick in' only later.

The /p/ which follows can then open up a channel into which its companion /ɑː/ and the succeeding syllables can pour. Each consonant supports the /ɑː/ connected to it, allowing it to radiate its soul nuance. When we have discovered how the consonant's activity can clothe a vowel and launch it into space, we are ready to tackle vowels unsupported by a consonant. This is what *asks* requires of us in the first line. Into the channel prepared by what has gone before, the clear streaming /ɑː/ of *asks* can pour, this time held in its course by the consonants at the other end of the syllable.

The transition from /ɑː/ (p<u>a</u>rcel) to /ei/ (m<u>ai</u>l) can be used to practise, either:

a) imbuing the final diphthong /ei/with the quality of /ɑː/.
b) achieving the shift in gesture from the vowel to the diphthong within the flow of a single line.

_____

[*]Americans may wish to replace some words with appropriate equivalents.

The second line rides on the completely different dynamic of the airy 'r', allowing the sequence of /ɑː/sounds to cascade in a light-filled arc through the space.

/ɑː/ (st<u>a</u>r) — stage 2

> A bra da ka bra
> Ra ba da ka bra
> Bra da ka ra ba
> Ka da ra bra ba

Rudolf Steiner

Here we have the opportunity to let each launching consonant reveal a different aspect of /ɑː/. Each vowel should be spoken in the long form /ɑː/ (st<u>a</u>r). This Speech-exploration is an opportunity to integrate the four elements and can be fruitfully combined with Chekhov's qualities-of-movement.[*] At a later stage it can be integrated with the Speech-explorations into character-creation and suggestions Steiner made relating to the temperaments.[†]

Floating/phlegmatic	A bra da ka bra
Flying/sanguine	Ra ba da ka bra
Moulding/melancholic	Bra da ka ra ba
Radiating/choleric	Ka da ra bra ba

/eɪ/ (d<u>a</u>te)

This English rendering of the German original requires us to play with a range of English diphthongs that gather around the pure vowel /e/ (m<u>e</u>n) which only appears in the English word *bending*. Aim for the pure placement first and then use this as a basis for broadening the related diphthongs.

> l<u>a</u>y b<u>e</u>nding v<u>a</u>rious tr<u>ay</u>s
> f<u>a</u>cing d<u>ay</u>s l<u>a</u>bour
> v<u>a</u>rious l<u>a</u>bour tr<u>ay</u>s
> l<u>a</u>y b<u>e</u>nding f<u>a</u>cing

---

[*] See *The Art of Acting*, chapters 1 and 4.
[†] See *The Integrated Actor*, Of Humans and Other Beings.

/ɪ/ (sip), /iː/ (me) and /eɪ/ (date)

These lines teach us to achieve the sharp edged clarity of the vowels formed in the middle of our instrument:

> quickly finished veered each
> it irritates labours phases
> it irritates labours phases
> veered each quickly finished

/ɔ/ (dot), /ɔː/ (awe), /ɔe/ (door), /ʊ/ (took) and /uː/ (shoe)

These lines are built around the range of vowels formed at the front of our instrument:

> storm wolf roars forth
> through door and tomb
> bold wolves bored
> through door and tomb
> doom taught wolves bored
> through door and tomb

/ɔɪ/ (joy) and /aɪ/ (life)

These lines ask us to move back and forth between two of our most common diphthongs.

> eye is viceless
> viceless is eye
> blithe is noise in Troy
> noise in Troy is blithe
> the night is broidered
> broidered nightly

These Speech-explorations are designed to help us learn how to en-soul the vowels, in accordance with their archetypal gestures. The next Speech-explorations invite us to en-soul the vowels, but now within a meaningful, specific content that calls forth one of the soul nuances or moods expressed by each vowel. Any text we speak is likely to contain a range of vowels, some of which suggest different and even quite contrasting qualities. Now we learn to recognize a dominant vowel mood, permeating all the other sounds with its unique vowel-colour, sustaining it throughout the text.

Speech-exploration 14 (DL)

/ɑː/ (st_ar)

> Be calm, O startled heart!
> Watch how the trees
> all hushed in wonder
> with star touching branches
> can do you no harm.

/æ/ (m_an) and /e/ (m_en)

> Lest we forget, remember
> that no man is bad that is not sad.
> He cannot tell the facts of why
> he is not well. Yet acts in hell
> have made him mad – if he could tell.

/eɪ/ (d_ate)

> Awaken to your own true name.
> Create your fate through self-hood's flame.

/ɪ/ (s_ip) and /iː/ (m_e)

> Greet the sun with feet that sing,
> ears that glisten, eyes that listen.
> See! the trees have leafed in spring.

/ɔ/ (d_ot), /ɔː/ (_awe) and /oʊ/ (n_o)

> Soft starlight falls from the skies vaulted dome.
> Love's candle warm is calling me home.

/e/ (m_en) and /eə/ (d_are)

> Where O where is a place so fair
> that there I may rest my head?

/ɛ/ (h_eard)

Tragic mood

> Where were you when the earth received its hurt?
> Murderous birds of death
> purging us, purging us
> to a further birth.

Comic mood

Things once bad, when turned to verse
can only go from bad to worse
making our expressions terse.

/uɪ/ (sweet)

Winter stars that wink and twinkle
make me wish a wish.
I wish that I could feel their twinkles
glowing sweetly
deep within.

/juː/ (few), /ɪə/ (ear) and /eə/ (dare)

Once they knew:
abused stupid senses
no more can hear
pure music of the spheres.
In perfumed air
listening ears
fewer and fewer.

/ʊ/ (took) and /uː/ (shoe)

Soon, too soon, the true music dies.
Once full, now faded, how gloomy the skies,
till through its pull, we choose to arise.

/aɪ/ (life)

In the sky spirits fly.
On the earth people die,
lovers sigh, children cry.
Why Oh why? Lullaby!

/ɔɪ/ (joy)

Say boldly, loudly,
'Ahoy!' with boisterous joy.
Then join the toil of the moist oyster;
the loitering beauty of its poise.

Julie Brodeur

/aʊ/ (<u>ou</u>t) and /aʊə/ (designated as a triphthong as in h<u>our</u>)

> ... Now!
> Hour by hour
> most delicate flower
> or mighty sun flower
> is drawn by your power.
> How? Wow!

Mixed

> Brighter wider wielding over this land.
>
> These leafless trees awaken in the spring.
>
> We are here, we are there
> we ride in the air
> in the flame of the sun beams dancing.
> We are white, we are bright
> we spirits of light
> on the shafts of the morning glancing   Maud Surrey

Speech-exploration 15 (DL)

The following sequences of common exclamations and simple phrases reveal the intimate connection between our soul-life and the vowels. Based as they are upon the octave of the vowels, we can practise them as scales which encourage our psycho-physical constitution (bodies, mouths and souls) to move through their whole range of experience and expression.

Exclamations arising out of the English vowel octave

> Ah! Ha!
> Drat!
> Hey!
> See!
> Whee!!
> God!
> Oh! Oh, no!
> Er!
> Sweet!
> Pew! Phew!
> Look! Pooh! Boo!

Exclamations arising out of diphthongs

Yeah! There, there!
Yai Yai Yai!
Hoy!
Wow! Ouch!

Sequence of common phrases based on the octave of the vowels

Ha! A star!
Drat! Take that!
Hey! Awake!
Silly Billy! See! It's me!
Going home.
Er! That hurt!
You absolute twit!
Phew! It's you!
True, too true!
Well, well, well!
Why that sigh?
O Boy! What joy!
Wow! It's now!

The total instrument: body, soul, spirit, voice

It is possible to experience a disconnection between the acting, Speech and movement modalities in which we train. Each requires its own discrete time and process, yet this should not lead to a situation where the emotional depth generated in an acting class, for instance, finds no organic connection to the way of working with the voice or text. Chekhov's psycho-physical approach creates an arena where these discrete streams of work can fuse; in fact, can be experienced as one. After all, we cannot make a sound without a movement; in the larynx and speech organs, at the very least. Within the context of a psycho-physical training, we shall learn how to experience that movement not only in our sensing, moving body, but also in our soul. Likewise, sensations in our soul will come to be experienced as movements in our body. This body may become so finely tuned that we shall sense those movements even into the micro-gestures of our larynx and speech organs.

In these initial stages we can nurture this awareness of ourselves as a totality composed of body, soul, spirit and voice, together making us an instrument for language by:

- The study of *eurythmy*; the art of movement introduced by Rudolf Steiner. His experience of eurythmy led Michael Chekhov to understand that full-bodied archetypal gesture is central to the actor's art. Through the practise of eurythmy, the whole body learns to consciously participate in archetypal gestures of the sounds of Speech and tones of music. Through these we may begin to sense that we ourselves have been created by them.
- Integrating *qualities-of-movement* with the consonants.[*]
- Integrating *qualities and sensations* with the work with vowels and body-soul gestalt, just now explored.[†]

Chekhov's goal was to create a path by which the actor's instrument might become that 'sensitive membrane' which can both receive and then transmit the subtlest impulses of soul and spirit. Our instrument for Speech, if integrated with the actor's total instrument, becomes part of such a membrane.

The marriage of vowel and consonant
With rare exceptions, we cannot speak a word without combining vowel and consonant. In the context of our current explorations, a word, and therefore meaning,

---

[*] See *The Art of Acting*, chapter 1.
[†] See *The Art of Acting*, chapter 3.

implies a marriage between outwardness and inwardness. If we impose a form without inwardness or soul, it leads to cold technique. We can equally observe how strong emotions not permeated by formative activity strike us as raw or sentimental.

What does this mean for speaking? Can we speak so that the inwardness inherent in the vowels is formed and penetrated by the active forces of the consonants? Or to express this in reverse: so that the strength and clarity of form provided by the consonants is both warmed and filled by the inner life inherent in the vowels.

To achieve this, we would need to bring a consciousness to speaking which is extraordinary. It would require that I AM present in every sound I utter. To strive for such a goal might appear to hold us hostage to some abstract demand requiring pedantic obedience. I hope the journey undertaken in this chapter might, rather, awaken both excitement and desire to plunge into an engaging world — a world I liken to white water rafting, which I have only had the courage to do once. Participants learn to surrender to an elemental power which is anything but dull and abstract. At the same time, they remain totally awake to make the highly skilled split-second choices they confront at every moment. There is no time to hold on to the past or dwell upon the future; only to be in the present moment, now and now and now and now and now.

The role of the syllable

To achieve the equivalent of white water rafting in the act of speaking, we need to understand the role of syllables. Generally, each vowel will form a syllable with the consonants immediately linked to it. O-ften a sy-lla-ble will con-sist of a vo-wel sandwiched be-tween two or more con-so-nants. But not al-ways. It might be a vo-wel which stands a-lone, or one which has a con-so-nant be-fore or af-ter it. Generally, the sounds that join, forming what we call a syllable, are those that flow together with a sense of ease, both in our mouth and to our ear.

To form a syllable with consciousness means two things:

1. The vowel is grasped by its accompanying consonants and held within the vessel that they form.
2. Those consonants are en-souled by the vowel for which they are responsible.

The vowel cannot perform its role unless it is free to reveal the nuance of its inwardness within the form the consonant provides; not only once in a single syllable, but continuously as demanded by the flow of language. We will accomplish this only if we can sustain our focus for as long as needed in a continuous act requiring us, again and again, to be present as we form each syllable, and let it go. For only when we free ourselves from what has gone before, are we available to grasp the next impulse. The quality of presence required for this seems almost beyond our present capabilities.

Until we experience each sound as a spiritual activity with the potential to convey not only information, but to communicate *experience* which unfolds in time and space, the goal of grasping each new syllable will seem pedantic. But, made as it is of sounds, a syllable is nothing less than a vessel *for* that experience. Syllables are the building blocks from which our words are made. They are the pieces without which we cannot shape the expanding jigsaw puzzle of experience encompassed by each word, phrase, sentence, paragraph, whole text.

One language

The story of the tower of Babel suggests there was a time when human beings spoke one language.[14] Is it fanciful to suggest that we have never lost that language but only forgotten it? Perhaps the sounds *are* that one archetypal language: the language spoken before Babel, and understood and spoken still by every child before its speech is shaped, sometimes exclusively, within the mother tongue? To work with speech in the way I am suggesting may well awaken in us a sense of such a universal language, regardless of the one in which we express our everyday experience. It may lead us to an Art of Speech that is not abstract and detached from the language we speak but arises organically out of it and leads us deeply into it.

To work with consonants and vowels in this way will sensitize our whole instrument. They will build in us a 'body of sensibilities' that can respond to an expanding range of impulses within the macrocosm and the microcosm; from the universe outside and that within. This 'body' will grant access to a broader, deeper range of experience than the actor's or Speech artist's personal biography, on its own, can offer.[15]

Speech-exploration 16

Experience the consonants and vowels through the art of eurythmy.

Speech-exploration 17

1. Go into the world of nature. Listen to the sounds of wind, water, fire and animals. Listen into the heart of rocks and trees. Touch the surfaces of things. Experience the different textures. Open as many different senses as you can.
2. Imagine you are Eve or Adam, with the task of naming things. Do not use known language. Discover which consonants express these phenomena. Which vowels most express your soul's response? Experiment with putting them together and creating names for your experience. Perhaps you will find different names for different aspects of the 'thing'. Is it possible to find one name that includes all aspects of the 'thing' ?

3. Go back to the names you know. Can you de-construct them and reconstruct the journey of experience that brought those names about. What experience has been condensed into the consonants and vowels of which each name is made? Can you release it?
4. Can you speak the word in such a way that re-creates that experience?

Speech-exploration 18

Take each consonant in turn to be a subject for your focus, for a day or week or whatever length of time feels fruitful.

1. Get to know it. Where does its gesture and dynamic, or its actual sound, express itself around you in the world?
2. Gather words that contain that sound, whether at the beginning, middle or end. Can you develop a sense for the way that sound contributes to your language?
3. Imagine your language without that sound. What aspects of experience could not find expression without it?

Speech-exploration 19

1. Create short phrases which convey the essence or spirit of each sound, such as:

   Fan flickering flames
   Sneak softly inside

2. Create a poem inspired by the spirit of each consonant; form it from words in which that consonant appears.

Speech-exploration 20

1. Observe the exclamations that we use.
2. Which vowel predominates? Can you discern the state of soul which finds expression in that vowel?
3. Take each vowel in turn and identify what inner mood gives rise to it.
4. Speak a word which has a strong clear vowel, such as *star* or *hate*. What mood of soul is expressed in that vowel?

   a) Let that mood of soul affect the way you speak that vowel.
   b) Let that vowel quality permeate the way you speak the word.
   c) Create and speak a poem based on the vowel of your choice and which communicates some aspect of that vowel's mood.

Speech-exploration 21

1. Find examples in poetry, drama or story where the writer uses a consonant or vowel in such a way that it conveys the experience.
2. Experiment with how to speak the text so that you reveal that sound's capacity to re-create experience.

INTERNATIONAL COSMIC ALPHABET (ICA)

Consonants and vowels

Rational consciousness observes that what we call a *consonant* is formed when the speech organs forming it, cause a momentary, partial or complete stoppage of the breath. The breath is then released and, along with it, the sound. It may be voiced or unvoiced. What we call a *vowel*, on the other hand, results when those same speech organs shape the breath without obstructing it. It is always voiced.

The explorations in chapter 1 are designed to awaken our experience of this difference at another level. At this level, I have made an *imaginative journey through the sounds* that compose our alphabet (not to be confused with the letters), though not in the accepted order. My guidance on this path has been an imagination Rudolf Steiner gave in the first lecture of the series, *Eurythmy as Visible Speech*.[16] There he invites us to contemplate the possibility that the totality of sounds comprising human speech embodies the range of activity that creates our universe. 'And God *said*: Let there be…'. I have called this range of activity, the International Cosmic Alphabet (ICA).[*]

In addition, Steiner invites us to imagine that these creative powers, spread throughout the macrocosm, express themselves as a totality within the microcosm of the human being. Of course, by 'human being' he does not mean the limited everyday consciousness an individual has of itself. Such consciousness perceives itself to be a separate 'thing', a material body enclosed within a skin. As such, it feels forever disconnected from the whole in which it 'lives and moves and has its being'. He is referring to the Human Being glimpsed in the opening verses of St John's Gospel.

The act of creation — an imaginative journey

With this in mind, I accepted Steiner's invitation to consider that the sounds of speech express activity of *divine creative beings*.[†] I have taken the most common English

---

[*] First suggested by Dr Alduino Mazzone.

[†] The order has not been chosen arbitrarily and in *The Integrated Actor* we shall recognize them as the Ones whose powers reveal themselves to our perception as the starry worlds that we have named the zodiac and planets.

sounds to be my starting point. Each one is a window through which I can experience an aspect of creation; in trust that my creativity is one expression of that greater macrocosmic creativity which becomes conscious of itself within the microcosm of my consciousness.

When we experience the world as object, we think we know it very quickly. This is because there is a limit to perception when we see only surfaces. When we open our heart, the journey to know another being is infinite. Like Bottom's dream in Shakespeare's, *A Midsummer Night's Dream*, it 'hath no bottom!'. It reveals behind the so-called finished world of nature, a world of infinite being; one that our 'cool reason', on its own, can never 'apprehend', dismissing it as 'antique fable' and of the same stuff as lunacy.[17] So it is with the beings of the sounds. It may seem impossible, on the basis of our everyday experience of speech, to have any conception of such things. Perhaps you are a reader who has never thought of sounds in this way. If so, I invite you to explore them with me, play with the magic *if* and entertain a 'willing suspension of [your] disbelief'.[18]

A meditative journey through the sounds

Short vowel /ʊ/ (t<u>oo</u>k) and long vowel /uː/ (sh<u>oe</u>)

Soon
Creator,
soon
it will be time to do what world-dreaming
asks of you,
gathering forever.
Foreboding looms, even terror
moves in you.
Fool!
Who are you
to think you could
to think you should?

World-breath
Creator,
pull oh pull
infinity inside of you;
its wind whistle through your cheek's narrow sides
into the finite nooks
the who of you.

Your actor-tongue
versatile, bows low, grants passage through.

Lips
guardians of outside and within
a small round precision tool
contract into —
inaudible to earthly ears —
vast canyon's unborn whistle.

You creator, you alone
can push it, push your own breath through,
vibrate the chords,
deliver from the silent tomb
birthing from your voice's womb
reverberate
against your cheek's narrow sides — contracted cave —
this primal ancient vowel Rune.

/uː/ illumining the doom,
reveals your mood, Creator,
the infinite inside
and truth of you.

Consonants /w/, /v/ and /ʍ/(<u>wh</u>en)

Creator makes a move.
Different energy takes hold . . .
Lips and tongue infused —
vigour of intention.
Breath
blow harder
/uː/ too long within
whip through cavern of contracted cheeks
brush past lips

turn /uː/ to /w/ to /ʍ/,
whip the wind and reign it in —
what was so long within will out —
breath, strong, drives upper teeth against the lip below —
Vibrate the chords!
Creator's voice unveil!
/v/

We who through vowel first become aware
of what Creator feels
are now aware through consonant
of what Creator does —

breath makes winds and waters, waves,
breath weaves, breath warms —
life breathes.
Creation has begun.

The long vowel /ɑː/ (st__a__r)

Ah!
We with lower jaw collapsing see
tongue surrender in its cradle
all the way, lips wide —
a path!

Breath's wonder wave breaks through —
almost /ɑː/ before we hear it,
woven we aware are in, within a greater /ɑː/
such vast within
are on our way at last!

No doubt what Creator feels —
we within Creator's heart.

In this imaginative journey two different kinds of sounds emerge. The vowels emerge from inside the perceiving, feeling soul, expressing inwardness. The consonants express the forces and dynamics we perceive are active in the outer world.

Rolled or trilled consonant r /ɾ/, vowels /e/ (m__e__n), /æ/ (m__a__n) and diphthong /eɪ/ (d__a__te)

On a roll!

Breath —
wilder warmed into vibration
how, discover how
to stir to wilder roaring torrents, churnings?
Roll the r! /ɾ/ P__r__onounce its __r__oughness!
Tip of tongue d__r__um ha__r__d on palate taut above.
But who that d__r__ummer?

Who the sort of person dare
so fierce to strive with nature's fierceness?
Struggle to resist
harsh northern air,
assert, survive annihilation,
reject lips softer comforts,
resist forever
weaker English /r/!
Refinement?
Never! rather be a Scot!
Let tongue's drum roll reverberate!
power to transform —
rise from the grave —
resurrect.

Not sit and wait.

Vibrate the chords!

Permeate with tension that's awake —
jaw flattens,
muscles tense along mouth's sides;
tongue rise up, flat and hard.
Aware of feeling different inside;
made of sterner stuff.

Substance evaporates,
becomes invisible.
See through it,
seeing through the rapidly vibrating airy element into transparent breeze and hurricane,
ourselves we breathe it in
and out again.
Cosmos is a bellows,
blowing, fanning, feeding warmth original.

As though the earth in fast thick pants were breathing

                                                        Kubla Khan, Coleridge

Consonant /h/

Hot,
hotter —
lungs a furnace

heaven to hell,
hell to heaven —

huge the hope —
huge the horror;
hardly heave of breath between them,

heart's heat heaped without defining.

Consonant /f/, short vowel /ɪ/ (sip) and long vowel /iː/ (me)

Teeth,
lips,
strike flint, transform,
intensify to finely focus,
fire
directed with precise intention,
manifest my first and future self
in flame.

Metamorphosis evolving me!

Cave's roof, hard palate, sky delete —
tongue strains against
pressing hard
would push it through to see,
to reach again that distant flame;

lips stretch
tighten;
sideways slit for self to squeeze through —

on its way to
each atom of me finely tuned,
precision shaped for sensing —
me —
/ɪ/ and /iː/,
birthed in necessity —
in need of being free.

If only I am keen and hard like the sheer tip of a wedge
Driven by invisible blows
The rock will split . . .

Song of a Man who has Come Through, D.H. Lawrence

Consonants /t/, /d/, /ð/ (voiced <u>the</u>) and /θ/ (unvoiced – <u>thing</u>)

Whereas when I
(thinks Creator)
feel myself more Deutsch,
in every /d/ of every der, die, das,
the light in every article has faded.
But yet a moving back and forth between
I sense a breathing between /t/ and /d/,
light and dark. I travel, easily, between
degrees of still un-manifest and manifest.
Blood moves through lungs,
oxygen enlightened,
distributing then losing light,
becoming dark – dioxide-carbonned,
breath delivering the darkness, death.
Creator breathes into exist.
The things exist, transform
then into darkness disappear . . .

Intent!
Fire and light drive down
into the void –
focused intensity, ferocity –

Matter generate!
Startle into light!

Have you heard in /t/ light tinkle
tip of tongue delicately trip on palate,
matter teasing from resistance?

Vibrate the chords!
Heard, as matter densifies, light die, in voice solidify?
In /d/the flame creating spirit disappeared.

What do you inhabit now –
Creator of the world,
of finished things?

What to call this –
pressing tongue tip firmly just behind the teeth,
satisfied creating boundaries between each dinge;

der, die das —
this tendency?

Deutsch decide on; step inside it.
But not yet completely do you dare Creator
utterly condemn that light to fade.

Experiment!
Tongue tip peep through teeth,
blow softly mist ethereal
endowing things with softer edge,
there ... there ... the ... the;
trying to describe, define
this tendency of thin diffuseness,
this ... what to call this ...
not letting things hit ground with thunder thud —
still let them have a little light,
a little breath,
a lisp of softness still at least around them.
retaining th at least for some things?
What to call this strange sensation?
Englishness.

Long vowel /aː/ (st<u>ar</u>)

Wonder-gasp! that light years fast —
from distant past
should come to rest, at last
condensed in matter —
all surrounding it —
still vast.

Short vowel /o/ (d<u>o</u>t) and the diphthong /ɔː/ (<u>a</u>we)

Wanting —
to embrace,
enfold,
lips —
like limbs to hold and mould—
hearts warmth pouring forth —
on breath from inmost soul —
/ɔː/

Consonants /b/ and /p/

But —
observing deeply world condensed, become —
object;
into being, pass away, oblivion.

Gesture of embracing /b/
enclosing,
bearing inwards —

Battle with —
eternally in tension with —

pushing outwards pressure; /p/ explodes into invisible;
build up substance —
bud becoming embryo and baby —
pushing outwards, bearing inwards; partners wrestling both with equal power,
being born, bring forth potential.

Diphthongs /ɛ/ (h<u>ea</u>rd) /juː/ (f<u>ew</u>) and /uɪ/ (sw<u>ee</u>t) /eə/ (d<u>a</u>re)[*]

Recurring universe
of stars exploding new into external fact,
withdrawing where?
Abstractions vacuum, flower
into poetry?

Empty atoms yearn for —
distant beautiful?

World's sweet breath emerging unattended?

Storms unfurling swirling round her fragile crust
a vacant whistling wind, not full of soul as we?

What vowels does she share with us —
of what is she aware, this goddess Gaia?
Birth and death's eternal turning —
can a planet care?

First shoots straining to emerge —
/ɛ/

---

[*] German oe/ö, German ue/ü, German ä.

/juː/ pursue —
push through to birth, to resolution, beauty's search.

Release, relief —
/eə/
a prayer of gratitude!

What dared was once
Sweet victory can now be shared!

Out of winter's heart, earth's rising spring!

Diphthong /ɔɪ/ (j<u>oy</u>)*

Creator's tongue
jaw
revolving,
holding —
lips at first enfolding deep acceptance of the /ɔ/
rising spirit of the /ɪ/, lips twist and coil,
squeeze into a sideways slit,
tongue ascends to sense the tension,
rounded lips no longer hold
this coiled spring
this choice
poised ready to release —
the diphthong /ɔɪ/!
Joy!

Review the sets of twins /d/ and /t/, /b/ and /p/

Ready to review creation!
two sets of twins
/d/ and /t/
alternate their gifts;
one dark,
the other, filled with light;
/b/ and /p/
wrestling,
striving

---

* Refer IPA (see page 18) /ɪ/ (s<u>i</u>p); /ɔ/ (d<u>o</u>t).

battling to upset – the balance –
of each other's power.

Within each pair, each
separate identity
one
earthy,
one, partaking of its partner's density –
yet tinged with fire.

Fused consonants /ts/ (pe<u>ts</u>)* and /ks/ (ro<u>cks</u>)

Experiments!
Fuse elements!
Bring together earth and fire!

fox eyes glisten in the night
earth and fire in balance tight
fire that makes and unmakes rocks
earth exploding with the shocks

fire fierce enough to sear earth's crust
first strikes at earth's resistance
bounces then
ignites!

single object
then another –
plural objects

see how /s/ unites!
mere accidents of chance perception –
or
results of clear intention?

Affricates /tʃ/ (<u>ch</u>ild) and /dʒ/ (<u>j</u>udge)

Press fire further into earth,
shower of spirits shine in /sh/
edging deeper voice engaging
pressures density of /d/
engraving, gouging into voice resistant,

---

* German /z/.

shine submerged in
merged in sludge completely,
from which will I ever budge,
to just in time
emerge from tragedy

knowledge,
judgement generate?

will children's cheerful mischief reach me?
childhood chatter chuckle at its chance of richness
flush of voice still undescended sh
and only on its way to
catch the t explode and
touch me?

Consonant /s/

Creator —
tongue tip presses subtle
so intense
against the teeth ridge,
senses —
slides inside the skin's most secret,
centre of its breath
a scalpel,
spirit's essence seeks itself in every aspect,
starting sensitive beware,
lest in certainty our soul slip —
steep abyss,
swift descent across ice surface,
slicing through the heartless waste.

In the stillness,
mercy soft as snowflakes stirs,
slides across the silken silence —

Vowel /ɛ/ (h<u>ea</u>rd)

Learning further —

Maker of the universe
firmly turning and unfurling,

burning galaxies,
universe extending further
ever bigger, ever greater,
/ɛ/
expressing certainty, no limits to eternity.
Can I keep my centre?

Doubt!
To hurt, to err?
Turn around, reverse, return.
Perception purged, rendered purer, finer.
/ɛ/now tentative, at first uncertain —

how to work on solar systems so minute,
so tiny molecules of snowflakes hurling,
wild-flower's petals whirling; murmur miracles!
first micro-galaxies emerging-filigrees of nerves for serving
consciousness to recognize —
itself.

Diphthongs /uɪ/ (sw<u>ee</u>t), /juː/ (f<u>ew</u>)

Phew!
/juː/
Close call!
So cold —
Unless —

love

humble searching of the /ɛ/
exquisite sensing of the /uɪ/
pure beauty of the /juː/

Without awe, without reverence, without soul,
mysteries exposed by scalpel,
seek and slice, reduced by /s/
to accurate analysis but lacking love.

Consonants /k/ and /g/

Creator recognizes: chaos calls, is coming closer —
technology can crack an atom.
Look Daddy! Cain can clever kill!

/k/

Consonant encapsulating cosmos uncontrolled,
can cause earth's continents to shake,
catastrophe and cataclysmic quake,
crash past guardians to risk, to take.

Guilt cracks open.

Conscience carves, agony engraves, engages, digging deeper into voice, gripping into
grave engulfing —

metamorphose through resistance,
gaining stronger ground of being,
gift of grain now golden growing,
grace of God's engraving me.

Can!

Controlled,
I can create again,
accomplish,
kiss, caress
creation.

Consonants /l/ and /ł/ (wall)

At last for life to blossom —
let me?
If I bombard, crack, attack with/k/,
resistant atoms,
can I ever get them back,
to link them, move them, ever make them into —
molecules,
make matter yield, like clay?

Dissolve all elements to water.
Liquefy,
melting all of fixed and hard,
malleable make
at last.
Evolve! I will.

Consonant /m/

Musing on my kingdom:
how I minerals might mould

and making into water mixing them to mud,
how I molten mountains out of matter,
making elements to mingle,
marry in my mind?
How I make my lips to warm and life-sustaining
then embrace their living form?
/m/ —
My home.

Diphthong /aɪ/ (li̲fe)

Arriving
sighing,
stroking sky
It's like...
Awe and wonder's /aː/ slides easily to
conscious presence of my
me
in /iː/

Soul,
spreads forever,
knowing now it cannot die;
feeling free enough to try, to fly, to question —
why?

To know myself an I.

Consonant /n/

Conundrum contemplate: how enter into
and invest myself entirely in my creation?
How, once invested can I know what I create?
Can I both be in and out myself at once?
At one with, yet observing;
conscious and yet willing
to surrender to unconscious hints, half whisperings; inspired beyond unknowing,
known?

Press tongue tip firmly, lean on
ridge behind my upper teeth.
Printing tongue tip, penetrating, sensing,
needing clarity and distance

strike back off its launching pad,
like lightning, push away.
Observe now
from a distance, understand.

Through /n/,

I can
united with my own creation,
vanish from my own perception.
Consider universe, phenomena,
finished, only void of being;
cannot recognize myself; no longer.

Yet, outside myself
entirely I look with love,
and never interfere,
wait patiently to be invited.

Aum Om: the beginning and the end...

In my beginning is my end. I give to you this mantra of my own becoming. Our
journey, encompassing the alphabet, Alpha and Omega, beginning and the end,
expresses its completion in the mantra *aum*. In *aum* the serpent bites its tail, the wheel
completes its circle.

Travel round.

Move from furthest back,
the /ɑː/ beginning past,
furthest forward through to
of what lies ahead;
focused consciousness of /uː/
Midway on the path from far to through
stop o stop and hold it
hold the centre /ɔ/
Behold and balance /ɑː/ and /uː/,
beginning, end,
and then pass through
resolve them into membrane /m/,
marking boundary yet passage through.
In my end is my beginning, /aum/

Chapter 2

The Breath of Life

...and to know the very breath of man
as cosmic substance actively at work within him...[19]

Any textbook on speech informs us of the way voice is produced, somewhat as follows:

> We expel air from our lungs. It passes through our larynx, or voice-box, which is situated in the wind-pipe or trachea, causing the vocal chords or folds to vibrate. These vibrations cause the stream of breath to vibrate. This vibrating air stream moves into the mouth where tongue and palate, teeth and lips shape it into different consonants and vowels. The resulting vibrations, subsequently reinforced within the resonating chambers of the throat and mouth and nasal cavities, transmitted through the ears to our brains, are perceived as sound. These sounds can be observed as wavelengths in laboratories of physicists. According to increasing or decreasing amplitude, these wavelengths will be heard as loud or soft. According to increasing or decreasing frequency, wavelengths will be heard as sounds of high or lower pitch.

From the physical perspective then, our voice and speech depend on breath. Yet breath is not only air-pressure which sets soundwaves in motion. At each stage, the physical aspects of speech are affected by our states of consciousness. A change in our emotions, for example, will affect our breathing and dramatically alter the degree of tension in the organs that participate in forming speech. These changed conditions determine the qualities of wavelengths heard as changes in the voice.

Transforming the substance of the voice

A student, still struggling to play the violin, draws the bow across the string. The tone pierces our ears and makes us wince. An artist plays the same note and the tone becomes transparent, piercing our hearts. So too, in normal speech our voices are too dense to reflect the myriad nuances of inwardness. To become expressive, they must be rendered into such a fine vibration that the earthly tone of voice becomes transparent, revealing only soul. We achieve such levels of vibration if we grasp the vowel with the spiritual activity required to form the consonants connected to it. The vowel will then be swept into the orbit of the consonant, so to speak, and move along with it.

The German word for 'word' is *wort*, pronounced as *vort*. When we speak both *word* and *wort* we sense the connection *words* have with what the English language calls a *vortex*.[20] Our aim is for a word to be transparent, revealing the experience it names. To achieve this, consonant gathers vowel and spins it into the vortex of its own activity, dissolving the opaqueness of the voice as it goes.

Figure 5 – Van Gogh (detail from Starry Night)

Transparency

Through mastery of the laws inherent in their chosen medium, the artist strives to render that medium transparent; for through transparency our inspirations are revealed. So it is that in the hands of Michelangelo, cold marble seems to live and breathe. In the painting of a Rembrandt or Van Gogh, the colours seem to shine with inner light, the life of being. By placing tones in various relationships, a Beethoven can move our souls.

The Art of Acting explores a path by which an actor's medium, the body/soul gestalt, might achieve its version of that same transparency — enabling it to be a mirror for the subtlest nuances of our experience. It is the purpose of *The Art of Speech* to indicate a path by which we might achieve this same transparency in speaking. The speaking voice needs no training to reflect the mundane, ordinary world of everyday reality. But what would be required to shape an instrument that could, through speech, communicate the spectrum of experience? If we sense that spectrum in the world of consonants and vowels, can we train ourselves to listen, to know, to be receptive to their qualities; available to let them stream through us, to join our wills with theirs?

Shaky vowels

This asks the ultimate activity of spirit from the speaker. Along the path to achieve this, the vibrations may not be fine enough. This may cause — horror of horrors! — the vowels to shake. However, once the activity which produces the vibration has been mastered, like the spinning earth itself, a word can move with such intensity that it appears still. As always, when that final stage of mastery has been achieved, it will seem effortless. Yet those who have attempted the impossible know it is:

> A condition of complete simplicity
> Costing not less than everything.

Little Gidding, T.S. Eliot

Such an Art of Speech requires a different use of *breath*.

Consequences for the theatre of present breathing habits

Breath and our feeling life

It is well-known in psychotherapeutic work that we become aware of our emotions when we allow ourselves to breathe. One way to protect ourselves from feeling anything too deeply is to suppress our breathing. In this way we stifle emotions and push them down into the subconscious.

The modern media's capacity to make us aware of what is painful in the world no doubt contributes to a cultural unwillingness to feel too much. Think of newsreaders, smiling reassuringly as they report the latest atrocity in a voice detached from emotion, using just enough breath to convey the basic information. The speech patterns that surround us in our western affluent world reflect this tendency. Because we do not want to feel too deeply, we do not breathe too deeply. We breathe just enough to stay alive and for our speech to convey, from intellect to intellect, the information we consider necessary to survive and function.

Of course, it is not possible to completely deny our feelings or emotions on the occasions when we wish to communicate warmth or passion; things which we consider to be significant. Without the fullness of breath that enables us to permeate our speech with fullness of intention and experience, we resort to stressing or emphasizing certain words. To convey a particular point with intensity, I push the vowel by tensing up my throat and, as though it is something separate to be added on, poke that intensity into the intended word.

What can actors do when an entire passage requires warmth of feeling? 'Emphasis' will not suffice. We do experience the need to communicate emotional intensity, yet language itself and importantly, our speech, seem emptied of it. The resulting frustration was certainly what in the 1930s led Artaud to mourn that actors no longer knew how to scream. I believe it is the same frustration, now, which has resulted in the increasing tendency for actors to shout. The consequence of this is a loss of subtlety, characterized by a more or less ongoing, unconscious subtext of aggression. This subtext may well indicate what happens in our souls when we suppress feeling or emotion. It may reflect additional frustration at our lack of capacity to finely differentiate and communicate the wider range of our intensities.

Breath and action/will

To carry out a vigorous action, we need to breathe deeply. To chop wood requires more breath than is required to sit and think about it. This engagement of our will with the resistance offered us by matter also results in a different relationship to time. Deeds take time. If we want our speech to express the effort and energy of action as well as depth of feeling and emotion, we must learn to breathe in ways that make this possible.

Breath and thinking

The development of intellectual thinking and our ability to form an abstract concept have led, on the one hand, to increasing alienation and detachment from the world in which we live and on the other, have given us the possibility of freedom. It is this freedom that enables us to tread the conscious path of re-membering we are connected to a greater whole.[*] This picture of our human journey is central to Steiner's contribution to our understanding. He has described how in recent centuries human beings experienced a separation of our faculties of thinking, feeling and our will.[†]

T.S. Eliot observed this separation and in 1921, published an essay, *The Metaphysical Poets*. In it, he described what he called a 'dissociation of sensibility' which had taken place in Western culture since the seventeenth century and from which 'we have never recovered'. Eliot observed how prior to this, the dramatists of the sixteenth century and the poets of the seventeenth century still functioned with a 'mechanism of sensibility' which 'could devour any experience'. They expressed their thoughts through their experience of feeling. In his insightful essay on Artaud, Jerzy Grotowski too observed:

> Civilisation is sick with schizophrenia, which is a rupture between intelligence and feeling, body and soul.[21]

How else, except by understanding that our thinking is no longer integrated with our feeling or our will (a condition so beautifully demonstrated by the character of Hamlet) can we explain the tendency many actors have to speak so quickly that comprehension is rendered almost impossible, even if as audience one is familiar with the text?[‡] In such cases, the intellect has raced so far ahead of its companions, will and feeling, that it has spun out of control. Words spoken at such speed are dissociated even from the thinking process of the characters and exclude the audience from access to their minds.

In the 1960s, a well-known and respected actor of the English stage and film achieved the feat of speaking ten lines of Shakespeare on one breath. At the time, I was a speech and acting student in Australia. What this actor had achieved was held before us as an ideal to be striven for. Ten years later, I was in England and speaking to a friend who was an acting student then in London. She told me that her class had been

---

[*] See *Speech-exploration 32*, chapter 3.

[†] See *The Integrated Actor*, 'The evolution of consciousness: the cultural epochs'.

[‡] See *The Integrated Actor*, 'The evolution of consciousness: the cultural epochs'.

encouraged to strive towards the goal of speaking 15 lines of Shakespeare on one breath. I imagine such a feat can elicit a desire for emulation only because words have lost their relationship to meaningful experience.

Texts which are themselves born out of our one-sided intellectual consciousness will not be so exposed to mutilation by actors who have trained their breath in such a way. Shakespeare, particularly, suffers from this modern tendency for speed. His language is so multi-layered and the thinking, feeling, will activities so interwoven in his words, speaking at high speed cannot but obliterate the complex layers which compose their richness.

Eliminating, thus, all but the breath to stay alive and utter sounds denuded of their life, we can but mourn:

> Alas!
> Our dried voices, when
> We whisper together
> Are quiet and meaningless
> As wind in dry grass
> Or rat's feet over broken glass
> In our dry cellar.

The Hollow Men, T.S. Eliot

Shakespeare's language thus rendered unintelligible has become uninteresting. Productions are 'made interesting' by the addition of sensational and clever gimmicks. Films of Shakespeare's plays made since the 1970s, also reflect this tendency. The feeling and will levels in the language are largely obliterated from the speaking. Actors can achieve such speed that even intellectual content may be difficult to follow. The elements of thought and will are replaced by graphic visual effects that relieve us of the need to understand or experience what is said. The feeling element is then injected back by underscoring whole scenes or speeches with emotive music.

Using music to express and stir emotion is not the issue, but it is worth considering at what point in our history music ceased going hand in hand with words and began replacing them as the means of affecting our emotions. Is it a coincidence that opera developed in Europe around the time T.S. Eliot observed that the 'dissociation of sensibility' began? Since then, music is increasingly called upon to express those deep intensities that spoken words are no longer expected to communicate.

The capacity to speak as many words on as little breath as possible certainly reduces the length of a Shakespeare performance. This is important because audiences increasingly are bored by all those words. What bores them, though, is that they can no longer understand what they are hearing. They cannot understand because the actors speak too quickly. Both audience and actors are caught in this 'revolving' door, strengthening the split between experience and language.

I have been, and observed others to be, increasingly unmoved at live performances of drama. Yet from time to time there still can be great moments, great performances, reminding us what theatre is about. They are moments when our whole selves are gripped and shaken, by laughter or by tears. It cannot be that words, great words which can unlock the mysteries of why we live and suffer, should be excluded from the theatre's power to shake us, thus, with recognition of our meaning.

Words will only play their part in healing us when they are healed of their participation in the split. This cannot happen unless our understanding of breath is healed. We cannot isolate our breath and the anatomy and physiology responsible for breathing from the rest of our experience and functioning. If we do so, we regard our lungs merely as a pair of bellows whose purpose is to pump air in and out. From this perspective, breath is an abstract thing just like the words we speak and we need only control it sufficiently for life to be sustained and to make the necessary noises in the larynx. At the time of writing, I observe the beginning of a reversal of this trend. Perhaps after 40 years of such extreme disconnection between our speech and breathing patterns in the theatre we are witnessing a move to integrate them once again.

A different way to look at breath

Breath as life

Before air was analysed in a laboratory and shown to be 'only' a combination of chemical elements, ancient wisdom taught a yoga of breathing. Breath was known to be a life-force in itself; a sacred substance that was not only life sustaining but when trained correctly, could lead to higher states of consciousness. Our skin has deceived us into thinking we are separate from the cosmos but every time we breathe air in and breathe it out again, we re-establish our participation in the universe.[*]

At the most obvious level, life depends on breath. We cannot live without it and it is possible to give the 'kiss of life' to someone who may have momentarily stopped breathing. In Old Testament mythology, God breathed life into the clay of earth and there arose a living being. We might imagine such a breath to be abundant, generous, not born of poverty or meanness. What if we applied this attitude to breathing when we speak? Not the mean attitude: how little breath would we need to squeeze out the largest number of the dry, empty shells we now call words. Rather, how can we access the breath that would enable us to breathe life into our words?

Breath as soul

We know the element of air to be the bearer of that thing we call *atmosphere*. We speak of air as being so 'thick with tension' that we could 'cut it with a knife', or 'heavy with sadness' or 'sparkling with joy'. Are these only imprecise expressions deriving from a naive remnant of the pre-scientific age, left over from a time when we, in our ignorance, assigned animate qualities to inanimate things? Or might it be that our 'cool reason' cannot totally succeed in obliterating our perception that air is soul?

When breathing in, we breathe not only life but world-soul. This, then, we transform, infusing it with our individual soul and through the spiritual activity of Speech, send it back to weave again with the great soul of the world. This world-soul will then be either warmed with our love or chilled by our hate and fear. Could the air we breathe be world-consciousness which we in turn affect with our own?

Speech-exploration 22

1. Choose a flower that you find beautiful. Consciously breathe it in, then speak its name ('rose' perhaps or 'flower'). Try to experience that what you breathed in is breathed out in the forming of the sounds which make that word. Can you experience that words are made of sounds and sounds are made of breath?

---

[*] See chapter 5.

2. Try this with other objects.
3. Try it with imagined things.

   In such a way, uniting breath with the consciousness of what we say, we strive to re-unite our breath with soul. When we create words out of breath, our voice is filled with life and soul. Without that life consciously breathed into them, words become hard little lumps that we hit out into space. We sound aggressive even if we do not intend to be. Conversely, if we are not committed to the act of speaking, of reaching someone with our voice, our colourless words drone on. Lacking life and soul, they die, almost still inside our throats. When we develop our perception, we will sense how words not filled with breath can also wound the space. We know how a harsh voice can slice through space, slicing us as well, causing us to wince and contract.

Healing the disconnection

Since our task is to heal the disconnection between breath and consciousness, we will practise breathing only in relation to our soul's experience and the spiritual activity of speaking.[*]

A meditative exploration of the primal act of breath in speaking

We read ... take world in, breathe it into us, consider ... hm! We listen ... take world in, breathe it into us, consider ... hm! We receive and digest what comes to us ... hm!

/h/ just a simple breath, not yet shaped further or transformed, chiselled, carved, moulded or caressed, just breath, as I received it, now warmed with my voice, returned to the world with me in it, integrated with myself.

And so that what we return to the world does not disappear, get lost in space; so we ourselves, united with it in our breath, do not disappear, lose ourselves in space, we close our lips, catch ourselves and the world in /m/, tasting, digesting, considering whether to make it part of us, return it to the world permeated with ourselves. A primal act of self engaging with itself. We speak it to ourselves.

To speak it to another, expand into the space. More world, breathe it in and now return it. Breathe /h/ out, away, far away, fling far away the /h/ from yourself, breathe yourself out into space. Catch yourself at the boundary in /m/ before you disappear. Bring yourself to stillness./m/. Stay centred even as you radiate into the world. Expanding by degrees further into space /h/, centering firmly /m/. Sense of ease, no pressure, no forcing, no unnecessary tension, your own voice nestling gently in the /hm/.

Speech-exploration 23

1. Revisit the heart-centre explorations in *The Art of Acting*.[†]
2. Working on your own, co-ordinate your full-bodied gesture for *giving* as you breathe out in /h/.
3. Co-ordinate your full-bodied gesture for *receiving* with /m/.
4. Work with a partner giving and receiving.
5. Give breath away in /h/. Receive in /m/.
6. Exchange these sounds at varying distances letting them unfold out of the gestures.
7. Work on your own again, now with both sounds. As you breathe out in /h/, arrest your breath in /m/ so you don't over extend. Sense how the /m/ holds and contains you in a membrane which is firm but not hard and impenetrable. It breathes with you.

---

[*] See *The Art of Acting* and *The Integrated Actor* for further discussion of the healing aspects of this integrated Chekhov/Speech Formation methodology.

[†] See *The Art of Acting*, chapter 3.

Speech-exploration 24

KEY: /ʌ/ (c<u>u</u>p) /æ/ (m<u>a</u>n) /e/ (m<u>e</u>n) /ɪ/ (s<u>i</u>p) /ɔ/ (d<u>o</u>t)

/hʌm/
/hʌm hæm/
/hʌm hæm hem/
/hʌm hæm hem hɪm/
/hʌm hæm hem hɪm hɔm/

1. Allow the short vowel /ʌ/ (c<u>u</u>p) to slip between the consonants: /hʌm/ (h<u>u</u>m) and release the syllable into the stream of breath within your gesture.
2. Give the syllable to your partner and receive it from them.
3. Increase and decrease the distances between you, checking that you have a sense of ease and that your breathing and voice is never tense.
4. Insert the short vowels between the consonants. Build the sequence up one at a time.
5. As your stream of breath increases to carry the growing stream of syllables, let it swing easily in and out with your gestures. Can you respond to the faster tempo that each longer line requires?

Speech-exploration 25

KEY: /ɑː/ (st<u>a</u>r), /eɪ/ (d<u>a</u>te), /iː/ (m<u>e</u>), /oʊ/ (n<u>o</u>), /uː/ (sh<u>oe</u>)

/hɑːm/
/hɑːm heɪm/
/hɑːm heɪm hiːm/
/hɑːm heɪm hiːm hoʊm/
/hɑːm heɪm hiːm hoʊm huːm/

Do the same with the long vowels: exchange them with your partner. Build up the stream from one to five, increasing your breath and tempo as you do so.

Speech-exploration 26
k, l, s, f, m
Speech-exploration 26 requires us to fuse the breath stream with the act of making consonants.

1. Stand, receptive and with energy available. As you imagine /k/ coming to you from the space, around, above, behind, and attuning yourself to its unique requirements, breathe it in and let its quality and energy take hold of your whole instrument.

2. Express /k/ with your whole instrument in the space, so that the speaking of it is integrated with your bodily gesture, so that the breath it organized in you is totally absorbed in the revelation of its being in the space. Create/k/ out of breath. *With one breath, I cleave the space.*

3. Do the same with /l/.

4. Now repeat steps 1 and 2 but collecting both sounds as a sequence to be spoken on one stream of breath. Create /k l/ out of breath, letting them absorb all of it. There should be no breath left over in the lungs. *With one breath, I cleave the space and then I soothe the space.*

5. Repeat steps 1 and 2 with /s/.

6. Include 's' in your sequence: /k l s/ *With one breath, I cleave then soothe then penetrate the space.*

7. Repeat steps 1 and 2 with /f/.

8. Include 'f' in your sequence: /k l s f/ *With one breath, I cleave, then soothe, then penetrate, then burn the space.*

9. Repeat steps 1 and 2 with /m/.

10. /k l s f m/ *With one breath, I cleave, then soothe, then penetrate, then burn, then heal the space.*

The aim is fourfold:

a) To experience that the sounds you speak are not separate from the breath each one requires to manifest itself.

b) To experience that the sounds will organize the breath they need, if you invite them to.

c) To learn how to pour all of your breath into the speaking.

d) To unfold, a continuous progression of sounds (experience) within one stream of breath.

Any word is just such a continuous progression of sounds which can unfold within a single breath-stream in this way. Notice how this sequence of consonants (klsfm) requires that we form our breath through the range of placements in our mouth, from back to front.

Speech-exploration 27 – combining explorations 25 and 26

KEY: /ɑː/ (st**ar**), /eɪ/ (d**a**te), /iː/ (m**e**), /oʊ/ (n**o**), /uː/ (sh**oe**)

/kɑːm/
/kɑːm keɪm/
/kɑːm keɪm kiːm/
/kɑːm keɪm kiːm koʊm/
/kɑːm keɪm kiːm koʊm kuːm/

/lɑːm/
/lɑːm leɪm/
/lɑːm leɪm liːm/
/lɑːm leɪm liːm loʊm/
/lɑːm leɪm liːm loʊm luːm/

/sɑːm/
/sɑːm seɪm/
/sɑːm seɪm siːm/
/sɑːm seɪm siːm soʊm/
/sɑːm seɪm siːm soʊm suːm/

/ʃɑːm/
/ʃɑːm ʃeɪm/
/ʃɑːm ʃeɪm ʃiːm/
/ʃɑːm ʃeɪm ʃiːm ʃoʊm/
/ʃɑːm ʃeɪm ʃiːm ʃoʊm ʃuːm/

/mɑːm/
/mɑːm meɪm/
/mɑːm meɪm miːm/
/mɑːm meɪm miːm moʊm/
/mɑːm meɪm miːm moʊm muːm/

1. Continue to use gesture to create a pathway in the space between yourself and your partner and exchange the sequence of consonants you have just worked with. Insert the sequence of vowels worked with in exploration 25 to create an expanding stream of syllables with a corresponding increase in breath and tempo. On one stream of breath, let each consonant launch each vowel in turn in the sequence.
2. Exchange them with your partner. Build up the stream from one to five, increasing your breath and tempo as you do so.

3. On one stream of breath let each consonant in turn in the sequence launch the same vowel.

> /kɑːm lɑːm sɑːm fɑːm mɑːm/
> /keɪm leɪm seɪm feɪm meɪm/
> /kiːm liːm siːm fiːm miːm/
> /koʊm loʊm soʊm foʊm moʊm/
> /kuːm luːm suːm fuːm muːm/

4. On one stream of breath launch the stream of syllables that arise when each consonant is partnered with the vowel formed in the same place in the mouth (back, middle, front) as itself.

> /kɑːm leɪm siːm foʊm muːm/

These sequences encourage us to achieve an easy flow of syllables on the stream of breath, ability to adjust our breath and tempo according to how much we need to say, and massage our entire instrument as we move back and forth through all the major placements of vowels in combination with all the major placements for consonants. By now you will realize that such complex activity is not about increasing technical agility for its own sake. In harmony with all we have explored in chapter 1, we know that agility in isolation is empty unless in the service of the specific qualities of all the sounds. Qualities which we are learning to sense and mediate, and weave together in a flow.

Two fundamental uses of the breath — declamation and recitation

When we are gripped by intense emotion or sensation, we tend to express ourselves with immediacy that demands simplicity. For example: *Wow! Hell! Incredible! Awesome!* And, of course, the one and only f-word, and its colourful companions. When we respond like this, what matters is that our intensity can pour itself through sounds and gestures unimpeded. The visceral levels at which we seek release and satisfaction are connected with the powerful release of consonants and vowels that is a feature of our 'naughty' and forbidden words. Such moments are remnants in our everyday speech patterns of this intimate relationship between experience and sounds.

On these occasions, we seem instinctively to know just how to organize and integrate the increased intake of the breath we need, the direct outpouring of it to achieve the maximum affect and, of course, the satisfying gestures. It is just this integration that we wish to recreate in an artistic context when, for example, Hamlet vents his rage in short bursts of single words and phrases. With emotions and breath-stream running hot, just uttering the sounds is exhilarating.

> Bloody, bawdy villain!
> Remorseless, treacherous, lecherous, kindless villain!
> O vengeance!

Compare those words with the end of Hamlet's same soliloquy:

> I have heard,
> That guilty creatures sitting at a play
> Have by the very cunning of the scene
> Been struck so to the soul that presently
> They have proclaimed their malefaction.
> For murder, though it hath no tongue, will speak
> With most miraculous organ.

They require a very different use of breath; one that allows us to express a thinking process that unfolds itself in longer, more grammatically complex sentences. A comparative coolness seems to be required, which makes detachment possible. This allows the speaker to grasp the thought and follow its thread through the labyrinth.

Speech-exploration 28

1. Imagine something that inspires the exclamation, *Wow!* Speak it and observe the full outpouring of the breath.
2. Do the same with something that inspires the exclamation, *Shit!*

3. Work with a partner. Take a few moments to decide how you will explain to your partner something that you, yourself, understand very clearly, for example: how to solve a maths or computer problem, ride a horse, hold a violin bow, etc.
4. Take turns to explain your area of expertise to your partner.
5. Observe, both as speaker and listener, the qualities involved in clearly expressing a thought process: breath, gesture, speech, etc.
6. Share your observations.

Steiner observed that the impulse to speak arises in our astral body; the aspect of our constitution that allows us consciousness of our experience within our souls and which we also share with animals.[*] Like the animals, we also share the impulse to express, by making sounds, the emotions connected with our bodily sensations and impulses of will.[†] Into this arena of our souls can also stream the thinking which connects human beings to the realm of spirit and by means of which we can also penetrate sensation and emotion, refining them into our finer feelings. We need our breath to express the whole range of our consciousness.

As always, observing what we do instinctively allows us to extract its elements and use them to create a conscious process. Our two examples from Hamlet's soliloquy reveal two fundamental ways in which we need to organize and use our breath:

1. When our sensations, feelings and emotions are so intense that they strike directly through our will into the sounds without engaging our cognition.
2. When length of line and meter guides our will to render our sensations, feelings and emotions into thoughts via the mental picture and the concept.

Speech-explorations 28–29 teach us how to organize our breath so we can achieve the first way consciously; this is the basis of the style that Steiner referred to as *Declamation*. *Speech explorations 30–33* teach us how to organize our breath so we can achieve the second way consciously; this is the basis of the style that Steiner referred to as *Recitation*.[‡]

---

[*] See, Terms of reference, page 23.
[†] See, *The Art of Acting*, chapter 3.
[‡] See *Poetry and the Art of Speech* listed in Appendix B.

Use of the breath for Declamation

Speech-exploration 29 — breath pours sensation and emotion directly through the will into the sounds.

Reforging gales
Through foghorns
Hails through surges
Through whirlpools
Whirlpool wails
In wavering[*]
Wails in quavering
Waves veiling
Waving breathing
In freedom
Freedom winning
Kindling.   RS MH

This rendering of Rudolf Steiner's first breath exercise invites immediate participation in the powerful weaving of sensation and will that is the feature of this first use of the breath. The lines are quite compact consisting of the same short phrases and explosive words as characterized our Hamlet example.

We learned in *Speech-exploration 26* to unfold a continuous flow of consonants within a stream of breath. Notice how many fricative-breath-fire sounds weave through the lines of our current text. The powerful energies these elemental images evoke inspire us to use our breath fully in order to create them. We aim to completely absorb one out-breath as we plunge into the seething vortex of each line.

Now images and elemental energies combine as the sequence of consonants unfolds in the stream of breath. Notice how many early lines conclude with /s/. To ensure that the ending of each line remains an active part of our creation we need to breathe life into that last sound. This enables us to use up all the air in our lungs and be ready to receive more breath from the universe. Thus our breathing in and out is organized by an organic necessity in harmony with all the other elements; imagination, language structure and the sounds.

Once we are accustomed to such complete investment of our breath, we can experiment with this alternative rendering of the opening lines. It will teach us how to bring that same activity to content that is quieter and, on the surface, less dramatic.

---

[*] See Appendix E for Mechthild Harkness's rendering of the exercises.

Fulfilling goes
Through hoping
Goes through longing
Through willing
Willing flows
In wavering
Wails in quavering
Waves veiling
Waving breathing
In freedom
Freedom winning
Kindling

Remaining active

The necessity to actively create even the last sound of a line rather than just 'saying' it confronts us with a common tendency to pull back or withdraw from the last words of a sentence. We seem instinctively to slow down or to cease activity as we prepare for a conclusion.

A creator must be active to the very end, if the creation is to be complete. We learn to sustain activity beyond the ends of lines and create an end that is the culmination of all that preceded it. In doing so, we discover that every end is also a preparation for a new beginning; one that is contained within that end.

None of this is possible if we run out of breath as we approach the end. As clay is to the potter, so breath is to the speaker. No matter how significant what we would communicate, without breath we are like the potter who does not have enough clay to complete the work. This lack then forces us to compromise the vision that inspired us, in order to 'get through'. 'Getting through' in context of our breathing, means just managing to 'say the words'. 'Saying words' is very different from creating an experience.

An artist always has a sense of ease and of abundance; a feeling there is 'plenty more where that came from'. Without this, we're like a gymnast who executes a form, but only just manages to land, somewhat off balance and not available for what comes next. So it is for us when a speaker just manages the breath required to 'get through to the end' of a phrase or sentence but is not in control of what follows.

Not able to command my instrument, my breath is no longer abundantly available. This leaves me with a sense I am 'behind', rather than 'on top' or 'in the centre' of what I create. Later in this chapter, I discuss how we can learn to dwell within the constantly renewing fountain of our breath.

Intensity and tension

Another challenge presented by this Speech-exploration is how we may increase intensity without unhealthy tension. The words demand intensity, yet if we achieve intensity of Speech by becoming tense, a sore throat will result. If this condition becomes chronic, we damage our instrument. There are healthy ways to achieve vocal intensity but without a strong foundation in the healthy way to use our breath, we will not be able to make use of them.[*] The following process is suggested as a way we might approach healthy expression of increased intensity. It should unfold in gradual stages, as each successive step is able to be taken with a sense of ease.

Speech-exploration 29 – stage 1

> Reforging gales
> Through foghorns
> Hails through surges
> Through whirlpools
> Whirlpool wails
> In wavering
> Wails in quavering
> Waves veiling
> Waving breathing
> In freedom
> Freedom winning
> Kindling.

1. Stand, with a sense of ease and available. Reach up to receive the first line from above, drawing it from the infinite space.
2. Speak the line with no attempt at effort, quiet and relaxed with no concern for being 'heard'. You should experience no tension as you let the words 'slip through your throat'. Let the line come through you. As it does, surrender to it. Allow your upper body to collapse, going with the line as it pours through you to the earth. The degree of collapse which accompanies each line need only be what is possible while standing.
3. Repeat the process with every line.
4. When you can experience the sensation of full-bodied surrender without the need to collapse full-bodily, raise just your arm, letting it collapse as you let the words 'slip through you'. This can be helpful, for a time, to remind you that words and breath come from beyond your instrument. Not *I speak,* but *I invite the words to speak through me.*

---

[*] See chapter 3 for specific ways to build vocal intensity.

The important thing at this stage is to let speech flow in a condition of complete surrender and simplicity; we insert no will of our own into the free release of words into our breath stream. It is important to recognize this sensation: how it feels to speak without tension, in a state of surrender. This is another aspect of what Chekhov called the *sense of ease.*[*] When this sensation becomes familiar, we make it our barometer, to detect when we are tense. This will be necessary as we move into the next step of our process; for only when we know how not to push our own will into what we speak are we ready to learn how to *use* our will. To bring the sounds to life requires complete commitment of our will without imposing it. We want to use our will in the service of the words we speak. Words are made of consonants and vowels; we learn how to let our will serve theirs.

Speech-exploration 29 — Stage 2

1. Apply the principles explored in *Speech-exploration 26* /klsfm/ to each line. Allow each consonant to reveal itself as movement and gesture in your stream of breath. It can be helpful to eliminate the vowels completely for a time until the consonants can unfold in their sequence, as do /klsfm/. The vowels can be slipped back in when they no longer have the tendency to interfere with the continuous stream of consonants.
2. As you develop confidence that each line can reveal its life and movement as the consonants unfold on one complete out-breath, check your sense of ease.

   - Step-by-step commit more *energy*.
   - At each level, check there is a corresponding increase in *activity* to grasp and form the consonants.
   - With each such increase, check there is a corresponding greater availability of *breath* to serve those consonants.

This balancing of all three factors should prevent your voice from hardening as your speech increases both in strength of form and volume. Our basic principle should be that greater volume and intensity require more breath to cushion their entry into space. Keep checking that all you do is permeated with the sense of ease.

'Breathy' speech versus speech that is fully breathed through

This approach uses more breath than would ever be required for everyday speech because the creative activity required to bring consonants and vowels to life demands that breath. It is their activity which calls forth that amount of breath and all of it will be

---

[*] See *The Art of Acting*, chapter 5.

absorbed into the speaking. We are learning to think of, and to collect, breath not as some abstract commodity that we can have 'too much of' but as the means by which the sound can come to life through us. Breathy speech is the result of using more breath than our speaking can absorb. This can never be the case if we allow the sounds to organize the breath they need. Intensity in speech need not result in greater volume, but if greater volume is required, then we need more breath and more activity to form that breath.[*]

The infinite source of breath

On the one hand, we always need sufficient breath; on the other, our goal is for our speech to use up all our breath. This apparent contradiction conceals a basic law: the more I give, the more I can receive. Having enough breath does not mean having breath left over; rather, we learn to be in contact with the source of breath, which is as infinite as space itself. I call it *world-breath*. In this sense, holding on to breath out of fear I will not have enough prevents me from fully breathing in what follows.

There is no end to what can flow through us if we do not keep what we already have, so do not try to make that one breath last as long as possible. If a single word needs one breath so that it can fully come alive, do not be afraid to offer it. There is plenty more where it came from.

> My bounty is as boundless as the sea,
> My love as deep; the more I give to thee
> The more I have, for both are infinite.

> *Romeo and Juliet*, Shakespeare

As we learn to harmonize our breathing and speaking, so too will the listener's breathing soul be brought into that harmony. Have you noticed how a speaker whose breath is cramped, can produce cramped breathing in the listener? That is because we share the same space and air and are not as separate as we think ourselves to be.[†]

> It is world-breath we share
> the tree outside my door
> the tree within –
> their branches, bronchi, bronchioles, capillaries,
> their leafy lungs a sponge
> for soaking up infinity
> earth's atmosphere
> exchanging life for death
> and death for life.

---

[*] See chapter 3, pages 147–164 to further examine the connection between breath and volume and intensity.

[†] See chapter 5.

Easy commerce when trust is there
supply is plentiful —

no need to fear,
hold on, forget to breathe,
withdraw from the exchange.

World-breath filling all of me;
trees' feet treading tendril toes
are spreading deep as far
as earth's firm grasp can hold our roots —
so anchored between earth and star
between us
breathes infinity.   DL

Stage 3 of *Speech-exploration 29* will help us to transform the idea that our lungs are just a bellows, whose function is to merely pump air in and out.

Speech-exploration 29 — Stage 3
Since breath is not an abstract commodity that we quickly inhale at the last moment after we have thought of what we want to say, we train ourselves to breathe in experience condensed in words which, in their turn, are made of sounds which, in their turn, are created out of breath.

Reforging gales
Through foghorns
Hails through surges
Through whirlpools
Whirlpool wails
In wavering
Wails in quavering
Waves veiling
Waving breathing
In freedom
Freedom winning
Kindling.

1. As you prepare each line, let it organize you so you breathe in what the line needs for you to bring the words to life.
2. Imagine it's your whole body breathing in. Raise your arms as though they are wings, expanding up and out from your shoulder blades on each side of your body. Imagine the surface of your body is a permeable membrane through which the

sacred substance of the universe, world-breath, can stream. In this way, the act of breathing will lead to a sense of ease.

This is important for the well-being of both artist and audience. If an audience becomes aware of difficulties in an actor's breathing, it may well interfere with their experience. Of course when an actor plays a character that is out of breath, for instance, it might be artistically appropriate to demonstrate the labour. Even this, the actor can do in a healthy way. Otherwise, it may arouse anxiety and tension in the listener, whose own body cannot help but resonate with the tensions of the speaker. Practising this way, we ultimately sense how our own breath connects us to world-breath: we are breathing in not just air, but light and life.

Speech-explorations 28–29 teach us how to pour out our breath in the declamatory style, with the immediacy demanded by the intense emotion and sensation generated as the soul soars and plunges between the heights and depths. Now we learn to measure it out, not holding on to it yet conserving it so we can reach our destination. This does not necessarily mean expressing an entire thought in a single breath but rather, that we breathe knowing how far we need to travel and where to renew our breath along the way.

Use of the breath for Recitation

Speech-exploration 30 — the measuring out of breath supports the will to render sensation into thought via the mental picture and the concept

> In the vast unmeasured world-wide spaces,
> in the endless stream of time,
> in the depths of human soul-life,
> in the world's great revelations
> seek the unfolding of life's great mystery.

Speech-exploration 30 trains our breathing so that we can give expression to a thinking and image-making process. A thought can organize our breath so it can reveal itself one step at a time and reach its culmination at the end. Here, one complete thought unfolds in five successive stages of a single sentence.

The strong trochee rhythm launches us into each successive stage on a long stress.[*] This 'puts the brakes' on that immediate sensation-impulse for expression which *Speech-explorations 26* and *29* encouraged. Instead, we are invited to transform that impulse into the mental pictures and the concepts that characterize our thinking. This deliberate tempo, the result of rhythmic regularity, prepares us for the sustained mood and activity required by thought and image-making.

If we step the rhythm first, we shall not be tempted to bypass the real experience of measure by which we teach our breath.

1. Step the syllables of each line as you speak them. Breathe in each successive stage and find out how to measure its release so that an entire line is able to unfold in the course of each complete out-breath.
2. As you become confident in co-ordinating breath with speech and stepping, gradually reduce the stepping. Replace it with a sweeping arm gesture that helps you experience collecting each line from behind and letting it unfold in front of you. Each syllable now becomes a step in the unfolding stream of breath.

There is a difference between releasing the breath stream in a measured way and attempting to complete the whole sentence on one breath. Were this last our aim, we should be rushing to get through. To keep our instrument relaxed throughout the unfolding thought, we must know our breath can be renewed as often as required. Most sentences expressing thoughts, if we pay attention to their structure, will show us where best to breathe. *Speech-exploration 30* provides us with a natural opportunity to

---

[*] See chapter 4, rhythm and meter.

do this at the end of every line. We grasp the whole thought and commit ourselves to progressively intensify at each stage of the journey so that we can bring it to completion.* This will be achieved with a sense of ease if we allow the unfolding concept in each line to organize us to provide the breath it needs.

3. When you are at ease with step two, experiment with integrating the formation of the sounds out of your breath as described in *explorations 26* and *29.* Now the formative activity serves to imprint the thought into the space and thus into the listener's consciousness.

To consistently imprint the sounds while we are held within a strong rhythmic impulse that is regular means that we develop the capacity to fuse sound, breath and thought, and recognize they are not separate. Such an experience may well awaken further intimations of that mystery to which we keep returning and which the Greeks expressed as LOGOS: that if thought is made of words and words are made of sounds, then thought is nothing other than the sounds themselves in their creative power. Thought is made word, is made deed, is something of what LOGOS indicates.

> In the Beginning was the Word
> And the Word was with God
> And the Word was God.
> The same was in the beginning with God.
> All things were made by Him
> And without Him was not anything made that was made...

Steiner refers to thinking as the spiritual activity that enables us to think a thought; the active process that takes place in the mind when we create a thought.[22] In this context, what we normally refer to as our thinking is merely the passive reflection of already finished thoughts. It is the former, active thinking that *Speech-exploration 30* requires of us. We learn how to get inside the active thinking which creates any sentence that we speak. Such activity can only be willed consciously and demands commitment, energy and fire. Rodin recognized this and in his famous sculpture depicted the thinker as a muscular figure, lean and athletic.

Speech-exploration 31 (partner work)
Imagine the first time a human being thought through the mathematical calculations which could explain the irregularities of planetary movement, and came to the con-

---

* See chapter 5 regarding the means by which we manage this.

Figure 6 – The Thinker, Rodin

clusion that our planet earth was not the centre of the solar system. What activity was required to think that thought? An equal energy and commitment are required to think the opposite – that based on our everyday physical perception that the sun revolves around the earth, the earth must be the centre.

1. Giving yourselves room to gesture across the space, exchange the following lines, becoming increasingly heated as you express your conviction.

   a)   The sun goes round the earth!
   b)   No! The earth goes round the sun!

2. Repeat this as often as you like, allowing intensity to grow as the clash of convictions increases. When your thinking is alive and energetic, apply that energy to *Speech-exploration 30* (*in the vast* ...). Use that energy to form the sounds out of your breath.

3. Play with transforming the intensity of holding doggedly on to a conviction into the intensity required to think a thought.

Recitation and Declamation in the dramatic style

Our entry into the two fundamental ways of using breath was recognizing how the two sections of Hamlet's soliloquy each require to be spoken differently, and that to achieve this we need to organize our breathing differently. Thus recitation and declamation can be important tools in the actor's revelation of a character through language. In chapter 6, we shall learn not only how to layer them with the dramatic style but also with the epic and the lyric styles.

Breath moments

Whether words express a thoughtful or emotional content, we seek an organic relationship between our breath and what we say. As a rule, the laws of grammar instruct us as to when we need to breathe.[*] Phrasing and punctuation guide the speaker into each distinctive moment of the soul's experience; each with its own integrity within the whole. As a rule, each demands its own breath if it is to convey not just information but living experience. To provide this we must breathe more often than our intellect requires which is content to cram as many words as possible on to a single breath. The task of weaving these 'breath moments' into a wholeness is explored later.[†]

Only in rare moments are we exclusively emotional or rational. So too, most language requires that we weave the two extremes in differing degrees. Only when we have mastered the ability to express each one are we free to mix these tendencies in whatever combinations seem appropriate.

I have marked the likely places for a breath in the following lines which Romeo speaks as he observes his Juliet in the famous balcony scene:

---

[*] See chapter 7, Grammar.

[†] See chapter 5.

But soft! * What light * through yonder window breaks? *
It is the east * and Juliet * is the sun! *
Arise, fair sun, * and kill the envious moon, *
Who is already sick and pale with grief, *
That thou, * her maid, * art far more fair than she:*
Be not her maid, * since she is envious; *
Her vestal livery * is but sick and green,*
And none but fools do wear it; * cast it off. *
It is my lady; * O! it is my love: *
O! that she knew she were. *

If we think of breath as merely a physical commodity that sets the wavelengths in motion that result in the hollow noises we normally accept as speech, it makes no sense to breathe as frequently as indicated here. Only when we free the letters from the page and turn them into sounds which embody Romeo's experience can we bring to life the ecstatic love that floods his soul. This we can only do if we breathe into them the breath of life.

The death and resurrection of the word

A sound not breathed into cannot reveal its life or being. It is an empty shell. Most of our experience of spoken language consists of empty shells. On this basis then, the following conclusion arrived at by current theories of philology can come as no surprise: language is a set of arbitrary symbols and for convenience's sake, meanings which are commonly agreed have been ascribed to them. T.S. Eliot laments this predominant experience of language in our present culture:

Words strain,
Crack and sometimes break, under the burden,
Under the tension, slip, slide, perish,
Decay with imprecision, will not stay in place,
Will not stay still. Shrieking voices
Scolding, mocking, or merely chattering,
Always assail them. The Word in the desert
Is most attacked by voices of temptation,
The crying shadow in the funeral dance,
The loud lament of the disconsolate chimera.

Four Quartets

Eliot's words were written in the 1940s, while Artaud was still alive. We considered how, arising from his desperation, Artaud's ideas have profoundly changed the expectations that we bring to a theatrical event. He gave birth to the concept that for theatre to fulfil its task to change the world by changing people's consciousness, it must be cruel. He justified the need to shatter audiences' psychological defences with massive doses of sensation. In film we see the same desperate bid to generate experience in audiences numbed by an increasing overload of sensory impressions; significant words are replaced by piles of sensation which in turn distance us still further from the act of language.

Rudolf Steiner hands us the key to language's rebirth and resurrection. It is not a path that pounds us with sensation. It is a path of patient working at discoveries that slowly waken future faculties in us. Along it lies the life that will one day be breathed again into the heaps of dead words littering our culture.

The Word is dead! Long live the Word!

It is sacred substance that we breathe. We receive it from, and can return it to, the world-breath; enlivened and ennobled with the living words which tell us of our meaning.

Chapter 3

Where Does Speech Come From?

A spiritual scientific exploration of further aspects of our Speech technique

To everyday perception, speech originates in our anatomy. For sounds and voice to manifest in physical space to physical ears, they do indeed *pass through* our physicality but our technique is predicated on the fact that sounds *originate* beyond the physical. This is no new idea. Referring to the musicians represented on the Grecian urn, Keats expressed:

> Heard melodies are sweet, but those unheard are sweeter.
>
> *Ode on a Grecian Urn*

Mozart insisted that he first *heard* the music which he then wrote down. The existence of a 'music of the spheres' claimed by Pythagoras, is expressed by Shakespeare in *The Merchant of Venice*:

> Sit Jessica; look, how the floor of heaven
> Is thick inlaid with patines of bright gold;
> There's not the smallest orb which thou beholds't
> But, in his motion, like an angel sings,
> Still quiring to the young eyed cherubins;
> Such harmony is in immortal souls;
> But while this muddy vesture of decay
> Doth grossly close it in, we cannot hear it.

If actors wish their speaking to be integrated with a spiritual path, they learn to listen to such 'unheard' sounds. How we do this and how this changes our approach to speech is what makes this path distinct; forever separating it from approaches based only upon an anatomical conception of the human being. For we learn, while still inhabiting our 'muddy vestures of decay', how to consciously and actively participate in the world of our 'immortal souls'.

An academic textbook on botany identifies and names the features of plants dissected and examined with a microscope. Knowledge gained in this way tells us many things we could not know otherwise. Nevertheless, what makes the plant a living organism cannot be understood when the plant is dead. Ripped out of its relationships with earth, water, air, light and warmth, the plant is no longer what it was. A study of the aspects of anatomy involved in speaking can teach us much but on its own will not serve as a basis for a technique and Art of Speech that seeks to reconnect us with the greater universe.

What Speech Formation offers is not some vague, mystical idea that we are spiritual

Based on the drawing by Leonardo da Vinci of the 'Human Being in a Circle: Illustrating the Proportions'

Figure 7

beings who must do the best we can to work within a methodology that contradicts that thought. It offers a technique that down into its every detail provides a path to reconnect us to the spiritual nature of the human being and the universe of which we are a part. Of course, if we are to speak in physical space our voice and the sounds we make must be formed by our speech organs. But what are they in the perspective of a supersensible reality and why do they function as they do? Later we shall look at these questions. For now we want to learn how to receive sounds from the realm beyond.

Speech-exploration 32 — for inhabiting two worlds

1. Prepare with the gravity/levity explorations until you reach the stage where you are standing upright and feeling balanced.[*]
2. Imagine your feet are rooted in the earth and that those roots reach down to the centre of the earth. At the same time, your head is in the stars and bathed within their light. Imagine your body streamed through by these powers.
3. Absorb the imagination that your existence is embedded in both realms.
4. Allow these powers to draw your limbs towards them, gradually growing you into a pentagram (see Figure 7).
5. Sustaining the sensation that your whole body is aligned with earth and stars, let your body return to normal uprightness. When you are ready, move around the space. How long can you sustain the sensation you belong to both these worlds?
6. When you are confident you can recapture the sensation, let it go. Keep moving but now returning to your normal state of everyday awareness.
7. Observe the difference between that former state and your everyday consciousness of being in your body.
8. Choose a moment to return to the former state. Observe the difference.
9. Practise going from one state to the other until you can move confidently back and forth.

The central challenge in this new approach to speaking lies in this: we work, simultaneously from the centre of ourselves and from the periphery of the greater universe. This requires retraining our perception of ourselves and the source of our activity. Approached in this new way, what might seem on paper just another speech-exercise appears quite different.

Speech-exploration 32 teaches us that dwelling in the consciousness of our connectedness is a choice we can make. Although it might be relatively simple to experience that consciousness once we have made that choice, it is not easy to always

---

[*] See *The Art of Acting*, chapter 2.

remember to choose it. Yet unless we do, our work will differ only theoretically from a purely anatomical approach. The practical suggestions for training voice and Speech that arise out of that connected consciousness will, in turn, confirm and strengthen it. We now have a basis for experiencing that sounds can come not *from* our mouths but *through* our mouths.

If we revisit the meditation on the beings of the sounds, we might sense that before we speak them, we allow them to approach us.[*] From beyond physical space, from infinity, each sound, with its own specific qualities and energy, requires something different from us. We attune ourselves to this and make ourselves available. When we are ready, it wills to move through us and we allow it passage. Gradually, we learn to know what it requires in order to reveal itself through us. Once freed into the space, it is no longer bound up with the speaker. It is a joint creation in which the subjective substance of the artist is both held and permeated by the objective, spiritual activity of consonants and vowels.

---

[*] See pages 71–85.

Articulation

Articulation, as traditionally understood, refers to our capacity to precisely co-ordinate the specific combinations of tongue, teeth, lips and palate, in order that each sound is accurately reproduced. Lack of clarity may be caused by physiological malformation, inability to imitate correctly, or laziness in any of the organs of articulation. A range of issues, from remedial diagnosis to societal expectations about what constitutes 'good' speech, may be involved.

Until the latter half of the twentieth century, what was judged to be 'good' English speech was what was referred to first as the King's and later Queen's English: the 'BBC voice'. Since then, a revolution has removed the once enthroned values of 'posh' speech. Now speech patterns from the whole spectrum of society are relished. The increasing adoption of English as a world language further complicates determining what constitutes 'good' articulation.

From our perspective, an actor's speech is judged by its capacity to express the broadest, deepest range of human experience. Articulation is not a matter of outer accuracy or correctness; we understand it as an inner receptiveness to the being of a sound and the capacity of the organs of articulation to manifest that being.

The purpose of articulation explorations, then, is to expand our Speech capacities until they can express each nuance of experience. This is achieved by mastering the relationships between the consonants and vowels and the spectrum of experience they embody. We strive towards an approach to articulation for which Steiner, in his *Speech and Drama* lectures, used the German word *intonieren*. This was initially rendered into English as 'intone'.

Because the word 'intone' has specific connotations in the English culture – the songlike sustaining of tone within a narrow range when speaking ritual texts – I was delighted when, many years ago, a student suggested the alternative *attune*. I have used 'attune' ever since as a more helpful rendering of *intonieren*. To attune ourselves to a consonant or vowel is to wait upon the being of that sound and let it organize us into what it needs to manifest itself. From this perspective, all the Speech-explorations offer the opportunity to practise some or other aspect of articulation.

Our primary purpose may not be to achieve 'correct' speech for its own sake, but this doesn't change the fact that our instrument needs to be capable of executing and co-ordinating complex movements. Speech-exploration 33 is designed to help articulation by waking up our organs which, through simple lack of exercise, have become lazy.

Speech-exploration 33

> Hist! Strategy stern
> masters mystical stages
> stale states earnest stripling
> stern stresses steadfast
> for stooping straightened striplings.

We marvel when a champion hurdler runs the length of a field of hurdles. The hurdles create resistance to be transcended, so the run is not impeded. In just the same way, /t/ confronts the organs of articulation with the necessity to form a boundary. The frequent combination of the /t/ with /s/ creates a further challenge. The speaker continually arrests the otherwise ongoing /s/ in order to create that boundary. At the same time we learn not to be impeded by, but *use* the boundary in such a way that it supports the easy streaming of the whole line.

We can achieve such effortless unfolding in spite of the hurdles if we collect an impulse that can drive through the resistances. With practice, the complex functioning required by our organs of articulation can be organized so it doesn't interfere with that impulse. Their activity must be so focused, agile and precise that they can do what they need to do and 'get out of the way' of the line as it comes through.

1. First, achieve clear articulation with each single word. The consonant must cleanly grasp the vowel or voice, so there is no 'fluffiness'.
2. When two or three consonants precede a single vowel, grasp them as one vessel which already holds the vowel. The awake consciousness that this requires will be as necessary to our clear articulation as will the multi-tasking and precise co-ordination of the organs which perform this feat.

Such skills are needed in *Speech-exploration 34*, but now required of the lips.

Speech-exploration 34

> piffling fifer
> prefacing feather
> phlegma fluting
> fairground piercing.

The very fine and focused interaction between lips and teeth required to produce 'p' and 'f', alternated at such tiny intervals, makes us agile in managing these rapid micro-movements. Because 'p' and 'f' are unvoiced consonants, conscious activity is needed to fuse them with the voice, so that the vowel will not be left behind in the throat. These sounds can teach us to balance the volume provided by the vowel (voice) and the consonant, so they form an integrated whole. The loudness of the voice shouldn't weigh so heavily upon the consonant that it cannot grasp the vowel and carry it out into the space, clean and free.

The result will be a very fine articulation; one which lends itself to shaping images that require such delicate precision, as:

> the winged seeds where they lie, cold and low,
> each like a corpse within its grave...
>
> *Ode to the West Wind*, Shelley

> What heart could have thought you?
> Past our devisal
> O filigree petal...
>
> *To a Snowflake*, Frances Thompson

> Sunk in an airless night they neither slept nor woke
> but hanging on the tree's blood dreamed vaguely the dreams of the tree
> and put on wavering leaves, wing-veined, too delicate to see.
>
> *The Cicadas*, Judith Wright

We learn what is required of our articulation organs so we can release the *being* of each sound into space, in its uniqueness, *free of the physical instrument that gave it form*. *Speech-exploration 35* provides us with further opportunity to practise this.

Speech-exploration 35

> children chiding
> chaffinch chirping
> choking chimneys
> cheerfully chattering

> children chiding and fetching
> chaffinch chirping switching
> choking chimneys hitching
> cheerfully chattering twitching

> beach children chiding and fetching
> reach chaffinch chirping switching
> birches choking chimneys hitching
> perches cheerfully chattering twitching

Here 'ch' appears in all possible positions in a word; beginning, middle and end. In chapter 1, we saw that the unvoiced affricate 'ch' arises from a fusion of two unvoiced sounds: the unvoiced plosive /t/ with the unvoiced fricative /ʃ/ (<u>sh</u>oe). The awake activity required for 'sh' to sear into the resistance of the 't', igniting both into a white-hot flash, is both delicate and mighty.

Only if we stay awake can we sustain the commitment required to form a 'ch' at every point demanded. We can only create 'ch' according to its nature if we are fully present; *in the driver's seat*, I like to call it. *Speech-exploration 35* affords no opportunity to escape into passivity, no single moment where we can withdraw our consciousness.

The task of fusing unvoiced consonants with vowels demands commitment. If the voice is too opaque, the transparent 'ch' won't be able to fully grasp the vowel. If the voice is fine enough, each 'ch', received from the periphery and created with necessary strength and precision, contains the energy to launch and keep our voice out in the space. There it will be free to play. Mastering *Speech-exploration 35* results in Speech that dances in the space with energy and sparkling, light-filled clarity.[*]

Speech-exploration 36

> judicious genial jar
> giant gentian jacket
> joyous jumble gender

To develop density and weight in the voice, we use the voiced affricate 'j' = /dʒ/ (plea<u>s</u>ure). Willed intention is needed if the voiced quality of the plosive /d/ is to be burned into by the fire of the /ʒ/ (plea<u>s</u>ure). The nature of this fusion resembles slow and deep combustion and makes 'j' into a strong vessel for the voice. Unlike the unvoiced 'ch', the voice is already contained in both /d/+/ʒ/ and no effort is required to make the consonant 'j' unite with it. The speaker is free to focus on carving each line into the substance of space and by doing so, create a vocal experience of weight and *density*.

Density of voice resists the flow of language. To create a dynamic strong enough to engage with and drive through that resistance in order for each line to flow, means we collect an impulse that can launch the sequence of sounds from which each line is made. We launch that impulse with the *leading sound*. For example, that first 'j' of *judicious* will be responsible for launching the impulse of line 1 into the space.

> judicious genial jar

Thus 'j' becomes responsible not only for its own word, but the whole line. The movement and dynamic that constitutes the flow of language is then achieved with ease, without the speaker resorting to the need to push.

---

[*] See chapter 5 for a consideration of other aspects of this exercise.

Letting the sounds do the work

This brings us to another central principle of our technique: learning to apply our effort so we do not invest energy unnecessarily. We might state our goals in this respect, as follows:

- To do the work that I can do in order to allow the sounds to do the work that they can do.
- To be as fully present in the *act* of speaking as in the *content* of what is being said.

With practice, we shall experience no separation. Until then, we may be frustrated by that split between the words we speak and the content we are seeking to express. In these explorations, we are not responsible for any content beyond the sounds themselves. This means we can afford to give ourselves entirely to creating sounds. This practice results in our ability to achieve maximum intensity with a sense of ease.

Let us imagine I am playing Romeo and speaking to Juliet on her balcony. I want to be fully present in the intensities of his relationship with Juliet and what is happening around him. This is not possible if my energy and focus are still engaged in achieving the magic of the language by navigating the complexities of sentence structure and producing all nuance of expression with the appropriate volume. Only when those requirements make no demands on my attention am I free to create, to be available artistically.

Every Speech-exploration presents an opportunity to learn the work each sound can do for us. One important function that the sounds can relieve us of, if we allow them to, is responsibility for the flow of language. We learn to recognize the *leading sounds*: those responsible for the dynamic. We learn how to gather them from space in such a way that they become the bearers of the impulse within which the dominant dynamic rides. Other sounds can then ride within that dominant dynamic and make their contribution to sustaining it.[*]

Flexibility, mobility and presence of mind

These next Speech-explorations demand flexibility and mobility from our organs of articulation. As our skills develop, we practise our art with the consciousness that the beings of the sounds work upon our instrument as a totality of soul and body in service of the spirit.

Huge contrasts are required both *within* and *between* each line of *Speech-explorations 37* and *38*. Only utmost presence of mind enables our organs of articulation to achieve these vastly different qualities within an overall dynamic. This mobility and flexibility

---

[*] See chapter 5 for an exploration of the leading sound in relationship to the theme of wholeness.

required in the mouth is much more easily achieved if it is not regarded as separate from the rest of our instrument. It is fruitful, therefore, to prepare for explorations 37 and 38 with Chekhov's full-body explorations which render our whole instrument available and sensitive to changes of texture, tempo and dynamic.[*]

Speech-exploration 37

curtsy betsy jets cleric
lastly light sceptic
curtsy cressets betsy jets cleric
lastly plotless light sceptic

Within each line we meet a shift from the sharper, staccato qualities of /ts/ which ignites the space with an incendiary flash, into the legato liquid quality of /l/. This shift then alternates with its reversal in the next line. We move from sharp flash into flow and then from flow to sharp flash, and so on. To achieve this shift so that each line unfolds as an unbroken dynamic that connects it to the next, we must warm up to the mobility and flexibility that such a shift, such a transformation, asks of us. The consonants exercise their power to permeate the vowels, determine the dynamic and, thus, shape each line expressively.

Speech-exploration 38

towhit twinkle twas
twice twigged tweaker
to twenty twangy twirlings
the zinnia crisper
zither zooming shambles
this smartened smacking smuggler
sneezing snoring snatching

The character that dominates the first three lines is built from the staccato tendency of /t/ continually softened by the lip sound /w/. This firm yet delicate interaction encourages dynamics which are playfully awake, projecting them into the space with a fine cutting edge that is unthreatening.

towhit twinkle twas
twice twigged tweaker
to twenty twangy twirlings

---

[*] See *The Art of Acting*, chapter 2, staccato and legato.

Then /z/ takes over as the leading sound.

> zither zooming shambles

Being a voiced fricative, /z/ immediately impresses greater density into the next two lines, slowing the tempo. The dynamic with which breath is released for the duration of the /z/ is steady, legato, and carves the space smoothly, imparting a sense of gravitas.

In the last two lines the combinations /sm/ and /sn/ perform as leading sounds.

> this smartened smacking smuggler
> sneezing snoring snatching

The first, /sm/, with its combination of clarity from the teeth and warmth and softness from the lips, enables us to sink into the texture of the line. The latter, /sn/, has a strong edge arising from the combination of the two sounds formed on the hard palate, just behind the teeth. Together with the character of /n/, this invites us to bounce or spring back from the earth.

This Speech-exploration encourages a sense of playfulness. We can imagine a mischievous child or adult speaking, or an elemental being like Puck who torments and taunts its victim with a sense of fun that is without malice.* We learn to manage every shift of quality and texture within the overall dynamic which in turn develops flexible and mobile instruments. Each line must be true to its own nature and yet arise organically out of what has gone before, at the same time creating the basis for what follows. Presence of mind will grow along with confidence, as we discover and join the unique activity with which each sound permeates a phrase or line.

Speech-exploration 39

> moisten mason mine essence
> lamer lightness liza loiter
> buy beaten bowers bide brave
> come crooked craftiest cur

The qualities of the four contrasting consonants shape language according to their nature, enabling us to express a range of nuances in an artistic context. Accurate formation for its own sake of /m/, /l/, /b/ and /k/ is not our goal. We want to know how each sound can contribute its specific 'gift' to our range of expressiveness. We

---

* See *The Integrated Actor* for its application to the comic style.

shall immerse ourselves in each one until we understand what it requires of us that enables it to do its work.

> moisten mason mine essence

The /m/, in combination with the qualities of /s/ and /n/, enables several strongly distinct syllables to flow in a smooth, legato sequence.

> lamer lightness liza loiter

Through the qualities of /l/, we overcome resistances provided by the /t/, once again creating a continuous legato flow of syllables.

> buy beaten bowers bide brave

The /b/ now teaches us how, within an overall dynamic, to enclose and make distinct each separate form within a sequence.

> come crooked craftiest cur

The 'c' (/k/ as in king) requires courage to enter space with the intention to divide and separate. Yet, to accomplish this division of the syllables within the ongoing movement of a line we need to launch an unvoiced consonant, formed in the very back part of our instrument, so that it takes the vowel forward into space. Such a challenge is typical of how Steiner often places a hurdle in our path which, in overcoming it, develops an enhanced capacity.

Speech-exploration 40

> narrow wren
> mirror royal
> gearing grizzled
> noting nippers
> fender coughing

These short sequences of sounds require the organs of articulation to pick their way, with utmost care, from one placement to another. This arouses a sensation of meticulous precision, appropriate for texts that require a delicate refinement or a mannered quality. It can be fun to try this with a partner and imagine that you thread a needle with each line. If you can make each syllable sheer enough to penetrate the eye without its edges fraying, it will enable your partner to pull it through to the other side.

Even in this exploration, where our focus is precision, our aim is still to free the voice and achieve transparency. This cannot be achieved if we shrink our consciousness from its participation in the infinite. We still remind ourselves that the syllables we thread through the needle's eye do not originate in us. We receive them from the greater space, like finely chiselled, feathered darts, and send them on their way. Notice too, how we are challenged to achieve such fine precision not only from the naturally suited teeth and ridge behind the teeth but from every placement possible. We learn how to engrave the forms of the softer lip sounds and the chunkier ones formed at the soft back of the palate delicately, like jewellers or those legendary artists who can carve a grain of rice.

A word about accents

The pronunciation, rhythms and patterns of inflection with which a group of people speak a language we refer to as an *accent*. In our context, the reproduction of an accent is not exclusively about the skill to imitate those qualities. Rather, those qualities provide us with the opportunity to feel our way into the consciousness which has expressed itself in them. From a psycho-physical perspective, the ways human beings experience the world produce the different accents.[*]

Let us place *world*, under the microscope. When we speak *world* in these five generic accents and allow the actions and sensations in our mouth to permeate our whole body, we sense the unique perspective of experience embodied in each accent.

A full-bodied meditation arising from the micro-gestures of five accents

Queen's English: *I am very conscious of my head, detached and stiff in relation to the rest of my body. I observe the world in a detached way. To roll the 'r' demands a level of engagement that is too confronting. Better to ignore it totally!*

Irish: *To speak the soft 'r', I bring it forward to my lips; this permeates me with warmth and makes me lyrical and dreamy; softer altogether.*

Scottish: *In order to roll the 'r' /r/, my tongue tip is very active, drumming against the hard palate. I am awake, ready to confront the world and the harsh northern climate.*

American: *I speak 'r' and my voice stays with it, back inside the throat. I am supremely confident, 'laid back'. I sense the world is mine, owes me what I want and I can have anything I want.*

Australian: *It's an effort to enunciate the consonants. 'r' disappears completely and 'l' almost disappears along with it. It is as though the consonants dissolve into some generic diphthong. I am aware of dryness in my throat. In a country with so little water, survival has priority and encourages a culture without pretensions. Why waste effort opening my mouth*

---

[*] See *The Art of Acting*, chapter 1, psycho-physical, also, chapter 4, gesture.

in the heat. Vowels droop and flatten, spreading out forever across vast plains. Without much breath they grate, like the harsh cries of galahs and cockatoos.

These few observations suggest a path of research for those who wish to work with accents.

Placement

Exploring the different ways of saying *world*, my sensations changed, reflecting differing relationships to my capacities for thinking, feeling and for action. These changes in sensation resulted from changes in the micro-gestures performed by different organs of articulation. There is a close connection between these three soul functions and the organs and structure in our mouths.

We can distinguish three main regions in our mouths:

a)   The front, forward of the teeth, up to and inclusive of the lips.
b)   The middle, the area behind and inclusive of the teeth.
c)   The soft palate at the back.

Approaching the anatomy of placement with imagination

Since our premise is that nothing in the universe is arbitrary, we assume that wisdom is at work in the sounds produced by the tongue interacting with lips, teeth and palate. For those who have learned to read such mysteries, the whole human being is imprinted in a single drop of blood, or in the palm or foot, or iris of the eye. Why might not the range of human functioning be equally condensed, with microcosmic intensity, into the structure of our mouth? Such a reading confirms that articulation is not mere mechanical proficiency isolated from what makes us human.

The mastery of speech arising from an understanding of the three placements provides us with the basis for creating speech of different characters, and the key to unlock the secrets of artistic style; the origin of different styles and their relationship to our spectrum of experience.[*]

The feast — I'll eat my words

> For we shall not live by bread alone,
> but are nourished by the word of God . . .

based on Gospel of St Matthew, 4:3

Can it be an accident that the parts of our mouth that enable us to shape the sounds of Speech are those with which we eat? What can our imagination make of this connection?

> I take the bread,
> hold it in my hands,
> this bit of world outside to be invited in.

---

[*] See chapter 6.

First cross the threshold of my lips.
In hatred, will they spit it out, or in love with,
will they soften, long for, kiss creation's crumb,
this hold it to my lips, caress, and feel
I want to let the world-bread in,
its labour to become
a part of, mingle, merge, be made of me?
I open them.

I break the bread.
Teeth between their edges, biting into, crushing, chopping, cutting into fragments,
breaking down, remorseless!
If you want to make them, turn them into you,
reduce, destroy these bits of bread, you must.

Receive them.

Tongue senses, stirs, tastes all is ready,
moves no longer bread already mingled with my juices, part of me dissolving
into bread no longer bread dissolving into me
no longer what I was,
moving back towards the dark abyss, the after this
no turning back.
Dark throat I can no longer follow
into, where mysteriously saying final yes
I take the world inside,
this crumbly bit of earth outside,
this once was bread into my unknown dark
to disappear,
to make into myself
a part of me.

I swallow.

Lips

Our lips form a boundary that separates what we perceive to be *inside* or *outside* of us. This imparts to them a special function. They are like the curtains in the theatre, or a veil that can be lifted. When we open them to speak, we expose what lives inside us to the world. They are soft and flexible, although the muscles can be tensed. When the lips interact, they form the consonants /b/, /p/, /m/ and /w/.

Their flexibility allows them to change into almost any shape. They can stretch in different directions, supporting and framing the vowels formed back in the mouth, nearer to the throat. They can protrude, helping to round and shape those vowels formed at the front: /ɔ/ (d<u>o</u>t), /ɔː/ (<u>awe</u>), /u/ (t<u>oo</u>k), and /uː/ (sh<u>oe</u>). In helping form these latter sounds, they contract almost to a point.

The micro-gestures with which our lips shape these forward consonants and vowels arouse sensations that remind us what we feel when we kiss and express love and intimacy. When we listen to consonants and vowels formed by and in the region of the lips, we sense a quality of *warmth*.

The teeth and teeth ridge

Set behind the curtains of the lips, the walls of the teeth are hard, inflexible and have a clear, sharp edge. Their function in eating serves as a metaphor for intellect, which breaks down our experience with its sharp, ruthless edge, chops it into concepts and allows us to chew over an idea. So too do the sounds we produce on the hard palate just behind the teeth (the alveolar ridge) have this clear edge to them and give precision to our speech: /n/, /t/, /d/, /l/, /s/, /r/, /ɾ/ (rolled /r/), /ʃ/ (<u>s</u>ugar), /tʃ/ (<u>ch</u>ild), /dʒ/ (<u>j</u>udge), /z/, /ɪ/ (s<u>i</u>p), /iː/(m<u>e</u>) and /ei/ (d<u>a</u>te). These sounds express our capacity to analyse, make clear distinctions and to think.

Soft palate

Almost inaccessible to conscious control is the threshold at the back of the throat. Hovering around this threshold enables us to gargle, gurgle, and if we transgress, the guardian at the gateway to the oesophagus causes us to gag. Once we have swallowed, what was once outside us is within. The fact that when we touch that place the gag reflex is aroused, shows that this region of our speech instrument is organically connected to our metabolic system, normally outside our voluntary control. We have no consciousness of how the catabolic forces break down food, transforming it into energy which enables us to act. Nor are we conscious of how the anabolic forces are constantly creating us anew. Yet the sounds formed in this region, /g/, /k/, and /ɑː/ (st<u>a</u>r), if we can learn to work with them consciously, allow us to express the quality of will in action.

Combinations

Some sounds arise when our organs of articulation play with crossing the borders that separate the areas of placement. For example, /f/ and /v/ require the teeth to interact with the lips, infusing precision and clarity with warmth.

Tongue

The tongue is the muscular, sensing actor, at home on the whole stage of the mouth, able to move anywhere and play any part. Its function as a tasting organ means that it can sense out what is needed and, chameleon-like, respond. It can harden into a blunt edge or one that has a fine point. It can arch, flatten, curl or roll, stroke or be soft and receptive. Its tip can sense its way, probing tenderly and delicately forward between the hard edge of the teeth towards the softer lips; creating, as it does so, /θ/ (thing) or /ð/ (the). In this aspect, it plays a special role in the consciousness of those who speak the English language.

Imagine that aspect of consciousness which in the seventeenth, eighteenth and nineteenth centuries pioneered discoveries that led to the industrial revolution. Through the contributions of Locke and Newton, it moved us nearer to materialism. And now the consequences have exposed the need to learn a new perception of the beingness of things; a heart-intelligence which already senses that the edges of these things are not so firm as had been thought.

Turner, painting them, shows how they dissolve into pure energy and movement. Science begins to confirm that these are the truth of matter. What sound could embody such a subtle blend of thinking moving towards feeling; in every 'the', we paint it with our tongue; the softening of edges, the recognition that the separate thing already is dissolving?

Hopkins writes:

> These things, these things were here and but the beholder
> Wanting; which two when they once meet,
> The heart rears wings bold and bolder . . .
>
> *Hurrahing in Harvest*

Is the English language giving us a hint of future sensibilities that will arise when thinking is not separate from love?

A purely physical conception of anatomy suggests the organs of articulation are the arbitrary consequence of cells dividing and combining over vast aeons of time. The Art of Speech Formation considers the activities of vowels and consonants to be expressions of divine creative beings whose creating includes the organs that enable us to utter and express those same activities. For example, the creative power which gathers and condenses energy to substance in forms that are embracing and protecting, has created lips which are capable of that same formative activity. The result is our capacity to speak /b/.

A view of articulation resonant with these thoughts invites us to be conscious co-creators with divine creative beings so their work can unfold through us. To participate in our evolving; to penetrate our thinking, feeling and capacity for action consciously in order to embody them in speaking; to begin the long journey back to an integrated Self that might some day give birth to an integrated word; a word which not only conveys information but *creates*.[*]

Speech-exploration 41

> by miner wafer
> by boom
> by vie
>
> see fee shielding
> reeled far
> full reeled needy
>
> noon air lark anger ink
> ink ringer growl
> ink ringer grows shaft

These lines teach us how to express, in Speech, the thinking, feeling and willing functions of our souls.

Stage 1

> by miner wafer
> by boom
> by vie

Our aim is to let the forward consonants of this first set of lines, /b/, /m/, /w/ imbue our voices with the warmth of feeling that is the special gift imparted by our lips. That warmth and softness can then penetrate the sounds that come from further back, the /f/ and /v/ which involve the harder teeth, and the /n/ which is formed on the ridge behind the teeth.

Allow the warmth of the forward vowel /uː/ (b<u>oo</u>m) to permeate the diphthong as it moves from back to middle in the /aɪ/ (b<u>y</u> and v<u>ie</u>). From these three lines, we learn to colour a whole passage of text with our feelings' warmth; a sensation that the sounds we speak are spilling gently from our lips, warmly caressing all they touch.

> see fee shielding
> reeled far
> full reeled needy

---

[*] Huge implications for a new approach to working therapeutically arise from such a way of looking at the art of Speech. References are given in Appendix D for those who wish to find out more about this work in English.

The heart-centre

Practise the explorations for the *heart-centre.*[*]

Figure 8 – Heart-centre based on the image of Apollo

---

[*] See *The Art of Acting*, chapter 3.

Can you sense a connection between your lips and heart?

Figure 9 – connecting lips and feeling 1

Now let the forces from your heart stream through your lips and speak the first three lines:

by miner wafer
by boom
by vie

Figure 10 – connecting lips and feeling 2

The head-centre

Practise the explorations for the *head-centre.*[*]

Figure 11 – head-centre based on the Charioteer

---

[*] See *The Art of Acting*, chapter 3.

Can you sense a connection between the region of your teeth and the centre in your head?

Figure 12 – connecting teeth and thinking 1

Now let your clear thinking forces stream through the region of your teeth and speak the next three lines:

see fee shielding
reeled far
full reeled needy

Figure 13 – connecting teeth and thinking 2

The will-centre

Practise the explorations for the *will-centre* (centre in your belly).[*]

Figure 14 – will-centre based on the warrior 1

---

[*] See *The Art of Acting*, chapter 3.

Can you sense a connection between the centre in your belly and your soft palate?

Figure 15 – connection between the belly and soft palate 1

Let the forces of your will stream through that region of your mouth and speak the next three lines:

    noon air lark anger ink
    ink ringer growl
    ink ringer grows shaft

Figure 16 – connection between the belly and soft palate 2

The second set of lines centres on the consonants and vowels formed in the region of the teeth and teeth ridge or hard palate. To support our striving for the clarity and definition, which is the gift of sounds formed on or near the teeth, practise each line with a gesture of releasing an arrow through the space.

Having let these sounds teach us their qualities, we can permeate the other sounds with the teeth's sharp edges and colour text with the distinctness and clarity we associate with thinking. We can learn to permeate even the broad and open /ɑː/ (f<u>a</u>r), formed at the back of the instrument, with something of the narrow, streamlined gesture of the /iː/ (s<u>ee</u>, f<u>ee</u>, etc).

> noon air lark anger ink
> ink ringer growl
> ink ringer grows shaft

The last three lines are anchored in the consonants formed on the soft palate at the back. We are led there first by sounds formed at the front and middle; only finally arriving at the back with the last sound of *lark*. Thus we are guided step-by-step to awaken our will in 'g' and 'k', which then keep us anchored firmly in the back even while the other sounds require us to range across our instrument. Each time we speak the combinations 'ng' and 'nk' we are required to shift our activity from middle to back.

Through these consonants, which awaken the forces of our will, we learn that Speech has the power to create. Then we return to the sounds formed at the teeth and lips (*grows shaft*), but able now to permeate them with the forming and condensing power of the will.

The sounds teach us to imbue our speech with qualities specific to their region. This can only happen when we start to sense not just how to *form a sound correctly* but how to *enter its activity*; how it takes hold of our instrument, shaping our voice as well as words. When we have a sense of this, we can apply that activity to sounds with different qualities. Then, in relation to our thinking, feeling and our will capacities, we can achieve and sustain our quality of choice.

A text may demand sharp clarity in order to express its rational content. In this famous quote from Shakespeare's *Hamlet*, there are several words with warm lip sounds, particularly /m/, /b/, /p/, /ɔ/(n<u>o</u>t), the diphthong /ɔʊ/(n<u>o</u>bler, opp<u>o</u>sing), /uː/ (t<u>o</u>) and the diphthong /ɔː ə/ (<u>or</u>, f<u>or</u>tune)?

> To be or not to be that is the question.
> Whether 'tis nobler in the mind to suffer
> The slings and arrows of outrageous fortune,
> Or to take up arms against a sea of troubles,
> And by opposing end them ...

Practising the second set of lines in stage 1 teaches me to form those lip sounds (feeling) with the clarity of those formed at the teeth (thinking), and to sustain that clarity throughout the passage.

Variations on stage 1 – integration with Chekhov's work on the three archetypal centres

The Art of Acting, chapter 3, assists the integration of our whole instrument in achieving the qualities of warmth, clarity and strength in our speaking.

Stage 2

> by miner wafer
> reeled far
> noon air lark anger ink
>
> ink ringer growl
> reeled far
> by boom
>
> ink ringer grows shaft
> full reeled needy
> by vie

When confident that you can activate each distinct capacity within each set of lines, divide each set and intersperse them so that you learn to change the quality from one line to the next. Your speech organs become flexible, able to shift in their response as you move between your faculties of thinking, feeling and of will. Gradually, you will learn to travel seamlessly from one soul function to another.[*] Your speech will be grounded because it has been integrated with your whole instrument.

---

[*] See chapter 6 for how these become the basis of the epic, lyric and dramatic styles, and *The Integrated Actor* for application to our work with character.

Figure 17 – will-centre based on the warrior

Figure 18 – The charioteer

Speech-exploration 42 – placement of the vowels

KEY: /ɑː/ (st<u>a</u>r), /iː/ (m<u>e</u>), /uː/ (sh<u>oe</u>)

Version 1

(a)   Ah there! she will teach dear, archers capers

(b)   O stir you moor, for me with milk, fruit to mousse.

(c)   harder strata /ɑː/ – – –
finger seemed /iː/ – – –
by vagrant /ɑː/ – – –
loitered shown /ɑː/ – – –
too fiendish /uː/ – – –

The vowels of line (a) require us to be active at the back of our instrument, only moving as far forward as the middle. The vowels of line (b) require us to be active in the regions of the middle and the front of our instrument. Section (c) requires us to weave back and forth between the placements.

Because English usage turns so many vowels to diphthongs, the specific, clear sensations engendered by the pure German vowels and their related consonants are not so easy to experience as in Steiner's original version. In version 2, I have attempted to find sounds which are closer to the German.*

Version 2

(a)   Ah ba<u>re</u>, itch fill nicked dea<u>r</u>, amen gay Ben.

(b)   O shell push mo<u>re</u>, mule foal, me<u>re</u> mit milk, news zoo moose.

(c)   hea<u>rt</u> air sta<u>r</u>k air /ɑː/ – – –
thing ai<u>r</u> sinned /iː/ – – –
by far ke<u>r</u>n /ɑː/ – – –
loiter shorn /ɑː/ – – –
zoo fiend dig /uː/ – – –

RS DL

---

* The decision to do so came from working with Speech-exploration 38 in German and the clear sensations that arise from the less mobile placements of the German vowels. In doing so I have sacrificed that aspect of the original which is the impulse and dynamic that arise because the sequence of syllables belong ultimately to a single sentence and are threaded in that stream.

Aber – ich will nicht dir – alle geben.

O schäl und schmor – mühe voll – mir mit milch – nüss zu muss.

It helps to experience the closest approximations to the German placements if the 'r' is rolled /r/ in places indicated by the phonetic symbol. It can be fun to explore this by playing with a Scottish accent.

We are not aiming only for correct articulation of the vowel; our goal is to free the vowel into space so it can reveal the soul-gesture it expresses. We don't speak the vowel until we've attuned ourselves to the appropriate inner state. This allows the vowel, in turn, to work back on that inner state.

The vowel is released into the space through the consonant's activity. When lines begin with vowels, the activity of consonants can already be present in the way we speak those vowels. We let the consonants draw the vowels towards them from the future, as it were.

In section (c) the strong activity of consonants with which each phrase begins carves a channel into which we pour the vowel.[*] Then, the possibility for that free-streaming vowel is contained in our collection of the phrase. The resulting dynamic provides a 'pulse' in which the vowel may stream into the space. This pulse is represented by the triple stroke following the symbol of the vowel.

The activity of the consonants is what prepares the appropriate micro-gesture in our mouths to support the vowel's journey into space. We have achieved this goal when we experience that the vowel does not come *from* our mouths but *through* our mouths, from infinity: it manifests in finite space and time for the duration of its pulse of three, and disappears again into the infinite.

When parts (a), (b) and (c) are mastered, work according to the sequence below, repeating each line and combination ten times:

Line (a)	− 10 times
Line (b)	− 10 times
Lines (a) & (b)	− 10 times
Line (c)	− 10 times
Lines (a), (b) & (c)	− 10 times

When we practise this sequence, we may observe that our sense of life is quickened. We start to understand that it is not our mouths alone with which we speak, and sense a deepening experience that the structure of our chest and head is engaged, supported by the lower half of our body. It is our whole body that supports the miracle that what we become aware of in our soul can be expressed in speech. *Speech-exploration 42* can cultivate a sense for the sacred mystery of speech: the human form has been created so that we might speak and there is not one cell of us that is not engaged to make this possible.

Ah ba_re, itch fill nicked dea_r amen gay Ben.

---

[*] See chapter 5 regarding the collection of each line in its totality.

In line (a) we form the vowel /ɑː/ (ah, amen) at the back and move forward only to the middle of the mouth in /iː/ (itch, fill, etc). The sensations awakened in us by this activity make us aware of forces that shape the lower region of our instrument, from chest to throat.

O shell push more, mule foal, mere mit milk, news zoo moose

Line (b), on the other hand, requires that we work with vowels that lie forward of the middle boundary but move no further back than that. The sensations awakened make us aware of forces active from the throat through to the top of our head.

heart air stark air, /ɑː/ - - -
thing air sinned, /iː/ - - -
by far kern, /ɑː/ - - -
loiter shawn, /ɑː/ - - -
zoo fiend dig, /uː/ - - -

The lines of section (c) invite us to move back and forth through both these possibilities. The sensations thus awakened make us aware that higher powers massage and permeate us when we speak. From this evolves a deepening sense that it is not we who make the sounds, but they who make us, and we are co-creators with them.

Volume, Resonance and Projection

Nowadays, perhaps because of film and the reliance on electronic amplification on the stage, the ability to increase volume in a way that does not cause stress to the throat has largely been lost. Consequently, when actors are required to speak more loudly, they shout. This increase of pressure in the throat is so traumatic for the larynx that it is common for actors whose roles are vocally demanding to suffer from chronic laryngitis. There are throat specialists who devote themselves to finding ways that will enable actors to preserve their voices.

In the years before electronic amplification, voice projection involved an understanding of the function and use of resonating chambers in the head. 'Old school' actors prided themselves on having rich and velvety 'actors' voices. They could fill large theatres without the need to shout, but that rich and velvety voice was often achieved and maintained at the expense of flexibility. Limited to a single timbre, it reflected but one aspect of an actor's personality and could lead to a preoccupation with pursuing the 'beautiful voice' for its own sake. Speech Formation allows an actor to develop the resonant possibilities of the voice in a way that serves the expressive nuances for which such resonance might be appropriate.

A new look at resonance

Our voices would be barely audible were not the wavelengths caused by vibrations of the vocal chords amplified within the resonating chambers of the head. These are located mainly in the throat or pharynx and the nasal and oral cavities. What is referred to as the distinctive timbre and texture of a voice is the result of these same resonating capabilities. Qualities arising from each person's individual anatomy, such as surface texture, density of substance, and size and shape of chambers, combine and interact to produce an individual's distinctive resonance. The distinctive resonance which makes a violin sound like a violin, a trombone like a trombone, is determined by these same variable factors.

There are two consonants, /n/ and /m/, whose gifts to our voices are the qualities we most associate with resonance; warmth and musicality. These are the sounds identified as *nasals*, formed when the breath obstructed in the oral cavity or mouth, is allowed to pass through the nose. The resonating chamber of the nasal cavity can then reinforce the original vibrations, imparting a characteristic richness of timbre to the voice.

The following lines awaken in the listener or reader an experience of musicality. It seems entirely appropriate that they should be spoken with a musical quality of voice.

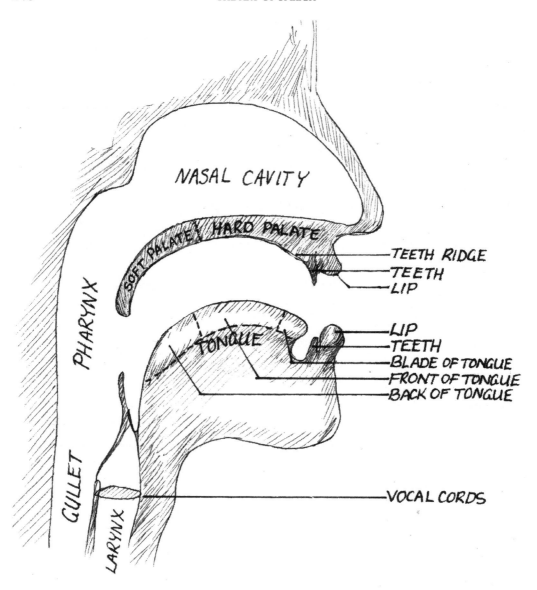

Figure 19 – resonance chambers

There is sweet music here that softer falls
Than petals from blown roses on the grass;
Music, that gentlier on the spirit lies
Than tired eyelids upon tired eyes.

The Lotus-Eaters, Tennyson

Another example is the famous 'moonlight' speech from *The Merchant of Venice*.* Or, these lines of Romeo, when he first sees Juliet at the ball:

---

* See page 115.

If I profane, with my unworthiest hand,
This holy shrine, the gentle sin is this:
My lips, two blushing pilgrims, ready stand
To smooth that rough touch with a tender kiss.[*]

In contrast to the 'old school' actor's voice, what we are aiming for is vocal beauty that does not draw attention to itself, but serves the beauty of the image or character's emotion. This can only happen when resonance is selfless.

In the traditional technique, an actor achieved resonance by a conscious sounding and sustaining of the tone of /n/ and /m/, allowing their vibrations to be amplified within the resonating chamber of the nasal cavity. That resonance became a base tone through which the vowels could be sounded. The actor's voice resounded in its own tone and, rather like the function of the drone, imparted it to all the vowels. Such a tone could not help but be self-centred, dependent as it is upon sustained reverberation of the voice *within* the instrument that is producing it.

Instead of encouraging our voice to ring and vibrate within our instrument, Speech Formation teaches us to let the resonance move through us so that it can sound in the space outside the speaker. Instead of holding on to /n/ and /m/, we reach into our back space, collect them from infinity and allow their gesture to flow through our entire instrument. As we actively move with and through the consonants, allowing them to appear from and disappear back into infinity the vowels travel inside their living stream and move along with them. Instead of resonating in its own tone, the voice becomes transparent, the vowels suffused with delicate radiance. The audience is not aware of the beauty of the actor's voice, but appreciates instead, the beauty of the image and the soul's feeling manifesting in the space.

Speech-exploration 43 – resonance in contrasting tempos

name neat norman/on nimble moody mules

Each of the first three words wants to occupy the fullness of the space. To achieve this, the line is spoken with a slower tempo. The speaker's challenge is to let each syllable achieve full resonance but not hold onto it. In contrast, the sequence of syllables in the second section needs to move through the space with a faster tempo, while still achieving resonance.

Some of the vowels do not naturally encourage the fullness of tone we associate with resonance. For example, (n<u>ea</u>t) /iː/ and (n<u>a</u>me) /ei/ tend towards a sharp-edged clarity. When such vowels appear in texts that require a warm, rich, full voice, they

---

[*] Some versions suggest 'This holy shrine, the gentle fine is this'.

present a challenge. The consonants /n/ and /m/ lend their rich resonance to those thinner sounds while they in turn enhance and define the movement in between the mellow sounds.

When resonance has been achieved in each separate part of the exercise, both can then be grasped as an entirety and, as though they form a single sentence, unfolded in an overall dynamic which includes the change of tempo.[*] When the desired quality of resonance has been achieved, apply it to the text examples from Tennyson and Shakespeare.

Speech-exploration 44 – to overcome nasality

> Cockney, look not!
> Seek no nicknames

One timbre in particular, the one referred to commonly as 'nasal', elicits a uniform response; unpleasant and difficult to listen to. Surprisingly it is the consequence not of too much nasal resonance, but too little. Lack of nasal resonance can be caused by a lack of tonicity in the muscles of the throat or pharynx which provides access to the nasal cavity. As with any muscles this is very often caused simply by lack of activity. *Speech-exploration 44* stimulates precisely such activity.

Throughout the exercise the muscles of the soft palate required to form /k/ are called on to be active, leaving no chance for passivity. Thus strengthened, they provide the tension necessary to support the opening of the resonating chamber of the nasal cavity. If each line is gathered as a whole, the resonant /n/ and /m/ can then occur within the context of the strong activity required at the back of the mouth. This activity then serves, not only the forming of each /k/, but the projection of that resonance in the space.

Volume and projection

There are times when a louder voice is necessary and/or artistically appropriate. Speech Formation offers us a healthy way to increase volume; one which will not harm the throat and which is able to equally project the tenderness and reverence in Romeo's words as Tybalt's hatred and aggression.

It is not uncommon to hear actors forced to sacrifice delicate feelings and emotions in the interests of being heard. If we allow the consonants to be our teachers, they will show us ways to project a range of vocal nuances and how to increase volume without

---

[*] See *The Art of Acting*, chapter 2 to prepare for such mobility by working with the tempo and dynamic explorations.

shouting. The following exercises especially benefit from applying the process described in *Speech-exploration 57.*[*]

Speech-exploration 45 – freeing the voice

> clip plop pluck cluck
> clinked clapper richly
> knotted trappings
> rosily tripled

To build the steps to our goal of increased volume without damage to our instrument requires patience. First we learn how to release our voice and free it from the body. If we can manage this, we need not depend on increased tension in the throat to push the voice out loudly. What we hear as 'voice' is always vowel. In our approach it is the consonant which takes responsibility to clothe the vowel and bear it into space.

The first two lines present us with sequences of vowels, each one enclosed by a string of compact little packages of consonants. Each package is grasped in such a way that it can be lifted cleanly across the threshold of the lips, carrying intact the vowel (or voice) enclosed within. The sequence of the consonants begins with an unvoiced plosive which grasps the voiced sound /l/. Try each syllable in turn.

> clip plop pluck cluck

Sense how /l/ acts as a lubricant. It smooths the vowel's path, enabling it to slip easily across the lips. The voice, thus loosened from the instrument, intact within its skin of consonants, is free to fall into the space. Like a ripe fruit dropping in its own weight, it lands on the firm surface of a /p/ or /k/. Because each syllable is sealed with the solidity of a plosive, our voice can bounce off it into the next syllable, which cascades down to the next level and continues dropping. If we do not demand greater volume before we are ready and are content to build a healthy foundation for achieving it, then this first step ensures that we let our voice emerge into the space *with a sense of ease.*

Absence of unhealthy tension does not mean absence of activity. We provide the impulse within which each little sequence of consonants can do its work and so attune ourselves to what each consonant requires to release its unique dynamic and activity. When the consonants emerge, they provide strong vessels for the vowels/voice.

We can work quite intimately, caring for each syllable as it emerges on the far side of our lips and drops down in its own weight, to the earth. Trusting gravity to do its part

---

[*] See chapter 5, page 206.

and take hold of our voice, we allow it to relax completely. Once freed in this way, we are ready to apply our effort to project it further.

The sounds /k/ and /p/ provide the beginnings and ends of syllables. This means we move back and forth through our instrument. The first syllable provides us with the greatest challenge: to send our voice all the way from the back of our throat, out into space. Having once achieved this feat, our task is to keep our voice out in the space in front; even as progressive formation of the sounds requires movement to the back of the instrument again.

The strong array of plosive consonants in the first two lines introduces us to yet another of our basic principles. Plosives can create a strong resistance or a barrier to the flow of speech and we make use of this resistance. Instead of being blocked by it, we use it as a base from which to spring. The second line confronts us with the multiple barriers of /k/ and /d/ in *clinked*.

> clinked clapper richly

If we approach these consonants with the intention and energy to bounce off of them, they will catapult our voices 'over the wall' into the space beyond. If we are able to collect the impulse of each single line, and ultimately all the lines as a totality, we shall find, across the wall, succeeding syllables awaiting us. We won't need to push them out by tensing the throat. Freed from our instrument and brimming with their own inherent life and energy, we can put our energy into creating *with* them what they would unfold.[*]

To project our voices in a range of qualities depends on our knowledge of how each sound moves in space and our part in releasing its capacity to do so. If we learn to make proper use of them, even sounds that offer us resistance serve the projection of our voices. In the third line, we make use of the firm staccato onset of the /n/ to grasp the forward vowel /ɔ/ in *knotted*:

> knotted trappings

If collected with the overall intention that it serve this task, the /n/ launches the voice into the line, condensed into a quality of strength and certainty. It is as though the very firmness with which we press this line into the space allows us to release into the final line.

The airy movement and dynamic of the rolled 'r' /ɾ/, can now unfurl its light-filled arc of syllables in contrast to the bouncing, earthy ricochet of the early lines:

> rosily tripled

---

[*] See chapter 5 for a further investigation of this principle.

When the potential for projection inherent in each line has been mastered, we can build their different streams and dynamics into a totality that unfolds as a single sentence might unfold. Even the dynamic of the final line will be contained within the energy and impulse of that first /kl/ of *clip*.

Speech-exploration 46

> Dart may these boats through darkening gloaming

We are now ready to project the structure of a single sentence into space. The first five words require us to move through the commonly accepted sequence of five vowels.

> Dart may these boats through

We move through the range of placements from the furthest back to furthest forward. Then they begin again at the back, move to the front, concluding in the middle. At the same time, the formative activity required by the consonants progresses from middle and front towards the back.

Speech-exploration 46 addresses a fundamental challenge. How do I keep my voice out in the space and moving forward when the activity required to produce a sound is occurring further back or moving progressively towards the back of my speech instrument? The last syllable *ing*, pulls our speech activity from the middle to the back again. We face this challenge twice as we draw near the end of the sentence, forcing us to find a way to avoid letting the last words of our sentence fade or disappear; a problem many speakers face.

To overcome this challenge, we explore three ways of physically projecting. The first is the javelin throw. Steiner suggests that of the five gymnastic exercises of the Ancient Greeks, throwing the javelin most prepares us for the act of Speech.[*] Why?

We know how frustrating it can be when speakers have so little commitment to reaching their listeners that we can't hear what they say. We cannot expect to be heard if we do not have the will to reach the listener. When we throw a javelin, we intend that the javelin should reach its goal and learn to commit the energy required to accomplish this intention.

If I do not gather my impulse from as far behind me as I wish to reach in front, I jerk the javelin from my shoulder. This produces not only an imperfect throw, but may well strain my muscles. Shouting is the speaking equivalent of jerking from the shoulder. When I shout, sensing I have nothing to draw on but my own physicality, that I have my 'back against the wall', I jerk my voice from my throat. This is why

---

[*] See *The Art of Acting*, chapter 2.

shouting always sounds aggressive. To project our voice in a way that will not harm our instrument we first step the syllables.

When I walk forward, each step occupies its own position, further forward than the last. Unless we make a choice to step forward to the next place, we are 'marking time', stepping on the same spot. But we cannot take a step forward and be present in the centre of it unless we relinquish the step just taken. So, too, a syllable can only move forward in the space if we let go of the one that preceded it and thereby free ourselves to step into the centre of the next. Not only does projection depend on this basic principle, but all aspects of artistic Speech. We cannot be in the centre of the new creation, creating it, if we are still holding on to what went before. We cannot receive anew, without first letting go of what we have. We need to stand balanced between what we send forward, and what we receive from behind, (see figure 18).

In *Speech-exploration 46*, /d/ provides the firm resistance from which to launch, not only *dart* but the whole line. Once out there, we find the way to keep each syllable progressing, one step at a time. Otherwise we shall be 'marking time', or returning home. This is what happens when we hear someone's voice fade at the end of a line or sentence. If we become conscious that our voice is fading, we may instinctively try pushing extra volume into any final words. Unfortunately, we achieve this by tensing up the throat and hardening the voice.

This is how to do it differently.

1. Take a step as you speak each syllable. To integrate the rhythm and dynamic of the sentence with the stepping, first sense them as the impulse with which to launch the /d/ and your steps.
2. To make the transition from stepping with your feet as you speak each syllable, to stepping only with your voice in the stream of breath, reach with your arm into the back space. This reminds you to receive the impulse of the line from infinity. Let your arm flow forward with the impulse as it unfolds in front, and mark the placing of each syllable with your hand.
3. Now utilize the principle of *continual renewal from the source*. If you gather enough impulse to launch the dynamic of the whole sentence, that dynamic will contain the second half within the first. But even though the impulse for *through darkening gloaming* is already on its way towards you, you still reach into the back space a second time to collect it and allow it to unfold. This time it will be 'thr' whose powerful dynamic carries the remaining words through to the finish, especially if the 'r' is rolled, /ɾ/.

Each sound appears from and disappears back into, infinity. How can we actively create and then accompany each sound as it appears and disappears? To be fully present in the final 't' of *dart*, means that we let it manifest its energy and create its resistance in the space. It means that we bounce off that resistance and catapult beyond its boundary into the waiting space. We are present in that waiting space, free to receive and join the impulse of the /m/ which is already on its way towards us from infinity.

This striving for constant presence in the activity of speaking is what makes Speech Formation so demanding. Yet only through such active presence can we awaken to that sense of co-creation with the powers that have created us. Only then can we begin to understand how through such co-creation, we continue to evolve.

The strongest opportunity for practising this principle lies in the transition to the second half of the sentence. If we launch the sentence with enough dynamic in the opening sound, /d/ will easily take us through the first four words. In addition it will deliver us with such an impact on to /ts/, the final sound of *boats*, that the dynamic will release the voice into the space and keep it out there. From this position, we can collect the impulse of the second half of the sentence while we are 'on the run', as it were. We can continue with the sentence where we left off, instead of needing to go back to the starting point.

In this way, we can compare the sounds to runners in a relay race. We are developing ability to utilize each sound's unique capacity to keep us moving in the space beyond what is audible. Thus, we are able to receive and join in the activity of each new sound while still remaining in the race.

These basic principles can be applied to all the explorations.

Speech-exploration 47

> march smarten ten claprigging rockets
> crackling plopping lynxes
> fling from forward forth
> fling from forward forth
> crackling plopping lynxes
> march smarten ten claprigging rockets

These lines provide us with three different ways of penetrating space. First is the action of the spear thrower, of which we have already spoken.[*] Line three will benefit from this approach.

We see that for the spear thrower to project the spear into the forward space, he must reach into the space behind.

---

[*] See The Art of Acting, chapter 2.

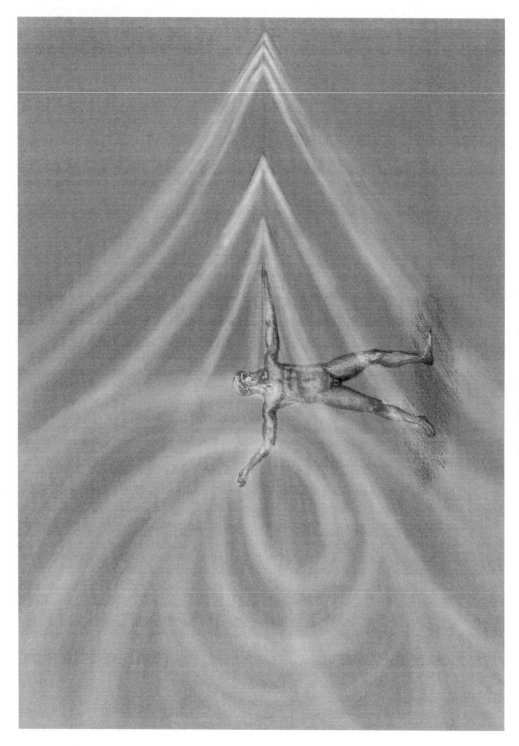

Figure 20 – the spear thrower

We see that when the impulse has been fully gathered, the spear is released to soar in an effortless, harmonious arc to its goal. Without this preparation in the space behind, the spear will be jerked from the shoulder and this same lack of preparation in the space behind when we speak is what makes us push our voice from the larynx. Our throat is then traumatized by being forced to bear complete responsibility for launching our voice into space. But that isolation can be traced to a deeper level of estrangement; one in which we can no longer sense that we belong to heaven and earth and that our instrument is a part of the greater context which surrounds it.

Stage 1

fling from forward forth

1. Imagine /f/ to be your spear. It is important that you aim at a specific target, not too far away to start with, so that you can practise gauging the amount of energy you need to reach your goal. Prepare with the gesture of the spear thrower, collecting from the space behind enough impulse to release /f/ to your goal.
2. Release your imaginary spear and, as you do, release /f/ in your stream of breath.
3. Repeat, increasing and decreasing the distance of your target and adjusting the strength of impulse collected from behind. The sense of ease with which you manage to send /f/ to its target depends on the right degree of impulse.
4. Try steps 1–3 again in pairs. Send /f/ back and forth between you and give each other feedback as to how effectively you reach your partner.

Up to this point we have not needed to engage the voice because the /f/ is unvoiced. This demonstrates that projection need not depend on the volume of our voice.

5. We are ready to engage the voice with the single word *fling*. Commit the increased activity and energy required to fuse the unvoiced /f/ with the rest of the word which is voiced. To increase volume healthily requires a corresponding increase in the power of/f/ to fuse with increasing density of voice. Project it to the target by releasing it within your gesture.
6. Try this with a range of volumes. You may be surprised to find that fineness and delicacy are just as easy to project as loudness.

Projection of a softer voice requires not less but more commitment and increased energy. Fire is needed to refine the voice into a spear or feathered arrow which can fly through space. Transparency and fineness are not to be confused with weakness or withdrawal of activity.

7. Build the line syllable by syllable until you can project the whole line within one overarching gesture. As more is spoken, more needs to be collected. Call upon the fiery being of /f/ to grasp your voice and leap with it across the chasm that separates you from another.

8. Project the line in varying degrees of volume and at varying distances.

Stage 2

   march smarten ten claprigging rockets

The line *march smarten ten claprigging rockets* is very different. Its dynamic is like a huge torrent, a flood of water sweeping everything along within its path: refrigerators, cars, houses, tree trunks, boulders. We learn to ride the flood. This line will teach us to project at maximum volume in a way that does not harm our instrument.

   It may be a surprise to learn we will not hurt our throat if we can totally release our voice. Paradoxically, the tension that damages our throat can be caused by holding back the full power of our voice, out of fear of doing harm. We gain control, not by holding back, but by understanding how to *form* the voice with power equal to the volume. It is the consonants that form the vessels that support our voice. We learn to increase the volume of our voice only as we strengthen the consonants to form and carry it. The first two sounds in this line are those released by newborn babies following that first intake of breath. Babies seem to have no problems sustaining maximum volume for lengthy periods without damage to their throats.

1. Attune yourself to the being of /m/. Like a mother, it has huge power and is at the same time able to caress gently. Formed by the gesture of the lips, the consonant 'm' gathers /ɑː/ (<u>march</u>) into its gesture and hurls the vowel from the back where it is formed. This /mɑː/ is a primal human utterance.

2. Find a gesture that helps you collect a great wave of power from behind, and a posture to support its passage through you. To the degree your effort to project is supported by your whole body, your throat is relieved of responsibility. Instead, it acts as a passage that lets the voice through freely and without strain.

3. Each time you release your gesture within the mighty stream of /m/, let go of each next syllable a further step beyond the last, until the whole line is released. Gather the syllables within the impulse of the /m/ and let them hurtle, with their awkward bulk and their protruding corners, in the inevitable surging tide. Can you remain awake throughout, to steer a clear path through the hurtling consonants and ride the impulse with them?

4. As always, our purpose in beginning with full-bodied gesture is to awaken strong sensations of the appropriate activity. When this feels secure, reduce your outer gesture while sustaining the original intensity.[*]

5. Although we use this line to increase volume without increasing strain to throat or larynx, begin softly. Only increase volume as you gain capacity to balance three essential factors. Increase of *volume* requires increase of *breath*, cushioning the louder tone, preventing it from wounding space and your throat. This, in turn, requires an increase of *activity* to form the consonants out of that breath, so they can grasp and carry forth our vowels/voice into space.

Stage 3

crackling plopping lynxes

If I hurl the right kind of projectile at a barrier with sufficient impact, it will bounce. Provided I launch it with enough dynamic, it continues on its way without any further effort on my part. This principle of ricochet or bounce is another means to project the voice through space.

This line makes use of the particular capacity of 'k' to explode with enough initial impact to provide an overall dynamic within which the other syllables can bounce. If something is to bounce, it needs to be firm as well as soft, resistant yet with some degree of flexibility. Here, the quality of firmness is provided by the plosives /k/ and /p/; the softness and the flexibility by /l/, /ŋ/(ing) and nx. The 'bounce' of each successive syllable is reinforced by each successive plosive. At last, while still in the original momentum, the final, softer, yielding *lynxes* 'bounces' to the finishing line.

1. Practise with bouncing varying degrees of volume at varying distances. It's important to discover how much bounce is needed to provide the momentum to support the unfolding syllables. How many smaller bounces are contained in the intensity of the initial bounce? Bouncing a real ball over varying distances will develop an instinctive sense for this.

2. Experiment with speaking syllables within the ball's momentum.

3. Try bouncing the whole line without the ball, but with full-bodied gesture.

4. Finally, when this dynamic is internalized, you can reduce its bodily expression and reproduce the line entirely in the stream of speech.

---

[*] See *The Art of Acting*, pages 46–47, Fully-bodied and naturalistic: our working principle, for a description of Chekhov's process for reducing full-bodied movement to more naturalistic on a scale of 10–1.

Stage 4

When the dynamic of projection specific to each line has been mastered, then practise making a transition from one into the other and back again.

1. march smarten ten claprigging rockets
2. crackling plopping lynxes
3. fling from forward forth
4. fling from forward forth
5. crackling plopping lynxes
6. march smarten ten claprigging rockets

As these three dynamics are internalized, embedded in the interaction of each sound's specific functioning, the voice begins to recognize its natural pathways of projection. Practising transitions in the order suggested builds the capacity to recognize which method will best serve in any context, and the flexibility of our instrument to respond to it.

Speech-exploration 48 (partner work)

> slinging slanging a swindler
> the wounding fooled a victor vexed
> the wounding fooled a swindler
> slinging slanging vexed

We explore the gesture and dynamic of the lasso and learn to ride successive waves of increasing intensity created by the fricatives released by the interaction of our lips and teeth.

> slinging slanging a swindler

1. The first and last lines can be explored with full-bodied gesture. Lasso your partner, who is attempting to escape. You need space to move and gesture freely. Aim to arrest your partner's flight with *slinging slanging*, discovering how /s/ and /l/ in combination enable you to swing your voice/vowels across the room, overcoming their tendency to be pulled back inside by *ng*. Consolidate your capture by swinging down on *a* and firmly grasping *swindler* as you take hold of your captive, in such a way that word and gesture fuse.
2. To prepare the middle line, experiment with full-bodied gesture, increasing the intensity and focus of the breath stream as you move from /w/ to /v/ to /f/. This time you are a skier who takes off down the slope in /w/ and builds up the intensity as the slope gets steeper in the /v/. Then, with /f/, ski off the edge and soar across

the space. In the final /v/, you can smoothly glide into a landing at the bottom of the slope and come to rest in /d/.

> the wounding fooled a victor vexed

3. Learn to ski from one consonant to another within a single breath stream.
4. Insert the vowels, so they too are carried in this stream.
5. The last two lines require a combination of the different ways of moving through the space.

> the wounding fooled a swindler
> slinging slanging vexed

We learn to shift from one mode of travel to another without returning to the starting point. *Speech-exploration 48* teaches our voice to soar into space and stay out there while we create; able to sustain and build an extended sentence structure without having to return again and again to our starting point. As well, it teaches us to ride on the dynamic of the launching sound; then, while we are out there, to let go. Still in full flight, and trusting the trapeze of the next words (sounds and breath) has already swung from our open back space to the place where we need to meet it, we grasp the next phrase and swing on it to the next place.

It is exhilarating, after such a flight, to 'land on our feet' and still be in control of that last *vexed*. How satisfying that we do not push or hit that final word! We have not barely managed to 'make it to the end' but are as agile, flexible and present in projecting our voices and riding on our words as our skier is at riding the slopes, our acrobat at riding the trapeze.

Romeo's speech when he beholds Juliet on the balcony requires just such capacity to let the words swing easily through distances of space. The speech in its entirety gives many other opportunities to practise this.

> ...for thou art
> As glorious to this night, being o'er my head
> As is a winged messenger of heaven
> Unto the white, upturned wondering eyes
> Of mortals, that fall back to gaze on him
> When he bestrides the lazy-pacing clouds
> Or sails upon the bosom of the air.
>
> *Romeo and Juliet*, Shakespeare

Speech-exploration 49

> Pow!
> Power

The gesture of 'expansion' provides us with yet another method to approach projection.* Expansion, combined with the gesture and dynamic of the /p/ can be used to 'explode' the voice into space with a range of volumes. Its gesture invites us to project our voices from a centre we can reach ever more deeply into for the source of its expansive impulse.

1. Practise a series of four progressively expanding /p/ sounds. Each should be supported with a full-bodied gesture moving from contraction to expansion.
2. Fuse /p/ with the diphthong /aʊ/ (p<u>ow</u>) so that as it travels, it takes the voice with it, as in the exclamation: *pow!* This syllable then evolves into the word: *power*. Each projection of the voice should be supported with a full-bodied gesture of expansion.
3. When ready, replace these preparations with the famous line from Shakespeare's *Julius Caesar*. Mark Antony is speaking to the Roman crowd:

> Friends!   – first expansion
> Romans!   – second expansion
> Countrymen!   – third expansion
> Lend me your ears!   – culmination to which the others have built

Once the words are able to expand, supported by your full-bodied gestures, reduce the outer gestures. This should ensure your voices are projected out of the dynamics of the gestures now transformed to inner life and energy and freed from tension in the throat.

Speech-exploration 50

The spiral that forms the basis of the discus throw is another useful preparation for projection.

> Friends!
> Romans!
> Countrymen!
> Lend me your ears!

Refer to *The Art of Acting*, chapter 2: adapt the discus exploration to a form that spirals four times inwards to a centre and four times out, with ever expanding dis-

---

* See *The Art of Acting*, chapter 2, Expansion and contraction.

Figure 21 – the discus thrower

tance. With each expanding spiral we release a word and at the culminating moment of the final fling, release the words: *Lend me your ears!* Our aim is to expand the sphere of our projection. We do this first through bodily movements which release the sounds into the space, free of the body and able to travel effortlessly to the listener. Such an expansion may well reveal itself in a louder voice but is not dependent on it or to be confused with it.

We are ready to explore another attribute of language which we need to understand if we are to master the ability to use our voice as an expressive instrument: rhythm.

Chapter 4

I am the Lord of the Dance

Approaching rhythm

Rhythm in everyday speech

We instinctively speak in rhythm when we wish to communicate, not just information, but our relationship to content. For instance, a mother speaking to a tiny child, might say: *Don't be scared! There's no one here! It's only your shadow!*

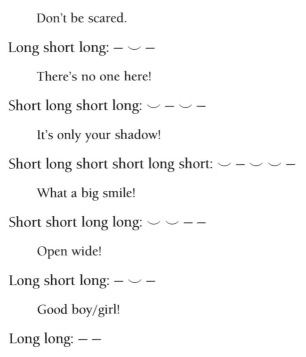

Don't be scared.

Long short long: − ⌣ −

There's no one here!

Short long short long: ⌣ − ⌣ −

It's only your shadow!

Short long short short long short: ⌣ − ⌣ ⌣ −

What a big smile!

Short short long long: ⌣ ⌣ − −

Open wide!

Long short long: − ⌣ −

Good boy/girl!

Long long: − −

Nursery rhymes and verses extend and build on these naturally occurring tendencies to speak in rhythm. They demonstrate how closely allied these spoken rhythms are to song. *This is the way we wash our hair, wash our hair, wash our hair.* Long short short long short long short long, long short long, long short long, etc. Even when communicating to adults, we turn to rhythm to convey significance. *How dare you speak to me like that!* Short long short, long short short, short long. *I never meant to hurt you.* Short long short long short long short. *I'm sorry. Please forgive me.* Long long short. Long short long short. *Careful!* Long, long. *Or you'll fall off!* Short short long long.

Rhythm reveals emphasis. Emphasis reveals our emotional/feeling relationship to what we say as well as what we want our words to do. Our feelings and emotions reach intuitively for the rhythmic interplay of long and short syllables, of which all words consist, to create the stress by which they draw attention to themselves. A second way to create this stress is to give weight to some words more than others by pushing deeply with our *will* into a word or syllable.

We also use melody, which arises out of patterns of inflection, to communicate *intention*. Melody and weight naturally weave themselves into the rhythmic interplay of long and short. These are the means by which we communicate the will and emotion/feeling aspects of our souls when we speak. If we understand what we do instinctively and identify the patterns that emerge, we can apply these consciously in an artistic context.

Two elements of rhythm; meter and weight

In the English language we can trace the source of two rhythmic impulses. The first arising from the interplay between long and short syllables stems from the contribution of the Greek and Latin languages to English.[*] The second, related to the interplay of light and heavy stress entered our language when Britain was invaded by Angle and Saxon tribes in the fifth century AD and expressed itself in the alliterative tradition of Anglo-Saxon poetry, with influence well into the fourteenth century.[†] It was revived again in the nineteenth century, in a metamorphosed form, through the poetry of Gerard Manley Hopkins.[‡]

These two elements of rhythm are the basis of traditional dance forms. There have always been dances whose character derived from length or shortness of a step executed with a glide or slide. Examples of these, in Shakespeare's time, were the Measure or Pavane. Dances such as the Jig or Lavolta, on the other hand, had their origins in the jump or leap, which rely on the interplay of gravity and lightness for their dynamic.

Distinguishing between rhythm and meter

Meter arises in language when a pattern of relationships between long and short syllables is repeated. The most fundamental patterns are explored, in detail, later in this chapter. The *rhythmical patterns* quoted in the earlier examples, that are a feature of our everyday speech are referred to as *irregular* and can also be found in prose and much contemporary poetry. Meter, isolated and extracted from the other elements

---

[*] See chapters 7 and 8.

[†] See chapter 8.

[‡] See Appendix A.

determining expressive speech, leads to lifeless repetition, mechanical though accurate. When, however, energy and life move through it, meter forms the basis of *rhythm* that is *regular.*[*]

Rhythm in the macrocosm and the microcosm

Rhythm weaves within our greater universe. The planets move in relation to the fixed stars with such regularity that it is possible to calculate, precisely, centuries in advance, what will take place, and when.

Let us look at the rhythms of heartbeat and breathing in the microcosm of our bodies. A healthy heartbeat is regular. It may slow down or accelerate, but the rhythmic relationship of diastole to systole is constant. For our everyday consciousness this fact of life remains outside of our control[†], and the healthy rhythm of our heart is determined by some law or wisdom that we have no freedom to determine. If we had to constantly decide when our heart should beat, we could not do it. Likewise with our breathing, which weaves its own rhythmic pattern into that established by our heartbeat. To be healthy, the relationship between our in- and out-breath also must be rhythmical, but whereas in relation to our heartbeat we have no choice at all, when we breathe our individual natures can express themselves to some extent because, within certain limits, we can decide to breathe in or out, and how long we hold our breath. At some point, however, if we are to stay alive, the cosmic wisdom takes control again.

---

[*] See chapter 5 for a thorough investigation of the difference between meter and rhythm.

[†] Certain yogis, through their training, can influence these functions.

The dactylic hexameter

Homer composed his epics, the *Iliad* and *Odyssey*, in the rhythm known as *dactylic hexameter*. English prose translations give us an idea of the content. This satisfies our intellect but cannot communicate what an Ancient Greek experienced; how through this rhythm quite other levels of our being are engaged and worked upon. It is important that we let this rhythm have the opportunity to work on us even if attempts to render it in English prove ultimately inartistic.

Homer and the dactylic hexameter

It is not known how much of the texts we are familiar with as the *Iliad* and *Odyssey* were original creations by an individual poet called Homer. Perhaps Homer was simply the one who was the last in a line of bards who had handed down the oral tradition in which they were immersed, and faithfully wrote down what he inherited. Or perhaps the inherited oral forms were significantly transformed by his individual genius. Whatever their origin, we cannot imagine that the poet sat down, like Odysseus, and 'racked his brains' to find the combinations of syllables and words that would make thousands of lines conform to the *hexameter*.[*]

In the *Odyssey*, Book 8, Homer tells us how the old, blind poet unfolds his tale in what he calls the 'voice of the god'. We cannot think that this did not bear some relation to himself. To begin each epic, Homer called upon this divine being to inspire him. We are at liberty to think of this as merely a literary convention; or we could imagine that what came to be thought of as convention originated in a real experience. If we accept the latter, we might imagine the blind poet listening to 'immortal harmonies'. We might picture him becoming a channel for the Muse to pour her voice through him; that very voice which itself gave birth to rhythms in the greater cosmos. And then, pouring itself out in an eternal river, it rendered those rhythms into human speech with unerring certainty; a certainty the human brain could only analyse in hindsight. We might imagine the community, gathered at its meeting place, held as much within that rhythm as by the content of the story; in the same way human beings on earth are held within the rhythm of the stars and planets.

How the dactylic hexameter works

The meter that underlies this form of hexameter is based upon a unit the Greeks called a *dactyl*. A dactyl consists of one long syllable (–) followed by two shorts (⌣ ⌣) One

---

[*] In the story of the Cyclops in Homer's *Odyssey*, Odysseus is described as 'racking his brains' to think of a way to rescue his men from the monster, in whose cave they are imprisoned.

line is composed of three spoken dactyls, a breath or *caesura*, lasting for the length of one, and followed once again by three spoken dactyls.

1: – ‿ ‿ – ‿ ‿ – ‿ ‿ | caesura – ‿ ‿ | – ‿ ‿ – ‿ ‿ – ‿ ‿ | – ‿ ‿
2: – ‿ ‿ – ‿ ‿ – ‿ ‿ | caesura – ‿ ‿ | – ‿ ‿ – ‿ ‿ – ‿ ‿ | – ‿ ‿

In order to speak each sequence of three dactyls, we breathe in for the space of one (for every four dactyls, three are spoken, one unspoken). Because we cannot speak except upon an outbreath, each half-line of hexameter expresses the ratio of speech to one complete breath (in and out) as 1:4. Every four feet of dactyl occupies one complete breath, in and out.

Research has shown that during the period of deepest sleep and at the optimum level of health a human being breathes approximately 18 times per minute and has a pulse of 72; the same ratio of 1:4.[*] We could say that in rhythmic speech the hexameter embodies the relationship our breathing and our heartbeat have when we are most in harmony with the cosmic laws that have created and maintain us.[23]

In one hour, at this rate, we should have breathed 1080 breaths. This number, multiplied by 24, tells us that in a day, we should have breathed 25,920 times. As the earth spins, the axis at the top spins more slowly than the axis at the bottom. This moves the axis slightly off its centre, causing it to face, progressively, different aspects of the heavens, making the sun appear to rise in different constellations of the zodiac. Could we perceive the sun to rise at the spring equinox through all twelve constellations of the zodiac, it would take us 25,920 years. This span of time is known as a *Platonic year*. Divided equally by twelve, it gives a period of 2,160 years. The idea that different cultures come into being and decline under the influence of each successive constellation is based upon this calculation.

Steiner confirmed this idea and according to his research, the Egyptian civilization was influenced by Taurus or the Bull for such a period of 2,160 years. The Greek and Roman era by the Ram, and so on.[†] We can, of course, dismiss these connections as coincidence. Or we could consider the expression of a cosmic rhythm in this ancient rhythm of hexameter. Perhaps we can imagine that the Ancient Greeks, speaking and listening to hexameter, would have felt that they were bathed in cosmic rhythms and once again brought into harmony with them.

Role of the dactylic hexameter in the Oracle at Delphi
Such imagining may give an insight into use of the hexameter by the oracle at Delphi. The priestess of Apollo, under the influence of fumes and gases rising from the earth,

---

[*] This ratio does not apply to situations of physical exertion.

[†] See *The Integrated Actor* to consider artistic style as it relates to different epochs and cultures.

uttered clairvoyant inspirations in reply to questions that were brought to her. These were then rendered in hexameter by priests who, in this rhythmic form, transmitted them to the seekers. We might imagine that those whose task it was to guide that culture, so that it could make its contribution to humanity's unfolding consciousness, did this for a purpose.

Replies to questions were often obscure and given as riddles. Riddles require seekers to be active in relation to the guidance they receive. We can imagine how important a part this played in the development of our capacity for independent thinking: one of the fundamental contributions of the Ancient Greeks to human culture.

We can equally imagine the anxiety of those who had lost touch with the cosmic wisdom which once had guided them. Seeking answers to the riddles of their destinies, they received them in a form which would have been incomprehensible without their own activity to understand, but at the same time the hexameter enabled them to feel that they were still held by the guiding beings of the universe.

Purpose of working with dactylic hexameter in today's world

We live in an epoch in which we are progressively less able to accept outside control because we are called by the evolution of our consciousness to achieve autonomy within. Then we will know the freedom that can only come from understanding reached by our own conscious will. Within the process of achieving this, from time to time, we can relieve ourselves from modern angst if we willingly submit our own will to the harmonizing rhythm of hexameter; surrender to its calm authority. It trains our breath and brings breathing and heartbeat into their optimum relationship. What a huge relief, for brief periods, not to have to make our own decision when to breathe because the hexameter decides it for us.

Dactylic hexameter texts for English practice

It is hard to sustain the match of form and content when rendering hexameter in English. The following texts nevertheless provide an opportunity to experience its value, before becoming ludicrous. The first is a translation of Homer's famous invocation from the *Iliad*:

> Sing, O Daughter of Heaven, | of Peleus' son, of Achilles; |
> Him whose terrible wrath | brought thousand woes on Achaia. |
> Many a stalwart foe | did it hurl untimely to Hades; |
> Souls of the heroes of old | and their bones lay strewn on the sea-shore, |
> Prey to the vulture and dog. |

This excerpt from Charles Kingsley's *Andromeda* describes Andromeda's experience before she is rescued by Perseus from being chained to the rocks as a sacrifice to the sea monster:

Over the mountains aloft | ran a rush and a roll and a roaring. |
Downward the breeze came indignant |and leapt with a howl to the water |
Roaring in cranny and crag | till the pillars and clefts of the basalt |
Rang like a god-swept lyre | and her brain grew mad with the noises. |
Crashing and lapping of waters | and sighing and tossing of weed-beds |
Gurgle and whisper and hiss of the foam |while the thundering surges |
Boomed in the wave-worn halls |as they champed at the root of the mountain. |
Hour after hour in the darkness | the wind swept fierce to the landward |
Drenching the maiden with spray. | She, shivering, weary and drooping, |
Stood with her heart full of thoughts | till the foam crests gleamed in the twilight |
Leaping and laughing around | and the east grew red with the dawning.

It is surely not coincidence that the units of which meters are composed are known as *feet*. Rhythm invites us to move our limbs. And so it is helpful to step the syllables as we train our instrument to co-ordinate breathing, speech and rhythm. We remember the distinction between meter and rhythm by invoking the Spirit of the Dance. Let us invite her, in the form of the Winged Victory (*Nike*), to awaken psycho-physical awareness as we step the rhythm.

Our goal is not robotic accuracy. It is to experience each line carried into space on an impulse gathered from infinity. Alive with such activity, it moves through the speaker on the wings of breath.

Speaking the hexameter

1. Prepare with the explorations for counter tensions from *The Art of Acting.*[*]
2. Stand and attune yourself to the impulse of each line. Clap the rhythm until it feels familiar. It's helpful if someone can speak it while you clap.
3. Allow the rhythm to pick up your feet and move them through the steps, ensuring your upper body is lifted and carried in that impulse.
4. Speak as you step. Until you are familiar with the rhythm, speak the archetypal line:

---

[*] See *The Art of Acting*, chapter 2.

Figure 22 – Nike of Samothrace

Archetypal line

> long short short long short short long short short (breath/caesura)
> long short short long short short long short short (breath/caesura)

5. When you are confident, step only long syllables.
6. Stand and use your arm to collect the line from backspace. Then swing it through into the space in front, letting your hand accompany your voice as you unfold each syllable.
7. Replace the archetypal lines with the excerpts from the *Iliad* and *Andromeda*.

Difficulties with the caesura

The form of hexameter does not determine when we breathe in order to obey some abstract rule. It is to guarantee that we breathe life into the feeling and will content of the words and images. Once we are in full swing, we shall have some sense of Homer's eternal river that holds and carries all deeds and events pertaining to the earth and heavens in its infinite path. When first learning how to speak hexameter, some people find that breathing in during the caesura is unnecessary because they still have breath in their lungs. This occurs when we haven't fully used the breath we gathered to speak the previous half-line. We will only experience what hexameter can teach us if we fully utilize our breath stream.[*]

---

[*] See chapter 2.

Four fundamental rhythms

The classical Greek poets, still under the guidance of the temple wisdom, worked consciously with different rhythms. Just as musicians knew which modes aroused anger or sorrow, courage or exultation in those who heard, so too, poets knew how to arouse a listener's emotions through the speech rhythms.

Today we may see this as manipulative, but the Greeks were just beginning to sense what was evolving through them; how huge could be the destructive forces of the individual self or ego as it wakened in each person. The power to master these forces from within had not yet come.[24] In the meantime, the guardians of culture could harmonize those forces through the arts, receiving inspiration from cosmic principles which could govern and educate the soul.

Basic meters
On the foundation of these four basic meters are built the rhythmic structures of centuries of Western poetry.

Iambic ⌣ —
The *iamb* consists of one short syllable followed by one long.

Anapaest ⌣ ⌣ —
The *anapaest* consists of two short syllables followed by one long.

Trochee — ⌣
The *trochee* consists of one long syllable followed by one short.

Dactyl — ⌣ ⌣
As already discussed in relation to hexameter, the *dactyl* consists of one long syllable followed by two shorts.

Falling or incarnating rhythms
Since we have already spoken of the dactyl (— ⌣ ⌣), let us now examine the other most common rhythm beginning with a long syllable; the trochee (— ⌣). It appears here in Longfellow's epic poem, *Hiawatha*:

— ⌣ — ⌣ — ⌣ — ⌣

On the **shore** stood Hiawatha,
Turned and **waved** his **hands** at **parting**.
On the clear and luminous water

Launched his birch canoe for sailing
And with speed it darted forward...
And the evening sun descending
Set the clouds on fire with redness,
Burned the broad sky like a prairie,
Left upon the level water
One long track and trail of splendour,
Down whose stream, as down a river,
Westward, westward, Hiawatha
Sailed into the fiery sunset,
Sailed into the purple vapours,
Sailed into the dusk of evening.

As with hexameter, we gain a clear experience of this rhythm by stepping it. Place one foot down for the length of the long syllable and then step the shorter syllable with the other foot. Immediately, our soul is stilled. We are quieter, more certain, more objective. It is as though that first, long syllable grounds us firmly here upon the earth and the short syllable gives us opportunity to catch up with it, gather and consolidate what it accomplished. This experience is reinforced if we step the long syllable with the heel and the short with the toes, as my colleague in Greece assures me is the custom in the Greek folk dances.[*]

When we translate this sensation into speaking, the trochee encourages us to form the consonants decisively, with definition. We imprint them into substance, creating out of them a three-dimensional reality. Consequently, speaking in trochee rhythm encourages the depiction of an image or event. The same is true of the dactyl. Because of this, both rhythms are particularly suited to storytelling and the epic style in poetry. The archetypal beginning of all stories is expressed in trochee rhythm:

$$— \ \smile — \smile —$$

Once upon a time...

Steiner observed that when we speak or hear a long stress on the first word or syllable, it conveys a sense of coming down on to the earth, into a world where physical events take place, where things appear solid. He referred to rhythms beginning with a longer stress as *falling* or *incarnating*.

---

[*] Katerina Vlachou.

Rising or excarnating rhythms

So, too, he observed that the iambic and anapaest rhythms, which both begin with a short syllable, arouse the opposite sensations: that we 'take off from the earth'. He called these *rising* or *excarnating* rhythms.

The preceding short syllable now acts as a springboard from which we launch into flight. Whereas when the long syllable *precedes* the short, it serves to anchor us and bring us down to earth, the sensation it arouses when it *follows* the short, sustains us in flight. The sequence of a short syllable followed by a long stirs our emotions, arousing our inner life. When I speak in *anapaest* or *iambic* rhythm, I touch the feelings or emotions of the listener with my own. The *iambic* pulse feels as intimate to me as my own heartbeat. It prepares me to reveal, or if I am the listener, to receive, the artist's inmost self.

When the long stress emerges from the short, the short syllable provides a gathering point for what is released in the long. The sensation of a quick contraction in order to expand into the length does not encourage us to form the consonants. The listener receives the content through the vowels and, consequently, becomes aware of the inwardness of what is spoken.

This does not mean that consonants are unimportant. As we discussed in the last chapter, the speaker always needs to form the consonants with the knowledge that they create the vessels within which vowels may reveal themselves. Vowels not clothed with the activity of consonants risk sounding sentimental, exposing emotion not penetrated consciously, not yet transformed into art.

Verse in Iambic rhythm

$$\smile \; - \; \smile \; - \; \smile \; - \; \smile \; - \; \smile \; - $$

O **wild** West **Wind**, thou **breath** of **Autumn's being**
Thou from whose unseen presence the leaves dead
Are driven, like ghosts from an enchanter fleeing,
Yellow and black and pale and hectic red
Pestilent-stricken multitudes . . .

Ode to the West Wind, Shelley

Verse in anapaest rhythm

$$\smile \smile - \; \smile \smile \smile - \smile \; \smile \; - \smile \; \smile \; - \; \smile \smile - $$

O the **wild** joys of **living**, the **leaping** from **rock** up to **rock**,
The strong rending of boughs from the fir tree, the cool silver shock
Of a plunge in the pool's living water.

Saul, Browning

These examples are filled with images of the outer world, yet the rhythms evoke the strong emotions awakened in the poet by the images. This is why rising rhythms are so suited to lyric poetry, teaching us to form the language in a way appropriate for pouring out emotion. In the following examples, these same excarnating rhythms conjure very different feelings and emotions.

2nd example of verse in iambic rhythm

˘   —   ˘   — ˘ — ˘ —   ˘   —

My **heart** aches, **and** a **drowsy numb**ness **pains**
My sense, as though of hemlock I had drunk,
Or emptied some dull opiate to the drains
One minute past, and Lethe-wards had sunk:

Ode to a Nightingale, Keats

2nd example of verse in anapaest rhythm

˘ ˘ —   ˘   ˘   —   ˘ ˘ — ˘ ˘ —   ˘ ˘ —

I be**gin** through the **grass** once a**gain** to be **bound** to the **Lord.**
I can see through a face that has faded the face full of rest,
Of the earth, of the mother — my heart with her heart in accord.
As I lie 'mid the cool green tresses that mantle her breasts
I begin with the grass once again to be bound to the Lord.

AE, George William Russell

The fact that the same rhythm can express such different moods as those evoked in the two different examples reminds us that rhythm and tempo are different things. The same rhythm at a faster or a slower tempo arouses very different feelings and emotions.

The Greeks experienced specific potency when one long syllable was followed by another. A foot might be composed of up to three successive long syllables. An English example is the first line of Tennyson's poem from *In memoriam*:

—   —   —

Break, break, break,
On thy cold grey walls oh sea
And I would that my heart could utter
The thoughts that arise in me.

Spondee – –

The foot that consisted of two long syllables was called a *spondee*. The spondee generates deliberate, considered, even ponderous sensations; such as when we step with an inevitable, inexorable, relentless drive in a funeral march; or when we climb a mountain and will to keep on going, one step at a time. But yet, the slow deliberation of our steps means we make a strong connection with the earth. The spondee is deeply connected with our will.

To speak more than a few syllables in the spondee rhythm sounds unnatural because at least one syllable in any word which is not monosyllabic will be already short. We are accustomed to combining words so we experience a natural flow arising from the alternations between long and short. We become aware of the particular effect the spondee has upon our souls when we consider everyday expressions of this rhythm. *Come here*! *Stop that*! *Go home*! *God Bless*! *Rest now*! Firm intent seeks expression in the long, equal stress we place on two consecutive syllables. A spondee chosen carefully for a specific purpose can have profound effect. Each line of the *Celtic Blessing of the Deep Peace* commences with a spondee:

> –   –
>
> **Deep peace** of the running wave to you.
> Deep peace of the flowing air to you.
> Deep peace of the quiet earth to you.
> Deep peace of the shining stars to you.
> Deep peace of the Sun of Peace to you.

Sometimes we try to signal significance by drawing out the length of every word but, after a time, this has the opposite effect. *If we emphasize each word, we end up emphasizing none.*

Most speech rhythms are based on interaction between short and long syllables, since spoken language is made up of both. A sense of real dynamic comes about when short and long relate. If a language could consist entirely of short syllables it would make us nervous. On the other hand, if it consisted entirely of long syllables, it would be interminably ponderous.

Contemporary relationship to meter

If, as Steiner's view of evolution would suggest, we are here on earth in order to develop freedom, it is understandable that at this present time our souls are not at ease within these stricter, more traditional, forms. We long to mature and choose our own rhythms. We may need to be a-rhythmical so we can experience ourselves as out of step with the universe. Much contemporary poetry is characterized by what we call *free* rhythm which enables and expresses the soul's need to find its own rhythmic pathway, moving and changing as demand arises. In his essay on Walt Whitman, D H Lawrence called this the 'poetry of the open road'.

Complex influences on the rhythm of great language

You may have observed in these examples two sources of rhythmic stress. One springs from our instinctive use of language to express our perceptions, thoughts, feelings and emotions, and the other is determined by the strict counting of the meter. There is a tension, even opposition, between the demands of each. In fact, if we were to speak in strict accordance with the meter, the verse would sound absurd. It would convey none of the vast treasure of experience buried in the forms of poetry.

This brings us to one of the secrets of great language. Its richness and substance, its subtleties and changing textures, arise precisely from the tensions between the differing demands of rhythmic stress and the need for expressive freedom; all of which must be respected and receive their due. Regular meter provides the ground to stand on, yet if we adhere to it pedantically language becomes absurd. In the following example we see how the writer himself, while basing his expression in the regular iambic pentameter, wants the freedom to be flexible, and where expressiveness demands adds an extra short syllable at the end of each line.

> To be or not to be that is the question.
> Whether 'tis nobler in the mind to suffer
> The slings and arrows of outrageous fortune...
>
> *Hamlet*

We see also how the natural stress that falls on a syllable in common usage, may be in tension with the stress determined by the meter and want to pull away from it. In the second line above, the iambic rhythm puts the short stress on the first syllable of *whether* while common usage makes it long. Also pulling on that meter is the actor's own artistic instinct, wanting to pour itself into the words in a unique and individual way.

It is just this very interplay between conflicting tendencies that creates the richest textures of expressive language. Verses not displaying such a tapestry of tensions may express clever wit and satire but cannot move us deeply. A writer, on the other hand, who tries expressing deep emotion in less textured verse, is in danger of sounding shallow or naïve.

In 1806, Coleridge wrote *Metrical Feet. Lesson for a Boy* to parody the basic rhythms inherited from Ancient Greece. We can enjoy his humorous attempts to match the meter with the content. At the same time, it makes clear that forcing language with pedantic accuracy into any meter puts it in a straitjacket. In doing so, the content is imprisoned instead of released into our understanding.

> Trochee leaps from long to short:
> From long to long in solemn sort
> Slow Spondee stalks; strong foot! Yet ill able
> Ever to come up with Dactyl tri-syllable.
> Iambics march from short to long —
> With a leap and a bound the swift Anapaests throng:
> One syllable long, with short at either side,
> Amphibrachys hastes with a stately stride:
> First and last being long, middle short, Amphimacer
> Strikes his thundering hooves, like a high bred racer.

Iambic pentameter, the English language and Shakespeare

The master of depth of texture in the English language is, arguably, Shakespeare. So skilful is he that we can read 154 sonnets and 37 plays and hardly be aware that nearly every line conforms to the rhythmic structure called *iambic pentameter*. That means each line consists of five iambs ($\smile - \smile - \smile - \smile - \smile -$). Of course there are exceptions; speeches written in prose and songs.

This rhythm, through the genius of Shakespeare, became the heartbeat of the English language, which came of age in the late sixteenth and early seventeenth centuries. It reached maturity in Shakespeare's work and in the Authorized Translation of the Bible. It cannot be a mere coincidence that this maturing coincided with the birth and mastery of unrhymed iambic pentameter also referred to as 'blank verse'.

Within a few years this flexible yet strongly formed line first appeared from the pen of Henry Howard, Earl of Surrey. It was quickly taken up by playwrights of the time who recognized its expressive possibilities. Dramatist and poet Christopher Marlowe, in particular, was able to perfect the vessel, handing it to Shakespeare who, in turn, expanded it to its maximum expressive capabilities. In his hands it became an instrument which could express every nuance of experience, still felt by many to be unsurpassed.

Evolution of rhythm in English drama

To appreciate the achievement of blank verse we shall examine three texts, each of which reveals a different stage in the development of English drama. Each demonstrates a further stage in the relationship between rhythm and the evolution of the English language; how it, step-by-step, became an instrument that could express the consciousness of a specific people.

The first is from the mediaeval play, *Abraham and Isaac*. The Brome manuscript is thought to have been written down only sometime during the thirteenth or fourteenth centuries and it was still performed into the early sixteenth century. For the purpose of our understanding, the Middle English has been modernized to some degree.

Abraham postpones the moment when, according to the angel's command, in order to demonstrate obedience to God, he must kill his son:

> *Abraham*: Lo, now is the time come for certain,
> That my sword in his neck shall bite.
> Ah Lord! my heart riseth there again,
> I may not find it in my heart to smite.
> My heart will not now thereto!
> Ah fain I would work my lord's will,
> But this young innocent lies so still,

> I may not find it in my heart to kill.
> Oh Father in Heaven, what shall I do.
>
> Isaac: Ah mercy Father, why tarry ye so,
> And let me lie so long on this heath?
> Now I would God the stroke were done also;
> Father, heartily I pray you, shorten my woe,
> And let me not wait thus for my death.

The rhythm of the language is awkward, like a garment that does not quite fit and the need to conform to a pattern of end rhymes limits the span of thought. Shortly, we shall see how Shakespeare's language renders a similar content. Between these two examples, blank verse, appeared.

A few lines from Marlowe's *Dr Faustus*, circa 1588/9, reveals a fundamental shift. The lines flow effortlessly. It is as though the soul is clothed, at last, in a garment of expression that fits perfectly. Faustus feels his death is imminent and regrets his wasted life.

> Faustus: Ah Faustus!
> Now hast thou but one bare hour to live,
> And then must thou be damned perpetually.
> Stand still, you ever moving spheres of heaven,
> That time may cease and midnight never come!
> Fair nature's eye, rise, rise again, and make
> Perpetual day; or let this hour be but
> A year, a month, a week, a natural day,
> That Faustus may repent and save his soul!

As intimate as our own heartbeat, this language can take us to the heights and depths our souls can reach. Carried on the strong wave of this rhythm and with no necessity to rhyme, the soul is freed onto a vast ocean of limitless possibility. A thought can stretch as far as the mind can travel.

Our third example comes from *King John*, an early play by Shakespeare, probably circa 1594. Hubert de Burgh, has been ordered by John to burn out the eyes of the king's young nephew, Arthur, whom he loves.

> Hubert: Is this your promise? Go to, hold your tongue.
> Arthur: Hubert, the utterance of a brace of tongues
> Must needs want pleading for a pair of eyes:
> Let me not hold my tongue; let me not, Hubert:
> Or Hubert, if you will, cut out my tongue,
> So I may keep mine eyes: O spare mine eyes,

	Though to no use but still to look on you:
	Lo! by my troth, the instrument is cold
	And would not harm me.
Hubert:	I can heat it boy.
Arthur:	No, in good sooth; the fire is dead with grief,
	Being create for comfort, to be used
	In undeserved extremes: see else yourself:
	There is no malice in this burning coal:
	The breath of heaven hath blown his spirit out
	And strew'd repentant ashes on his head.
Hubert:	But with my breath I can revive it, boy.
Arthur:	An if you do you will but make it blush
	And glow with shame of your proceedings, Hubert:
	– All things that you should use to do me wrong
	Deny their office: only you do lack
	That mercy which fierce fire and iron extends
	Creatures of note for mercy-lacking uses.
Hubert:	Well see to live; I will not touch thine eyes
	For all the treasure that thine uncle ow's;
	Yet I am sworn and I did purpose, boy,
	With this same very iron to burn them out.
Arthur:	O! now you look like Hubert, all this while
	You were disguised...

Mastery of the rules brings with it the authority and freedom to play with them. They become our servants, not our masters. We see over the next years, Shakespeare's growing mastery of this rhythm; how this declared itself in an increasing flexibility with the syllabic count. At the same time, he still depended on the broader structures it provided to create the foundation of his language.

Shakespeare's capacity to mould this evolving language to its full potential as expressive instrument reached maturity along with his mature plays. In these we detect no separation between the soul's need to express and the language that can do so. Language is now as intimate as our own most intimate hearts and minds are to themselves. We can no longer make distinction between thoughts we utter to ourselves or to another. This transparency is nowhere more reflected than in Shakespeare's perfecting of soliloquy as an expressive form:

To be, or not to be: that is the question:
Whether 'tis nobler in the mind to suffer
The slings and arrows of outrageous fortune,
Or to take arms against a sea of troubles,

And by opposing end them. To die, to sleep —
No more — and by a sleep to say we end
The heartache, and the thousand natural shocks
That flesh is heir to! 'Tis a consummation
Devoutly to be wished. To die, to sleep —
To sleep — perchance to dream: ay, there's the rub,
For in that sleep of death what dreams may come
When we have shuffled off this mortal coil,
Must give us pause. There's the respect
That makes calamity of so long life.

Hamlet

Iambic pentameter and the renaissance human being

The discovery of un-rhymed iambic pentameter released us from the need for the end of a line to coincide with the end of a sentence or thought. This provided us with a language of infinite expressive possibilities at a time when human beings were expanding into new horizons. During the Renaissance it seemed there was no new frontier that could not be crossed, no new territory that could not be explored. The spirit, bound for so many centuries in the prison of authority, was at last becoming free. It would measure itself against the infinite.

The ancient symbol of the Star of David, the six pointed star, was created from two equal interlocking triangles. This symbol embodied an old order expressed in the words: *As above, so below.* In that old order, human beings had been held within the strict form dictated by the heavens until we were mature enough for freedom. The hexameter, based on the line of six spoken dactyls, was one such reflection of this order.

Figure 23

Based on the drawing by Leonardo da Vinci of the 'Human Being in a Circle: Illustrating the Proportions'

Figure 24.

In the famous sketch of the *Human Being in a Circle: Illustrating the Proportions* by Leonardo da Vinci circa 1495–50, we see the human being stretched out in the cosmos as a five pointed star, a pentagram. The five pointed star unbalances the tightly constricted, interlocking pyramids of the six pointed star. It suggests the human being freed, like Faustus, to stretch into the universe and 'gain a deity'. To plumb the heights and depths of knowledge and to choose. Will we, like Faustus, choose damnation, or, like

Prospero, recognize the need to integrate the path of knowledge with the path of moral transformation?

When Leonardo, who drew the human being as the measure of the universe, painted *The Last Supper* in Milan, he left the head of Christ unfinished, '. . . convinced he would fail to give it the divine spirituality it demands . . . nor did he dare suppose that his imagination could conceive the beauty and divine grace that properly belonged to the incarnate deity . . .'[25] He was searching for the face which the Egyptian culture had represented in the face of the Sphinx: the I AM whose task is to transform and integrate the forces that do battle in our souls and in time draw us to our true humanity.[*]

Leonardo chose to paint the moment when the disciples responded to Christ's words, that one of them would betray Him, with the question: 'Is it I?' It is the question that confronts us when the truly human wakens in each of us and shows us how we constantly betray it. It is the question Faustus did not ask until the end. Shakespeare, like Leonardo, needed all his powers to depict this moment. He does so in *The Tempest*, when Ariel pleads that Prospero be merciful to those who wronged him. Shakespeare, with the delicate brushstrokes of his words, reveals in the human heartbeat of iambic pentameter that 'divine grace' wakens within Prospero:

> *Ariel*: Your charm so strongly works 'em
> That if you now beheld them, your affections
> Would become tender.
>
> *Prospero*: Dost thou think so, spirit?
>
> *Ariel*: Mine would, sir, were I human.
>
> *Prospero*: And mine shall.

We have seen how the iambic rhythm so readily allows our souls to soar. Now it is woven in a line resonant with the mystery of the number 5. The lines do not rhyme and therefore set no limit to the span of thought. They demonstrate in this example how the rhythm can be shared between two characters whose moral evolution is dependent on each other. We are held within the structure of each line and, at the same time, freed from its constraints. Unrhymed iambic pentameter mirrors, thus, the birth of the Renaissance human being, who felt:

- Still held within an ordered cosmos, the certainty of which would not
begin to crumble until the second half of the nineteenth century.
- But free to explore that cosmos to its limits, to challenge its boundaries and leave no corner of it unmapped.

---

[*] See *The Art of Acting*, chapter 3, The Sphinx.

Iambic pentameter and the modern age

Now, 400 years and two world wars later, iambic pentameter can sound too easy, too comfortable, too confident. One of the last great pieces written in this meter in the English language is the epic, *Le Morte d' Arthur*, written towards the end of the 1850s. Through his telling of the story of the Round Table's end, Tennyson laments the final collapse of that old order which had governed life and culture for so many centuries, but looks towards a new beginning. His unerring musicality has left us verse that rolls off our tongues with ease and harmony, touching us deeply with its grandeur and its scope. It inspires in us the noblest sentiments.

Yet it is this very ease of flow that now makes us uneasy. The civilization which fought in the trenches of the First World War, witnessed the holocaust and dropped the atom bomb was inspired by just such noble sentiments. Today we demand rhythms that do not lull us to sleep in the illusion that 'God's in his heaven. All's right with the world'.[26]

We sense that if we are to face the challenges before us now, we cannot afford to be too comfortable. T.S. Eliot was among the first who examined and articulated this dissatisfaction with the poetry of Tennyson which contributed to its going out of fashion in the later twentieth century. Now we can see it in a greater context once again and revalue its considerable beauty. These lines tell of Arthur's final words to Sir Bedevere before he is taken by three queens to die upon the island of Avilion.

> The old order changeth, yielding place to new,
> And God fulfils Himself in many ways,
> Lest one good custom should corrupt the world.
> Comfort thyself: what comfort is in me?
> I have lived my life, and that which I have done
> May He within Himself make pure! But thou,
> If thou shoulds't never see my face again,
> Pray for my soul. More things are wrought by prayer
> Than this world dreams of . . .
> For so the whole round earth is every way
> Bound by gold chains about the feet of God.
> But now farewell . . .
>
> So said he, and the barge with oar and sail
> Moved from the brink like some full breasted swan
> That, fluting a wild carol e'er her death,
> Ruffles her pure cold plume, and takes the flood
> With swarthy webs. Long stood Sir Bedevere
> Revolving many memories, till the hull

Looked one black dot against the verge of dawn
And on the mere the wailing died away.

It is interesting that Tennyson told his great epic in a rising rhythm. As we discussed, rising rhythms encourage lyrical outpouring rather than depiction of events,
yet Tennyson chose iamb to sing of the destruction of what had sustained our culture
for millennia. Does this intimate another aspect of transition into modern or post-Kali
Yuga consciousness?[*] In his play *A Sleep of Prisoners*, Christopher Fry suggests ours is
a time when 'events are now soul-sized'. Could it be that as our souls expand and with
the world becoming 'smaller' it is less possible to see our inner world as separate from
the world outside?[†]

---

[*] A more detailed exploration of the term Kali Yuga is found in *The Art of Acting* and *The Integrated Actor*.
The Sanskrit name means, the Age of Darkness. In Indian mythology this designates the evolutionary
stage when human beings lost direct perception of supersensible reality. Steiner adopted this terminology
for the age dominated by materialistic consciousness, which he dated as beginning circa 3101 BC and
culminating in 1899 AD. According to his view of evolution, human consciousness is now beginning to
expand again beyond material perception. See also, Appendix A.

[†] See *The Integrated Actor* for a discussion on imagism.

Rhythm and weight

Alliteration

In Anglo-Saxon poetry, alliteration involved the rhythmic repetition of a consonant or vowel that created a pattern of stress which formed the structure of each line. Each line was divided into two halves separated by a breath or caesura. Each half had two stressed syllables. Generally, the consonant providing the first stress in the second half determined the first or both stresses in the first half. This continuity of consonant forged the connection between the two halves of each line. Any two vowels could alliterate. The second stress in the second half was supposed not to alliterate.

> Grim and greedy | his grip made ready;

Here are a few further lines from the Anglo-Saxon epic, *Beowulf*. Although it originated in an oral tradition accompanied by harp, the written text is thought to date from the seventh century AD. This passage tells of the first visit of the monster, Grendel, to the great hall of the king.[27]

> ... | The fiend accursed,
> Grim and greedy, | his grip made ready;
> Snatched in their sleep | with savage fury,
> Thirty warriors; | away he sprang
> Proud of his prey, | to repair to his home,
> His blood dripping booty | to bring to his lair.
> At early dawn, | when day break came,
> The vengeance of Grendel | was revealed to all.

As we read *Beowulf*, each alliterated sound invites us to press deeper into it, achieving its stress through weight. This experience suggests how the consonants convey a sense of active participation in the life described and the connection of this form of verse to the forces of the will.[*]

The characteristics of alliteration arose out of the instinctive sense for rhythm. Only later would they be extracted and identified as *rules* which govern composition of alliterative verse. To enter into the spirit of alliterative speaking requires more than an abstract understanding of the rules. Unless we lift ourselves out of such abstraction and recognize the consonants as formative creative powers and the vowels as revelations of our inner life, it is difficult to imagine what may have been experienced through such forms.

When we actively attune our will to the will of consonants, we experience elemental

---

[*] See chapter 6 for more detail regarding this relationship of the will forces to alliteration.

powers whose activity has condensed the universe. Certainly, such lines as we have quoted suggest the harsh conditions of the Northern winters and a people whose will was forged by battle, with each other and with nature. When we think of an inner life in such conditions, we may imagine that delicate refinement of emotions had little place and that in such a culture, emotions would be bound to lives of action. This might help explain why vowels could serve as consonants in the patterns of alliterating sounds.

Our way of working can certainly provide insight into how alliteration might have been experienced by those whose consciousness gave birth to it. Flexibility was achieved within this seemingly restricted form, firstly by the irregular number and position of unstressed syllables and then by the acceptable variations in the alliterated consonants and vowels. Lastly, the absence of end-rhyme meant that beginnings and ends of sentences did not need to coincide with beginnings and ends of lines.

Hopkins and *sprung rhythm*

The transition from Victorian values into post Kali Yuga consciousness, as embodied in the poetry of Tennyson, would involve more than learning to accept the loss of what had gone before. Other dimensions of reality would come crashing through.[*] Our need to understand and integrate them would make new demands on language and smash the old familiar forms in which our souls had so comfortably settled.[†] As though in preparation for this necessity, Gerard Manley Hopkins (1844–88) had been experimenting. His investigations into rhythm and the nature of the sounds themselves led to an interest in the old alliterative forms that came into the English language through the Anglo-Saxon. So much Victorian poetry lamented, in a passive way, the passing of old glories and a world of faith. Hopkins intuited that strenuous effort would be needed to penetrate and integrate the spiritual realities which would increasingly pour into our consciousness. In these following lines from a sonnet, he reaches for the muscular stress of alliteration to express this quality of will.

> O the mind, mind has mountains, cliffs of fall
> Frightful, sheer, no-man-fathomed. Hold them cheap
> May who ne'er hung there. Nor does long our small
> Durance deal with that steep or deep...

We sense the hero or warrior's activity is shifting from outer conquest to the realm of consciousness. It is the shift Blake refers to in *Jerusalem* when he says:

---

[*] See Appendix A for the connection between the poetry of Hopkins and the event Steiner refers to as 'the second coming of Christ in the etheric'.

[†] See *The Integrated Actor*, imagism.

We shall not cease from mental fight...

Hopkins's life and work was permeated by his own supersensible experience of a loving presence, immanent, not only in human beings but in the whole earth and its atmosphere.[*] His early poetry reveals a growing mastery of the forms and rhythmic structures based on classical meters such as those considered earlier. He recognized how these forms kept the mind imprisoned in old thinking and perception, and would inevitably be broken open. He experimented with stress arising out of weight from the Anglo-Saxon alliterative forms. These became the wedge with which he could split open the smoother lines based on meter. Alliterated sounds created cracks through which the new could strike 'like lightning'.

His letters as well as his poetry reveal a mind deeply immersed within the birthing place of language, a cauldron in which the original elements of the English language had melted down.[†] There they could merge with the consciousness that was to come and rise together in a new form in the English soul. He wrote at length, to guide his readers into his new language. He demonstrated that alliterative use of stress based on the consonants and vowels could integrate with classical forms of meter.

It was for an audience he would largely not encounter in his life time. The theories appear complicated, yet his understanding sprang from his instinctive experience of sounds and rhythms. This, he observed, was no different from the energy and life of nursery rhymes and children's language. We can experience such joy and vigour if we dive into his words with the same delight and energy with which a child discovers language. We can relish the rich textures of its shifting tempos and dynamics without the need to fully understand the complex theories to which he gave the name *sprung rhythm*.

Hopkins' poetry was too revolutionary to be published in his lifetime. It evolved to express the realities that would break through into our consciousness, more widely, only after World War I. Hopkins is now recognized as the father of modern English poetry. Here is how this new consciousness came crashing through in its new language: the first two verses of *The Wreck of the Deutschland*.

> Thou mastering me
> God! giver of breath and bread;
> World's strand, sway of the sea;
> Lord of living and dead;
> Thou hast bound bones and veins in me, fastened me flesh,

---

[*] See Appendix A for the connection between the poetry of Hopkins and the event Steiner refers to as the 'second coming of Christ in the etheric'.

[†] See chapter 8.

And after it almost unmade, what with dread,
Thy doing: and dost thou touch me afresh?
Over again I feel thy finger and find thee.

I did say yes
O at lightning and lashed rod;
Thou heardst me truer than tongue confess
Thy terror O Christ, O God;
Thou knowest the walls, altar and hour and night:
The swoon of a heart that the sweep and the hurl of thee trod
Hard down with a horror of height:
And the midriff astrain with leaning of, laced with fire of stress.

And later, describing one of the nuns who drowned:

Sister, a sister calling
A master, her master and mine! —
And the inboard seas run swirling and hawling:
The rash smart sloggering brine
Blinds her;...

After this, the smooth numbers of Tennyson could serve, less and less, to sooth and comfort. In this poem, Hopkins brought to fulfilment, for the first time, his attempts to find a language that could integrate both rhythmic streams; the one arising out of weight, the other, meter. In doing so, he had revitalized, through the barbarian invasion of alliteration, the classical forms his mind had once so comfortably inhabited. This synthesis created a vessel tough enough to withstand what might be hurled at him from the new and uncharted territories of soul and spirit. At the same time it provided him with the means to explore and chart them, providing maps for those who would come after.

The miracle was that this new language, forged to be a weapon for Blake's 'mental fight', was equally fitted to convey tenderness.

Or night, still higher,
With belled fire and the moth-soft Milky way,
What by your measure is the heaven of desire,...?

Or later the delicacy of this, from his well-known sonnet, *Nothing is so beautiful as spring*.

Thrush's eggs look little low heavens...

The genius of Shakespeare's language

I have suggested that unrhymed iambic pentameter would become increasingly inadequate to express the consciousness of the post Darwin-Freud-Marx-World War-human being. Yet there still remains for us the mystery of Shakespeare's language. In its mature expression it has qualities that, I believe, we have still not understood and certainly not superseded. It is not too comfortable. It is not so 'smooth in its numbers' as the verse of Tennyson. It is still unsurpassed in its capacity to reveal thought, emotion, action, and the miraculous fusion of all three. Along with the Authorized Version of the Bible it has, until now, shaped the consciousness of the English-speaking people as nothing else has. I believe his language has the power to teach us still and to awaken sensibilities still dormant in us:

> ...the fabulous wings unused, still folded in the heart.
>
> *A Sleep of Prisoners*, Christopher Fry

Shakespeare's language teaches actors what to do and how to do it. It is the perfect fusion of speech and action. We are spoiled for any lesser teachers and yet inspired to bring the lessons of that greatness into all other work we may be called to do. Through the genius of Shakespeare's language, we experience the discomfort modern consciousness demands; to wake us up to present challenges. In his mature plays, the late tragedies and later comedies, while still a master of iambic pentameter, he begins experimenting with its limits.

> Tomorrow and tomorrow and tomorrow
> Creeps in this petty pace from day to day
> To the last syllable of recorded time.
> And all our yesterdays have lighted fools
> The way to dusty death. Out! Out! Brief candle!
> Life's but a walking shadow; a poor player
> That struts and frets his hour upon the stage
> And then is heard no more. It is a tale
> Told by an idiot: full of sound and fury
> Signifying nothing.
>
> *Macbeth*

These words enable us to examine his precision with meter. We see to what degree he played with it and stretched it, yet still it was the ground within which his language took root and grew to scale the depths of earth and the heavens. The language of *Winters Tale* is rougher still, and tougher. Some passages seem jagged with a strong alliterative tendency. It is as though, like Hopkins, he knew to reach for this when searching for a language to accommodate the growing wrestling with the shadow; a theme that increasingly occupied him in the final plays.

We cannot call the words from *Macbeth* old-fashioned. They have a quality which is neither past nor present, but seems to transcend time. At the stage of his life when Shakespeare wrote *Macbeth*, he had mastered the rhythmic form of unrhymed iambic pentameter, called *blank verse*. He could move both in and out of its strict syllabic count with ease. It seems he was already reaching out to what would only be identi-fied, four centuries later, as *free verse*; the rhythmic structures required by spirit which is self-determining. Yet his powers of expression were tempered in the furnace of blank verse. It is this tempering which grants each word its power to glow and reso-nate with depths of hidden treasure; compressing them in sentences of deeply tex-tured, incomparable transparency.

So, as in Ariel's and Prospero's exchange from *The Tempest* quoted earlier, we sense how language, schooled so many years within the structure of iambic pentameter, has evolved to something else. It is both modern in its stark simplicity and yet illumined with that undefinable and indescribable magic whose signature is in the stars.

Chapter 5

Speech and the Etheric

The Seamless Garment

The sense of life

Global ecology is showing us there can be no future for the earth or for humanity if we think and behave as separate things. Yet even knowing that it is not true, enclosed within a skin I easily succumb to the illusion arising out of physical perception: *I am separate from everyone and everything.*

Simply by means of the air outside my skin circulating, passing through me and then out again I am woven into all that lives and breathes. Space appears an empty vacuum, nothing, yet within the earth's atmosphere it consists at least of something — air — without which, we die. Although we cannot see the air that fills the space around us, it is still a physical phenomenon which can be analysed and measured physically. But space is filled with something finer still. If we behold a plant that is alive and flourishing next to one that's dying, or dead, we can observe the presence or absence of this 'something'. It is *life* and our ability to perceive it, a *sense of life.*[*]

> I know when one is dead and when one lives.
>
> *King Lear*, Shakespeare

We perceive when life penetrates an earthly form and we perceive when that form is no longer filled with life. Yet what we refer to as 'life' in either case is a concept, inferred from data, physically perceived. Our normal consciousness does not perceive the life itself, so once it has departed from the form it inhabited, we conclude it is extinguished and that death is real. This is the conclusion. Life, when it can no longer be perceived, does not exist.

This is Lear's experience when he finally accepts Cordelia is dead:

> She's gone forever.
> I know when one is dead and when one lives;
> She's dead as earth ...
> No no no life!

---

[*] See *The Art of Acting*, Terms of reference, The 12 senses.

Why should a dog, a horse, a rat have life
And thou no breath at all? Thou'lt come no more.
Never never never never never!

Our everyday consciousness is like Lear's when he first recognizes life has left Cordelia's body. What most of us perceive is not the life itself, but dead form emptied of its life. However, over the next centuries, as perception gradually shifts, it will expand to include such supersensible dimensions as that of life itself. Even now this shift can come about through shock or some event which loosens the etheric body from its physical sheath. Such loosening results in a capacity to see beyond the physical.

Lear's final moments show just this. The shock of Cordelia's death initiates his own dying process. His heart 'breaks'. Shakespeare's language, ever multi-levelled, indicates the loosening of his etheric body from its physical garment. *Pray you, undo this button.* As this happens, his perception loosens with it and he 'sees' Cordelia's etheric expanding out beyond her corpse. There in that invisible realm, her soul and spirit wait for him to join her so that she can guide him further. *Look there! Look there!* he says as he breathes his own life out.

Although to a mind schooled only in the physical perception of phenomena, Lear's experience is an illusion, an hallucination that arises in his soul because he cannot face the grief of losing her, yet it might equally demonstrate the scenario described above; the way our circumstances sometimes shift us into new perceptions, seemingly without our conscious choice.

When life is healthily at work in us, we are like the fish that does not know what water is. Unlike the fish, we can develop our awareness of this subtle realm of life that weaves both in and round us. The sense with which we perceive it can be trained. This life, which Steiner called 'etheric', occupies the whole of what we see as *space*. We share it with all other beings. Beyond the boundaries of our skin we weave within a seamless garment; One Body that contains us all; within which we affect and are affected by the all within which we are woven.

Time, rhythm and life

One attribute of LIFE is rhythm; breathing, heartbeat, sap rising and falling, the seasons, sleeping and waking, living and dying, dying and living, sunset and sunrise; life unfolding constantly in *time*. Although time can be measured and can seem as regular as clockwork, it is not itself mechanical. We may set a metronome in motion to establish regularity but if the notes we play are only strictly metrical, we cannot hear or play the music. J.S. Bach very often suffers from this treatment, easily degenerating into what was once described as 'kilometres of notes'. Verse written to be strictly metrical without the interplay of other tensions and dynamics is known as doggerel, not poetry.

When learning how to dance, we may need to clarify the beat with accurate precision in order to co-ordinate our steps. Yet we know the dance is something else; more subtle, less easy to define. That 'something' is what *flows through* steps and beat. Time is able to be measured, but it is not measure. And it is life itself that flows, manifesting in a form that appears but for a moment, or a week, or month or years before dissolving to release it once again, back to the invisible, inaudible. Beat and measure may be linear but time is mysterious: its end already there in its beginning, its beginning in its end.

> ...Words, after speech, reach
> Into the silence. Only by the form, the pattern,
> Can words or music reach
> The stillness, as a Chinese jar still
> Moves perpetually in its stillness.
> Not the stillness of the violin, while the note lasts,
> Not that only, but the co-existence,
> Or say that the end precedes the beginning,
> And the end and the beginning were always there
> Before the beginning and after the end.
> And all is always now...
>
> *Burnt Norton*, T.S. Eliot

And it is when the different rhythms interact and interweave that creation is most rich and complex.

Our ability to sense life can be blunted. Aspects of our present culture work against, even obliterate, our sense of life. As it relates to our own wellbeing, we may not realize we are ill until our symptoms are acute. And so, we are mostly unaware how our own speech, the speech of those around us, or that which bombards us through the media, quite apart from content, drains us of life.

Energy and life

To fill our speech with life is a central goal of Speech Formation. This is not merely a matter of more energy. Frenetic energy may express illness or may make us ill. Yes, energy is needed, but energy in harmony with what is healthily alive, with what breathes and unfolds itself healthily and rhythmically. At the basis of the technique for achieving this, lie the principles so far explored. It is the nature of our breath to be already finely woven with the ether that surrounds us. And only when a sound is formed out of breath, so that it is free to reveal its being, can it weave into the greater ether which we share.

Speech that expresses the whole human being

First we learn to do this with a single sound. Then we learn to weave its gesture and its substance with the other sounds, forming living structures that create a tapestry which has no end and no beginning. What we call beginning and end refer only to the boundary perceived by our five senses. This living tapestry woven from the infinite, is imperceptible to them, and yet can fill the space and enfold the listener in life-nourishing forms. Sentences become living organisms of more or less complexity, in which the will and thought and feeling content are embedded and in-woven. In just the same way are our souls and spirits woven into our etheric bodies when we are awake.

Spoken language will then be experienced as *like ourselves*. It will have at its core, a sovereign creator, the I AM, who then creates a complex vessel in which it can express itself. This vessel, human speech, will be woven, just as we are, of:

A *physical* body. This is what our ears receive and is interpreted by our brain function as *sound*. It can be measured in terms of amplitude and frequency of wavelength.

This will be permeated with:

An *etheric* body, or life substance that flows through the sound and which our own life body can perceive.

This, in turn, will be permeated with:

The *astral* substance of our soul experience; our feelings, emotions, thoughts and impulses of will.

Spoken language, constituted in this way, can only be created by the whole constitution of the one who speaks, and nourishes the whole constitution of the one who listens. When this is achieved, human speech moves a step closer to fulfilment of that aspect of its destiny at which those words from the gospel of St John have hinted: the power of the LOGOS to create.

Silence — the space between

Silence . . .
the veil our sense perceives
protecting us from finer worlds of sound
which, if we heard,
would draw us to their throne
or strike us dead.

In relation to Speech, silence is the space between spoken words or sentences. We call this space a *pause*. Without ability to perceive in the etheric realm, a pause is empty space; only the words considered real. As such, the spaces seem unnecessary, needing to be filled up, crammed with words by speaking quickly, or as arbitrary gaps, used here or there for emphasis. Yet a great artist can fill a pause with substance that speaks as strongly as the words that frame it.

The rest is silence.

Hamlet, Shakespeare

The Parthenon would occupy less space without the distance in between its columns. Yet when we behold this temple we know the spaces and their exact proportions are as much a part of its effect on us as are its marble forms. Just so, if we would work in harmony with the etheric realm and perceive our speech and actions to be woven in that greater whole, we know a pause cannot be arbitrary. The time between two living forms is not an empty gap. Its position and duration cannot be the consequence of whim, but arise instead from a deeper lawfulness. When this is the case it will fuse seamlessly with the action and the intellectual/emotional requirements of a text.

If we can achieve this fusion, a text becomes a living organism. The life in great language comes from that dimension in which word, rhythm, emotion, thought and action were originally fused in the genius of the creator. To reveal that in speech, I travel back along the pathway of those words to the life which is their source. From there I can return, bringing that life with me.

While a pause made arbitrarily is not part of that living stream but a dead gap, a silence that reveals itself within a stream of words which move etherically, is alive. We feel it is inevitable, even as it allows for what is new or unexpected. It is filled with the life of what has manifested in the world of time and space and disappeared again, and with what is preparing to be born. It is, in the true meaning of the word, a 'pregnant' pause.

To form a sound or syllable or word so that it lives, we must sense that its being has its source in silence and emerges from the realm of the invisible, inaudible. If we learn to accompany its movement and gesture as it manifests in space and time, we are able to stay present and accompany its disappearance back into the realm of silence. We are surfing, riding or flying into space, carried on the dynamic of the sound. Then, as if we swing on a trapeze, a moment comes when we can let go of the one sound, trust ourselves in space, and find the next sound on its way towards us. We will be in the right place to take hold of it and swing on its dynamic, once again into the audible realm. This ability to ride from one sound to the next is only possible if the stream of breath is free. To ride thus is to exhilarate in the inexhaustible flow of life itself, to experience our own life revitalized. In this way, even the longest passages are spoken with a sense of ease.

Hearing and weaving the tapestry of the inaudible

Speech-exploration 51 (partner work)

You are learning how to first create and then receive the impulse for a sound in order to reveal its nature. (Steps 1–5 can also be attempted by a single person speaking sounds for a whole class or group.)

1. Stand with a sense of being present and available. Let your partner speak a consonant into your back space.
2. Listen to the sound with your whole body. As its impulse moves through you, silently receive it and let it move your body in whatever way it wishes to respond.
3. Do the same again but when you have received the impulse of the sound, as it picks you up and moves you, speak it.
4. Do this with several sounds so that it becomes a habit only to speak upon an impulse you have first received.
5. Swap.

Speech-exploration 52

1. Work on your own. Now *imagine* a sound coming to you from behind. Move in response, then speak. Don't allow yourself to speak unless it's a genuine response to what you have received.
2. This whole procedure can be repeated with a word, a phrase, a whole line. Approaching *Speech-exploration 26*, (klsfm), or any of the other Speech-exercises in this way ensures that the layers of work we are presently exploring are integrated with what has gone before. We want it to be second nature that we speak only what we first 'hear'.

3. Try this whole process with a line of text. A good one to begin with is the opening line of D.H. Lawrence's poem: *Song of a man who has come through.*

   Not I, Not I, but the wind that blows through me.

Build it, phrase by phrase, until the impulse of the whole line can be received from the invisible realms of life where it began. Let it receive its body in time and space through your back, through your mouth. Then let the swirling vortex of its life return again to join the greater life of which it is a part.

Speech-exploration 53 (partner work)

Exchange roles at every stage. This ensures that you become adept at listening as well as speaking and understand that these two functions cannot be conceived apart.

1. A receives a sound from the 'unheard' realm.
2. A moves and speaks that sound strongly in the space. B 'listen' with your body, move the sound, follow its dynamic and stay within its impulse as it disappears back into the silence whence it came. Continue to move with its dynamic, sensing how it may begin to change and metamorphose into a different sound. Don't move beyond the life of that impulse. When you sense the impulse change and grow into another, respond. Let your whole body move into the sound that now arises out of what has gone before. Let it unfold in the space, directing it towards your partner and speaking it. This sound is your 'reply' to what you first received.
3. A now receives B's reply and follows with steps 1 and 2, emerging from them with the next response.

In this way, moving back and forth between you, you build up an exhilarating dialogue of dynamically interweaving sounds. In such a dialogue, the spaces in between the spoken sounds are experienced to be as much a part of the exchange as what is said. They are the unheard portion of that living tapestry of which the 'heard sounds' are but part.

4. Create an exchange of words, of phrases and of lines.
5. Build the etheric body of a scene you are working on by weaving the lines back and forth between you in this way.

Speech-exploration 54 (partner work)

For flexibility in our capacity to use the sounds in their differing combinations and dynamics, it's exciting to combine this etheric weaving of the sounds in dialogue with Chekhov's qualities-of-movement.[*]

---

[*]For explorations, see *The Art of Acting*, chapter 1.

1. My partner sends towards me a fiery /s/. I receive it, let it move through me, and follow its movement.

2. I sense that fiery movement wants to turn into a watery /l/. I let my body respond to its changing impulse and find that I am floating. I move with it until /l/ is ready to emerge as a sound in space. I let the sound move onto my stream of breath and send it to my partner.

3. My partner in turn receives its impulse and joins it, full-bodily moving it until it wants to densify. The floating turns to moulding and, in time, when my partner speaks it back to me, it will have turned into a 'd', and so on.

Speech-exploration 54 can be played with myriad variations.

• Experiment with planning the transitions in advance.
• Let the transitions arise spontaneously.
• Move from single sounds to working with the texts.[*]

> Heard melodies are sweet but those unheard are sweeter.
>
> *Ode on a Grecian Urn*, Keats

Through such practice we cultivate our sense for the life from which what we hear as sound emerges, and to which it then returns. This sense tells us when our work begins to be in harmony with all that lives and breathes. Such explorations train us to be conscious of our own etheric body. This consciousness becomes our organ of perception for the etheric dimension of spoken language. Without this, we cannot have direct perception of what enhances life or what is life-depleting and the whole idea remains, at best, an interesting theory.

---

[*] See texts provided in *The Art of Acting*, chapter 1.

The sense of the whole

The basis for developing the sense of the whole is laid in *The Art of Acting*.[*] We now extend this in relation to our understanding of the etheric and, in particular, as it relates to the act of speech and language. We have observed the strong connection between rhythm and life. The living universe unfolds itself in rhythm. So too, if language is alive, it is rhythmical. Rhythm is not always regular. It can be 'sprung', as Hopkins called it, or irregular, as in good prose and much contemporary poetry.

We cannot transform beat and meter into rhythm unless we cultivate our *sense of the whole*. This sense is constantly attacked in our culture, obsessed as it is with chopping wholeness into ever smaller fragments. A thing is seen to be the sum of its bits and this indeed is how machines are made. But the application of a mechanistic view to living organisms threatens our capacity to sense the whole and therefore life.

A living organism is conceived from the beginning as a whole within which what appear to be its separate parts then manifest in space and time. What appears first, contains what is to come. The mature oak tree exists as potential in the seed. That potential is not physically perceivable. We can chop the seed into the tiniest parts and still not find it. It exists outside of space and time, within what was once called the quintessence and we might call the *divine creative thinking*. There, the final oak, that which appears last in time, imperceptible to our physical senses, awaits its opportunity to engage with the perceptible. At that mysterious interface, it draws the elements of earth, water, air and fire with which to weave itself from first to last, in time and space.[28]

As this idea relates to language, we reach beyond both space and time into the divine creative thinking which has expressed itself in a specific text. We need to sense the wholeness in a word, phrase, sentence, paragraph: no less within a verse, poem or story, speech, scene, act, a whole drama.

Our modern intellect may be overwhelmed by the length and complexity of sentences in Shelley's poetry or Shakespeare's plays. Yet we know that Shakespeare's plays were popular in his time and his audience included those with little or no education, and who, no doubt, voted with their feet. Such sentences as these seemed not to trouble them:

> Besides, this Duncan
> Hath borne his faculties so meek, hath been
> So clear in his great office, that his virtues
> Will plead like angels, trumpet-tongued against
> The deep damnation of his taking-off;

---

[*] See *The Art of Acting*, chapter 5.

And pity, like a naked new born babe,
Striding the blast, or heaven's cherubin, horsed
Upon the sightless couriers of the air,
Shall blow the horrid deed in every eye,
That tears shall drown the wind.

Macbeth, Shakespeare

Sentence structure in relation to the *sense of the whole*

We want the speaking of such sentences not to defeat us but to be exhilarating. This will not be achieved without a sense for the whole, which we shall look at first in relationship to sentence structure. The following explorations are designed to lead to the experience that a sentence is not just the sum of its parts but that the parts unfold out of a greater whole.

Speech-exploration 55

1. Stand at point-A. Walk. On impulse, stop. You have reached point-B. Look back. Your journey consisted of those steps.
2. Go back to the starting point. Intend to travel to point-B, then walk there.
3. Observe your experience.

Speech-exploration 56

Apply the same process to the sentence: *I want to go there.*

1. Step the sentence taking one step with each word. If you add on one word at a time, you will probably observe that the sentence sounds robotic.
2. Step and speak the sentence with a strong sense that you know from the beginning exactly where you are going.
3. Explore this process until you start to recognize the sensation of fore-knowing and how to find its source beyond space and time, in 'infinity'. To reinforce this sense, find a gesture to remind you of this source when you speak: that you are reaching to collect from infinity an impulse which contains all that you intend to say. Then move and speak as it moves through you. We can do this even with a single word. Reaching for it in infinity we discover not an arbitrary gathering of sounds but a creative act in which the sounds are woven at their source.

You are a diver poised on the edge of the diving board, preparing to execute a complicated dive. A complicated sequence of actions, woven to unfold rhythmically, culminates in entering the water. Only then, release! All of that is present in the diver's consciousness. You cannot dive until your instrument has been prepared and gathered to itself what is needed to perform the whole dive. The more complex the dive, the more that must be gathered before taking off. Before you leave the board, you grasp the dive in its entirety. It will not work to leave the board and while in flight decide to add an extra turn or twist.

Learning the routine requires analysis; thinking out what might come next and how to arrive at that from what preceded it. Mastery of the dive involves a growing sense of ease in executing what at first seemed complicated. In time, intelligence or consciousness will be locked into the body's memory. Yet it is not our material body that remembers, it's the life or etheric body; the same that carries in its memory our human form and embodies it in matter.

By regular practice of a skill, we program its wisdom into our etheric body. When the skill becomes instinctive we no longer think it out, proceeding step-by-step, from first to last. We experience instead that its end, what lies in the future, is what leads us into action; the future pulling us towards itself, from last to first.

This process leads us to another mystery. Everyday experience leads us to think of time proceeding from the past to the future, and memory as storage of the past. Think again of how an acorn mysteriously remembers how to grow into an oak tree. Normal consciousness perceives that the tree grows forward from the past into the present. Etheric consciousness invites us to imagine how the future oak tree reaches back to the present and draws the substances it needs to grow towards itself.

> Time present and time past
> Are both perhaps present in time future
> And time future contained in time past.

Burnt Norton, T.S. Eliot

To train ourselves to speak according to etheric laws requires that we gain capacity to act out of this complex experience of time. For a sentence to unfold in space and time, from the first word to the last, we need to conceive its end in its beginning and sense how the last word is already present in the first.

> Learn from the cat!
> Body poised to pounce
> outwardly a stillness, finely tuned,
> a movement gathering –
> an act accomplished inwardly
> rehearsed invisibly.
>
> Underneath the skin
> the preparation, rippling, imminent
> unseen but palpable

from there to here
from then to now
faster than a fling
cat winds it in
with will's intense intention
winds in
the distance between there and here
then and now
till distance disappears
and there is here
and past and future
wound into the spring so tightly sprung
the wave withdrawn to suck the ocean in
the presence whole —
ONE MIND
and readiness complete
neither hesitation nor false start —
NOW
the act, effortless —
complete before begun
a liquid body pours into the mould,
invisible container, channel, pathway
from here to there
now to then
and distance in between them disappeared.

Prepare to speak like that.
Project a syllable, a word,
not push it out, but like the cat
a freed form
bodied forth
into world ether —
there to eddy in the oceanic breath
a tiny curl of sound, a ripple,
swirling whirlpool, living flame,
a wind, a pebble forming rock —
a human offering within the Word of Worlds.

Conscious Creator I
reach down into myself
dive into my own created form

the image making, word creating, sculpting
word made flesh –
condensed into my mouth and all its parts –
the I AM HERE in what I made.

Now to extend the making
THERE outside myself in sound.
Project it there!
First wind it in,
the distance in between,
from there to here or then to now
till there is here and future now within
and distance disappeared –
all wound into the tightly coiled spring, one mind, one self –
Now, speak!

The following exploration can be attempted with any single sound or syllable, or word. At some point this process should be applied to and integrated with all other explorations as it is basic to our whole technique.

Speech-exploration 57 – freeing the voice

1. Stand poised like a diver on the diving board or a cat, preparing to pounce.
2. Picture the space in front of your mouth where you want to place what you speak. Project your consciousness into it, take it back inside you and weave it into the following step.
3. Perform the entire activity of forming what you intend to speak, but without making sound. Experience not only the actions that take place in your mouth but also the engagement of the muscles and tensions throughout your whole instrument that support the movement in your mouth.
4. At the same time lift the whole sequence of action forward from your mouth out into the space.
5. When the etheric action is complete and delivered into the space, then let your voice drop effortlessly into the etheric form you have created.

Speech-exploration 58

We will work with the word, *rose*.

1. Imagine a rose.
2. Like the diver, you are poised on the diving board preparing to speak the word: *rose*.

3. Find a gesture which helps you to imagine plucking the rose. Do not speak before you have grasped the wholeness of the word; gesture, sounds, image, thought, feeling, breath. Then dive and, as you pluck it from infinity with your gesture, say the word. Try to fuse gesture, sounds, image, thought, feeling and breath together in one act.

4. Go back to your diving board. Poise yourself again and this time gather two words from your invisible source. This dive is more complex and requires increased preparation. Do as before, except that you will say: *the* rose.

5. Your third dive is more complex again. Gather it as a whole, then speak: the *red* rose.

6. Being careful not to take shortcuts with preparation and gesture, expand the sentence. Remind yourself that with each new dive you are not just 'adding something on' each time, but creating a new wholeness:

> The red rose *is on the bush.*
> *He sees* the red rose is on the bush.
> He sees the red rose is on the bush *and he smiles.*
> He sees the red rose is on the bush, he smiles *and he smells it.*
> He sees the red rose is on the bush, he smiles and he smells it, *then he bends down and plucks it.*

7. Work in reverse. Each time you reduce the sentence by one of its components, grasp it as a new whole until you return again to just one word. Try to experience that you do not simply add or take away a word. You are diving from infinity, the bearer each time of a different wholeness. Observe, when you succeed in this, how each new wholeness generates its own dynamic. Each dynamic has power to organize the syllables into their own unique and rhythmical relationship.

> He sees the red rose is on the bush, he smiles and he smells it, *then he bends down and plucks it.*
> He sees the red rose is on the bush, he smiles *and he smells it.*
> He sees the red rose is on the bush *and he smiles.*
> *He sees* the red rose is on the bush.
> The red rose *is on the bush.*
> The *red* rose.
> *The* rose.
> *Rose.*

8. Think of this one word (rose) as the seed which contains the whole sentence in it. Can you speak it with that sense?

Speech-exploration 35 (reprise)

The following Speech exercise appeared first in chapter 3 where we used it to develop nimbleness and flexibility in our organs of articulation, to achieve clarity and lightness in our speech. We use it now to develop our capacity for working with the sense of the whole.

children chiding
chaffinch chirping
choking chimneys
cheerfully chattering

children chiding and fetching
chaffinch chirping switching
choking chimneys hitching
cheerfully chattering twitching.

beach children chiding and fetching
reach chaffinch chirping switching
birches choking chimneys hitching
perches cheerfully chattering twitching

In the first stage of building up *Speech-exploration 35*, it is helpful to rearrange it so the first line of each group forms a sequence, then the second, then the third:

1. children chiding
2. children chiding and fetching
3. beach children chiding and fetching

Our purpose is to experience each line as a new and discreet wholeness that we gather from an infinite source. If we can do this, the word *beach* in the third line will contain the words that follow it. They can then tumble out of the dynamic *beach contains* without any extra effort on our part. Once we have mastered the metamorphosis of the etheric stream within the variations of each line, we can bring that mastery to the original arrangement.

This way of speaking, which participates in the etheric stream, is only possible when the breath is free. If we can make our breath available as the substance in which the sounds unfold, we will experience an exhilarating sense of ease when we tackle even long and complex sentences. That effortless sensation is always the sign that we have tapped the life source of the universe. Effort *is* needed in our initial act to grasp the whole and make our energy and breath available for what that whole requires to enter time and space. If we have trained our organs of articulation to respond, the words will organize themselves.

Emphasis and climax

It is natural to stress those words we regard as important. *If we do not work out of a sense of the whole*, we tend to give such words an extra push and leave the others unattended. A sense of the whole helps us recognize how each word plays its part within the overall intention. A specific word or words possessing such significance can organize and permeate the other words in the sentence, thus integrating them into the whole. Equally, 'less important' words can lend support. To manage both skills means we know how to create a climax. When we can do this in a single sentence, we are able to apply these principles to a whole passage, scene or play.

Speech-exploration 59

> The waves *crash* on the shore.

Because the function of a verb is to be the active part of any sentence, verbs serve as useful tools to determine the dynamic.[*] Here, the climax bursts within the middle of our sentence. This means we learn how to prepare for it with the preceding words, and then allow it to release its energy into the words which follow.

1. Find a full-bodied movement and gesture that expresses the word *crash*.[†]
2. Integrate the movement with the speaking of the word, so that the sounds play their part in expressing the experience.
3. Speak: *The waves crash*. See if you can speak *the waves* so that the activity of *crash* is already present in *the waves*. 'The' which is normally regarded as a boring word, now comes alive and, along with *waves*, is already moving on its way towards the verb. The first two words no longer 'hang around' until the verb, but play their part in building up to it.
4. Practise the whole sentence. To ensure that *on the shore* is not 'stuck on' at the end, let the energy and life in *crash* permeate those final words. When sh is able to reveal its own activity within the overall progression of the sounds, it will naturally create the sound of foam and water in commotion. It will do so twice; firstly, as it impacts with the rock in *crash* and, secondly, as it moves up the sand in *shore*. Experiment with alternative artistic choices by forming the second sh either with strength or gentleness. In the former, the water remains turbulent in the aftermath of *crash*. In the latter, the wave recedes calmly and serenely.
5. You can accomplish these effects only if you have learned to:

---

[*] We learn at school that verbs are 'doing' words. Refer chapter 7.

[†] See *The Art of Acting*, Terms of reference, full-bodied movement.

- grasp your artistic purpose and the sentence as a whole before you speak
- attune your instrument to the dynamic of the verb and of the sounds composing it
- sense how the other words are contained in it.

All of these constitute your preparation and only when it is complete, you dive.

6. Try this several times within a sequence of full-bodied movement. When you are satisfied that the whole sentence is alive, reduce the outer movement by degrees until you can recreate it in your speaking.

Speech-exploration 60

Crash, oh waves, on the shore!

In the first version, the function of *the waves* was to prepare the way for the climax. Here, the climax explodes at the beginning and the other words follow in its wake, swept along by the energy released.

Speech-exploration 61

The waves, on the shore, *crash*.

In this third version, the climax is the culmination of the sentence. Although it only makes its full appearance at the end, we learn to speak the preceding words so they participate in the build-up that leads to its explosion.

Exercising in this way, we awaken our capacity to sense the whole in language and apply this principle in different contexts. The climactic word may not always be a verb, but because their active nature reveals the central thrust of sentences so clearly, practising with verbs can teach us how to work with climax.

Speech-exploration 62

Repeat the steps of *Speech-explorations 58–60* using the following example:

The flowers *open* in the sun
Open, oh flowers, in the sun
The flowers in the sun, *open*

These sentences are based on the same structures as those in *Speech-explorations 58–60* but require us to imagine an activity of very different nature and apply it in a less outwardly dramatic context. Apply the same process. Can you sense as the verb shifts from beginning, to middle, to end, how the centre of the vortex of the sentence shifts, sweeping all the other words into its dynamic?

You may already have begun to sense how going to the source where the whole is gathered involves a willingness to dive into the cauldron of creative fire. To bring life into a sentence in this way, is to *create* it and creation cannot take place without fire. Without such fire, a sentence can only pass on information.

Speech-exploration 63

> Then quickly *rose* Sir Bedevere and *ran*
> And *leaping* down the ridges lightly, *plunged*
> Among the bulrush beds and *clutched* the sword
> And strongly *wheeled* and *threw* it.

We are now ready to apply this principle to a long and complex sentence. This one from *Le Morte d'Arthur* by Lord Tennyson describes the moment when King Arthur is dying of his battle wounds. Having realized that Sir Bedevere has lied to him, Arthur shames him into the fulfilment of his final wish; to throw the sword Excalibur into the lake, thus bringing to an end the order that was known as the Round Table. In doing so, he would prepare the way for something new; an order not maintained by the sword.

1. Prepare each verb with a full-bodied movement or gesture.[*] Integrate the movement with speaking the verb so that each verb's action is revealed through the sounds.
2. Speak the sequence of the verbs. Allow a whole breath for each one. Retain whatever movement you require so that each verb expresses its dynamic and activity. Find out how to build the sequence so that each one makes its contribution to the climax: *threw*.
3. Play with step 2 in a group. Each member takes responsibility for one verb in its order in the sequence and speaks it so that it contributes to the building of momentum; it must gather what has gone before, and build on it in such a way that it supports the next one to go further.
4. After each has made their contribution to the sequence, move the verb around one place until everyone has learned what is required at each stage on the journey to the climax. It is very different to speak the opening verb in such a way that it supports everything that follows, or to speak the one preceding the climactic verb. Or to be responsible to bring the sequence to its culmination in the final verb.
5. Take the word or words connected with each verb. Speak each section so that its component words share in their verb's activity.[†]

---

[*] See *The Art of Acting*, Terms of reference, full-bodied movement.
[†] See Speech-explorations 58–62.

Then quickly *rose* Sir Bedevere
and *ran*
and *leaping* down the ridges lightly
plunged among the bulrush beds
and *clutched* the sword
and strongly *wheeled*
and *threw* it.

Practising this way teaches the breath to organize itself as the phrasing suggests. Again, it's fun to practise in a group. Each member learns to provide, one step at a time, what each clause requires to serve its function in the whole.

6. Having mastered each stage of the journey, each individual can now attempt to build the sentence as a whole.

Movement or hurrying?

Identifying each successive stage of a sentence within the overall dynamic enables us to enter its etheric flow. One like that from *Le Morte d'Arthur* requires sustained commitment to achieve the necessary culmination. It provides the opportunity to learn how to stay centred as we enter that stream of living time for extended periods. For we can only surrender to the power of its current if we experience that we are anchored in it. Otherwise we panic and mistake the intensity required for urgency which tempts us to rush headlong through the sentence and lose control of it. Thus, we need to understand the difference between movement and hurrying. By working in the way suggested, we can start to sense a healthy energy; one which breathes and has, at the centre of its movement, stillness. We reach a stage where we can speak such a sentence with a sense of ease.

We may be amazed at how much time we actually have to organize ourselves, even as we speak within the flow. We have time for gathering. Like the diver on the board, we collect the whole, then move through each part, renewing from the source by letting go of what has passed in order to prepare for what is on its way towards us from the future.

We work towards Speech that integrates the thinking, feeling and the willing functions of our soul. Speech formed with such intent requires time to be prepared and gathered. When this time unfolds within etheric lawfulness, it will not seem excessive but natural. We are supported in its harmonious, organic flow, to speak as quickly as a text requires, without a sense of rushing.

The story of the hare and tortoise helps us understand. The hare is like the intellect. Because it can remain in abstraction, content with information, having no need for experience, it arrives first at the finish line. The tortoise wants to feel the experience and sense its action in the world. This needs time. If we want to speak what we imagine so that we communicate what *happens*, it has to be enacted by the body. If the body is to move and do a deed, it must engage with the resistance that the earth provides, and that takes time. This is why we work so much with gesture in the early stages. If we create in movement first, before and while we speak, we are not tempted to believe that the shortcut taken by the intellect can satisfy our need for experience.

Further thoughts concerning emphasis and climax

The need for intensity urges me to poke my will into the specific words that are significant; give them an extra shove, so to speak, to ensure they bear the weight of my intention. But such emphasis does not relate to the surrounding words. They continue on their empty way, conveying information with no life in it, until another word receives its dose of emphasis. Our attempt to build a climax will be reduced to 'giving emphasis' if what we speak does not arise from a sense of the whole.

Speech-exploration 30 for breath (*in the vast*) is one of the few exercises Rudolf Steiner gave that expresses a content of ideas beyond the sounds of which it is composed. When the aspects of *in the vast* described in chapter 2 have been mastered, then we can build it up out of its wholeness. We see it is a single sentence, structured so that the first four lines lead progressively to culmination (or climax) in the fifth.

> In the vast unmeasured world-wide spaces,
> In the endless stream of time,
> In the depths of human soul life,
> In the world's great revelations
> Seek the unfolding of life's great mystery.

Like our acorn, the first *in the vast* already contains its culmination *seek,* which not only penetrates and carries the whole last line within its wake but draws the other lines towards it, sucking them into its vortex. What we gather for the dive and which launches us into *in the vast*, includes the preparation of our instrument to take hold of the /s/ in *seek*. For it is the /s/ that must gather what has gone before and bestow on *seek* the power it needs to sweep us through the whole last line, bringing the sentence to its culmination.

Repetition or metamorphosis?

Machines repeat, producing static replica of what was made before. Living forms grow and develop further stages of their lives; there is no repetition. They are born. They grow into maturity. The outer form begins to crumble, wither and in time, it dies. While that form returns completely to the earth, its life is released into the

realm beyond what physical senses can perceive. Speech is alive when it participates in all the stages of that process. If a sentence is to be a living form, it must
evolve.

In *Speech-exploration 30*, *in the* is 'repeated' four times. What if we regarded these
not as repetitions but, enhancements? Experiment with how to speak the same words
several times *without repeating them*. Shakespeare provides us with many such
examples; moments which require metamorphosis, enhancement, not repetition.
Think of Lady Macbeth's three *Oh!*s in the sleepwalking scene. Or the five great *never!*s
uttered by King Lear as he digests Cordelia's death.

To do justice to such moments requires many layers of artistic process. The capacity
to create an evolving, living form, is but one of these. Yet without the life it weaves into
the whole, no matter how deeply felt, the words are dead. Nothing can be repeated.
Each detail, like each new leaf or bud, needs to be a metamorphosis, enhancing and
developing what went before. If what we create in space and time is to unfold with
increasing fullness, we need to receive it from the infinite, invisible source, in equally
increasing measure.

> My bounty is as boundless as the sea,
> My love as deep; the more I give to thee,
> The more I have, for both are infinite.

Romeo and Juliet, Shakespeare

Speech-exploration 64 (partner work)

1. A to stand behind and be ready to support B. B falls gently backwards and comes to
   rest against A's hands.
2. Now A, imagine you receive a gentle impulse from behind and, with it, gently push
   B out into the space, staying true to that impulse. B don't resist, but go with what
   you have received, just as far as A's impulse takes you.
3. Do this several times, each time with a stronger impulse. Your aim is to experience
   that for B to travel further, A must receive and provide an impulse correspondingly
   enhanced.
4. When you are at ease within the silent stages of the process, allow a word to unfold
   within the impulse, then a phrase, then a longer sentence. Sense that the ever
   increasing length of what you say is fed by the ever increasing strength of the
   impulse from behind.

You can choose to focus on a single word, letting it unfold each time within a stronger
impulse. The enhancement of each word or phrase results from the increasingly
enhanced impulses we gather from behind and serve with our breath and energy.

5. Change over. B now has the opportunity to send the impulse and A to receive. As you become practised in each role, your experience refines and you sense that to provide an impulse you must first receive it. And to receive it, you must first learn to give.[*]

6. On your own, work through steps 1–4, replacing the concrete impulse from your partner with an imagined one.

7. Now take Lady Macbeth's three *O*s or the five *Never*s of King Lear and work with the words as suggested above. When you are ready introduce the character's emotional intensity, letting it become the source of your impulse. Discover how the enhancement of the forms allows the time and space for the emotional intensity to build and pour itself into the words, instead, as often happens, of becoming disconnected.[†]

Speech-exploration 65

Another opportunity for practising enhancement or metamorphosis is Lawrence's poem, *Song of a man who has come through*. Work on the whole passage in this way. Discover how to turn each repetition of *if only* into an enhancement of the one before, culminating in the first climax: *split*. Don't miss the opportunities afforded by *not I* in the first line, or *we shall* in the last.

> Not I, Not I, but the wind that blows through me!
> A fine wind is blowing the new direction of Time.
> If only I let it bear me carry me, if only to carry me!
> If only I am sensitive, subtle, oh, delicate, a winged gift!
> If only, most lovely of all, I yield myself and am borrowed
> By the fine, fine wind that takes its course through the chaos of the world
> Like a fine, an exquisite chisel, a wedge-blade inserted;
> If only I am keen and hard, like the sheer tip of a wedge
> Driven by invisible blows,
> The rock will split, we shall come at the wonder, we shall find the Hesperides.

When we learn to reach into our backspace, we strengthen the sense that our source lies in infinity. Drawing our speech from there, what could so easily turn into a shopping list grows into a living form.

---

[*] See *The Art of Acting*, chapter 3, page 137, giving and receiving.

[†] See *The Art of Acting*, chapter 2, Expansion and Contraction. This Chekhov tool offers another approach to managing enhancement.

Speech-exploration 66

Shylock's speech from Shakespeare's *Merchant of Venice* provides us with the opportunity to transform several shopping lists. Shylock justifies pursuing his revenge against Antonio:

> He hath disgraced me and hindered me half a million, laughed at my losses, mocked at my gains, scorned my nation, thwarted my bargains, cooled my friends, heated my enemies; and what's his reason? I am a Jew. Hath not a Jew eyes? hath not a Jew hands, organs, dimensions, senses, affections, passions? fed with the same food, hurt with the same weapons, subject to the same diseases, healed by the same means, warmed and cooled by the same winter and summer, as a Christian is? If you prick us do we not bleed? If you tickle us do we not laugh? If you poison us do we not die? and if you wrong us, shall we not revenge?

Lawrence's and Shakespeare's texts reveal not just a simple progress to a climax but a series of enhancements. Each one builds to its own 'mini-climax' and contributes to the final one. If I were to tackle such a climb 'to the summit of the mountain' in one progressive mounting of intensity, I would very likely lose control of the speech. The hoped-for effect would thus be compromised.

The principles inherent in expansion and contraction teach us that healthy expansion is preceded by contraction and vice versa.[*] If we apply these same principles to speaking Lawrence's and Shakespeare's texts, each time we intensify we first 'contract' or gather what has been achieved so it can continue to expand. The contraction 'dams up', as it were, what was won so far in order to release it further.

We need a range of skills to orchestrate this interplay of contracting and expanding tensions. Increasing or decreasing volume, rise and fall in pitch, fast or slow tempo; all have a part to play but can only do so if the speaker has control.

Alpha and Omega

The impulse for each phrase or sentence comes from infinity. It then unfolds itself in space and time through the gestures and dynamics of the sounds. The spaces in between the words are determined by the sounds which have gone before and prepared for them and from the dynamics of sounds still yet to come. This is the Alpha and Omega of the living word.

With experience and mastery of these dynamics, the spaces in between become elastic, infinitely flexible and various; held within the greater membrane of the interweaving tapestry of sounds. The artist, too, is held within that membrane while at the same time, creating it. All the space the soul needs to feel, to sense each moment,

---

[*] See *The Art of Acting*, chapter 2.

play it differently, find a new nuance, be surprised by some new possibility, is there, interwoven with the living form.

For actors to pour out life upon the stage, as well as thoughts, emotions, actions, they need to experience their own etheric bodies to be woven with the life of what they speak, and of the audience; that what is spoken in the space interweaves with everyone, enhancing or diminishing their life. This will inspire them to draw life from that greater life and in turn, pour life back into it.

Our ability to flow with the life in language is blocked if we cannot navigate our way through complex sentence structures. This means we need to learn how to recognize and differentiate between main and auxiliary clauses in a sentence.

Main clause and subordinate/auxiliary clause

Speech-exploration 67 (for three people)

Before we can craft more complex sentences, we begin with one that has a simple structure — a main clause consisting of *subject* and *predicate*.

> Swords of lightning slashed the sky.

We expand it thus:

> Swords of lightning, flashing mightily, slashed the sky.

The main clause has been interrupted by an auxiliary or subordinate clause. This more complex structure presents the speaker with a challenge. The auxiliary clause, which has the purpose to expand on the original thought or image, shouldn't confuse the clarity of the original. To make the structure clear, the speaker needs to sense it as a whole.

1. Decide which of you will be *Swords of lightning* (A) and which *slashed the sky* (B).
2. A and B have been separated and now long to be reunited. Reach to each other across the room with full-bodied gesture. Build the tension to its utmost then release the energy and let it take you to your partner.
3. When you are at ease with the dynamics, speak the two halves of the main clause with the sense that each is incomplete until it joins with the other. Have fun with variations that occur to you. It may take practice before the words and movements co-ordinate. When they do, completion of the sentence can be consolidated with a hearty hug.
4. Enlist C as the auxiliary clause. C's role is to delay the meeting between A and B, holding the beloveds apart with the enthusiasm of what it wants to add to the conversation, until the intensity of their yearning overcomes C's dynamic. Again,

the aim is co-ordination of the words and movement, encouraging the speech through the dynamic and energy of the action.

5. Swap parts so each person can experience the dynamics of each role.
6. Reduce the outer action while retaining its dynamics as you speak.
7. The ultimate goal is that each of you internalizes the dynamic and energy of all three roles and can reproduce them, speaking the whole sentence.

Speech-exploration 68

Rattle me, *more and more rattles*, now rightly.

The sentence is meaningless in a conceptual sense.[*] Its structure provides us with the principles by which our organs of articulation may pick their way through any combination of main and auxiliary clauses; enabling us to delineate the structures of even the most complex sentences.

We use the qualities of sounds provided to create two different textures. These textures enable us to differentiate main and auxiliary clauses in a sentence. Using an architectural analogy, we imagine that main clauses provide us with the basic structure and auxiliary clauses with the decoration. Content aside, it makes sense if the primary structure is made of firmer, denser substance than the secondary.

The journey that this archetypal sentence takes us on begins with those consonants that provide clear structure because they are formed on the teeth ridge or hard palate. Then, just before the intervention of the auxiliary clause, /m/ requires us to move forward to the lips. Having shifted there as though in preparation, we stay in their warmer, softer realm for most of the auxiliary clause. Then, as though in preparation for completing the main structure, the consonants in *rattles* demand us to be active on the teeth ridge once again. There we remain, resuming our construction of the basic edifice and bring it to completion with the firmer imprint of its consonants.

Achieving the necessary firmness of our basic structure will initially be helped by rolling 'r' /r/. The forward /m/ and /ɔə/ (*more*) provide a fineness and a spilling-over quality that enables the auxiliary clause to weave between the two halves of the main without distracting from the central thrust of the sentence. Returning to the clarity and firmness of the final clause informs the listeners they have arrived back at the main structure once again. Ability to differentiate between two fundamental textures, one firmer and one finer and more mobile, means we can tackle complex sentences by

---

[*] Identification of the main and auxiliary structures in a sentence is not directly linked to the relative importance of the content of the words. Structure is about the organizing of that content for the purposes of clarity. I will say more about this in relationship to grammar in the final chapter.

identifying their structure and replacing their words with the appropriate parts of *rattle me*.

Another useful metaphor to be explored in a full-bodied way and integrated with the indicated speech delineations is *the journey*. We want to clearly reveal the pathway of a sentence. Imagine we are guides, leading the listener along that path. On the way, we enhance the main journey with all sorts of fascinating, scary, delightful and important detours, but our task is to make sure that if the audience does wander off in some diversion, they never lose their bearings and can always return to the main path. They are confidently led by their guide to their destination.

Yet a third metaphor that offers opportunity to integrate full-bodied exploration with the indicated speech delineations is that of *king and court jester*. The king treads upon the earth, confident in his authority while around him the jester dances, nimbly side-stepping the reactions of his master.

Approaching the components of simple and complex sentence structure in a living way suggest the theme of chapter 7; a new approach to grammar.

The stream of Speech

All the aspects of technique we have explored now flow together to create something we can liken to a stream or river. We know we are entering this flow or stream of Speech when we can:

- Reach beyond the words we want to speak, into their place of origin, their source.
- Grasp what we intend to say as a whole, with the end already active in the beginning.
- Reveal to the listener, through delineated sentence structures, that complex of thought/feeling/will embodied in the sounds the words are made of.
- Let the sounds reveal their being in a free stream of breath.

We are co-creators participating in a living sculpture of continuously weaving, metamorphosing sounds. Our speech begins to 'do itself'. If it is not pushed or forced in any way but rides on the etheric stream, it will have a power that seems effortless. Such power is sustainable for long periods without damage to the voice, even where greater volume is required. When our speech can tap the life force of the universe, it will eternally renew itself without cost to the speaker. Indeed, it will be life renewing.

The paradox of form and freedom

Where, in all this, is the artist's individuality? An artist strives to reach the moment where technique becomes invisible. When this happens, the audience is not aware how hard the artist works. When through practice, what once required effort is imprinted into the etheric body of the artist our capacity becomes instinctive. Only then are actors really free to concentrate on what needs to be expressed in any moment. Entering the stream of speech does not, as we might fear, lead to an automatic, stereotyped, predictable performance; rather, we're free to be spontaneous, to be available to fellow actors and the situation. Only then can we create, out of the unique conditions that have come together, a never-to-be-repeated artistic deed.

This is the paradox; that we are most free to be spontaneous, creating something altogether new, when the form that holds us is secure. Developing the sense for wholeness might seem to obliterate the possibility of doing something fresh. On the contrary, it creates the space in which the new can come about. Because it is a living space and not an empty 'gap', what is born within it will not fragment but nourish the life-forces of creator and beholder.

The paradox of form and freedom has always been acknowledged in the arts. The intense drive to express oneself can be unbearably frustrated by the time it takes to master a technique. Some actors escape with being talented or with a training that aims no further than polishing that talent. There have always been gifted people who seemed to enjoy the fruits of talent without their work appearing obvious. It is important too, to enjoy expression of ourselves at every level. To consciously connect our self which seeks expression, with the greater Self whose Presence is expressed in all that we perceive, requires a longer journey.

The formative aspect of Speech

What's in a name?

Sprachgestaltung was the name Rudolf Steiner gave to our approach to speech. There have been several attempts to render the German name in English. Each has proved unsatisfactory for different reasons. *Creative Speech* is used widely to mean quite different things. *Speech Formation* is often used. Its disadvantage is that it conveys a sense of something static. This could not be further from the nature of the forces with which the etheric world both penetrates and organizes matter to bear life.[29] It is this living, sculptural activity for which we aim and which the German word *gestaltung* suggests.

When we observe a dying plant, we perceive the material substance, previously organized into its form, gradually collapse. The substance itself has no capacity to hold that form. It is as though the invisible 'lines of force' which did the holding, withdraw. On complete withdrawal of these forces (which we refer to as *etheric*) the material substance returns to earth.

Advanced photography of the developing human embryo reveals the same relationship of the etheric forces to our human form. Our eyes cannot perceive the forces, yet we see evidence of their activity. In the mother's womb the invisible sculptor is at work. We behold it drawing substance from the mother's body, organizing it in patterns and configurations around different nodal points. In time these densify into the veins and arteries, the different organs, muscles, bones and so on.

This is the *gestaltung* we are striving for in Speech Formation. It is not some pedantically pursued insistence on precise articulation or meticulous pronunciation of the ends of words. It is a path of development that challenges us to understand and engage in the creative activity of the spiritual world.[30] We can only approach these mysteries with utmost reverence. This creates the mood in which we might begin to 'form' a sound.

Speech-exploration 69

I suggest that we begin with the exploration for opening the heart.[*] We could undertake this process with any sound. Let's use /b/ as an example.

1. Sit, stand or kneel, at ease and comfortable yet available and able to access your energy. Focus your listening. Begin to sense that /b/ is imminent, approaching. Attune yourself. You feel it surround and clothe you like a garment or a cloak.

2. Let /b/ take hold of you. Sense what it needs from you so it can reveal its being in the world. Let this awaken a new experience of breathing in. Breath is not something separate, to be snatched at in the moment just before you speak. Instead, know you are breathing in the sound. The /b/itself will organize your breath to be exactly what it needs in order to reveal its gesture and quality of being.

3. To assist the birth, surround the whole event with loving hands. They will help you gather from the great space all around, then mould, encourage and protect the emerging /b/. Sense that what you gather and form creates substance around you. Space, filled with that substance, comes alive.

4. You sense the sound is ready to be born. Your speech organs, in particular your lips, move slowly and surely into a loving gesture of embrace. /b/ moulds your emerging breath stream and imprints it with its form: /b/. Be attentive to this birth. Stay present with the form you have created, beyond its duration as a heard sound.

5. Explore this process.

6. Now gather and form a word. Choose one that you love. We want to sense and form, give birth to, the many qualities of substance created by the sounds. It is helpful to begin with denser sounds; because they ask us to engage in the activity of moulding, they encourage a slower tempo. In these initial stages, this gives us opportunity to thoroughly observe the formative activity.

In such a way, we develop the capacity to sense that we form *substance* when we speak. We do not yet possess the larynx or the powers that can affect and shape matter.[31] There are mythologies and dreamings though, that hint at this. We have already quoted the opening of the Gospel of St John. According to Celtic tradition, Merlin sang the stones of Stonehenge into place. In our babyhood in this respect, we practise with our breath and ether.

We have seen enough in the last century to know that words can wield destructive power when they are used to manipulate and dominate emotions and the will. It would be wise if we consider the consequence of wielding power in the realm of life itself or matter, without developing our power to love.

---

[*] See *The Art of Acting*, chapter 3.

In *The Wizard of Earthsea*, Ursula Le Guin considers such a possibility. In this myth, created for our time, she explores the moral implications of developing the magic powers of the spoken word. Ged, on his path to be Arch Mage, is tempted to use his gifts in service of his lower impulses. This 'baby Dionysus' is not dismembered by the Titans.[*] Instead, he is almost torn apart by the shadow he releases through his unconscious deed. It pursues Ged through the world, destroying all upon its path. Finally, Ged stops running and, like Prospero, turns to face his shadow and embrace it. This enables him to step into his true power. It is not the power of the 'rough magic' that he played with before, but the alchemy of love. Measured against the forces which would control and dominate this world, it does indeed appear 'most faint'.[32] This power, which does not need to prove or defend itself, is the I AM.

As performers we enact this drama in ourselves each time we stand upon a stage, of whatever size or shape. The greater our gift, the greater the temptation to stand, like baby Dionysus, on our Father's throne and wield his power in the service only of our own lower natures. These are the implications of a path of speaking that leads to the capacity to form etheric substance and, in so doing, hold the audience within our power. They behove us to set off down this path with full responsibility for what we do. For we have the choice to touch an audience with words formed from the substance of our love and heal them to new life. Or we may, like Ged, unleash upon them the power of our disowned shadow, our as yet untransformed lower nature. Touched, none-theless, they will be: by powers of healing or disintegration, according to the forms that we create.

---

[*] See *The Art of Acting*, 'Epilogue'.

Chapter 6

Epic, Lyric and Dramatic Styles

Speech placements and the archetypal styles

The Art of Speech would not be complete without considering the fundamental styles: epic, lyric and dramatic. A foundation has been laid in chapter 3 regarding the connection of the three archetypal Speech placements (lips, teeth and teeth ridge, soft palate) with Chekhov's way of working with the three archetypal centres (heart, head and belly).[*] To focus on one approach without the other is unsatisfying. If, by working from the centre in the belly in the way we move and experience the world we create a character whose will is strong, for example, but cannot express this in our speech, the character's voice will not be convincing – leading actors to resort to shouting which, quite apart from damaging the throat, distorts what we mean by 'will'. Conversely, to practise Speech Formation without engaging our total instrument produces a disembodied voice. If we now develop the integration of Chekhov's approach to the centres with the Speech placements, however, we build a firm foundation for artistic style.

Speech-exploration 70 – will-centre and soft palate

1. Warm up your will-centre as described on pages 140–146 of *The Art of Acting*.
2. Sustaining those sensations and allowing your breath and voice to engage organically, improvise strong will activities such as:

   > *chopping wood*
   > *combat*
   > *lifting something heavy*
   > *manning a boat in a storm*, etc.

Observe how your voice seems to come from the belly itself, and at the very back of the depth and cavern of your mouth, on what is called the *soft palate*, a hardening

---

[*] For further exploration of the Chekhov technique and use of the term 'archetypal', see *The Art of Acting*.

takes place which provides a firmer platform for your voice. You may observe greater vocal strength and density, a lowering of pitch and possibly a tendency to shout.

Our task is to achieve that strength and density by a conscious penetration of our speech with the forces of our will. We want to achieve this without damage to our throats, so that our speech can express a much broader range of nuance than shouting can communicate.

1. Warm up using *Speech-exploration 41*, pages 139–40 (noon air lark). We discovered in chapters 1 and 3 how the consonants 'k', 'g', 'h' and 'ng' are formed on the soft palate, and that their activity is strengthened and deepened by this exercise.
2. Keep checking that your movement is full-bodied so that the activity in your speech organs is supported by your whole instrument.
3. From time to time, jump back into your 'warrior' to strengthen that connection. As you land in the warrior gesture, gather your will-forces and direct them through your soft palate as you speak the words:

Strength in the limbs.

In the limbs works strength of will.

4. When you have achieved the appropriate density in your voice without unhealthy tension, apply this to texts such as Shakespeare's, *Henry V* or the Sir Bedevere passage quoted on page 211, chapter 5.

> Once more unto the breach dear friends! Once more!
>
> *Henry V*, Shakespeare

Speech-exploration 71 – head centre and teeth

Exploring speech placement in the region of the teeth with full-bodied work with the head-centre allows us to express the quality of thinking through the sharp and clear edges of the sounds formed in that region. We are not only after clearly defined consonants but aim for their activity to permeate the voice itself, so that the vowel element also takes on their sharp-edged clarity. It is important not to confuse clarity of speech with speaking in a higher pitch which creates a sense of unnaturalness, of something stuck on from the outside. Rather, the clarity should penetrate right through the centre of the voice, transforming it from the inside. Then it will radiate into the space like a beam of light piercing the darkness.

1. Warm up the head-centre as described on page 151 of *The Art of Acting* and integrate it with *Speech-exploration 41* on pages 133 and 136–7 (see fee shielding).
2. Weave in the words:

Light in the thinking

In the head lights up thinking

3. Sustaining these sensations, direct them into some appropriate text, as in these words from *Hamlet**, for example:

> how noble in reason...
> ...what is this quintessence of dust?

Or passages of extended thought, such as the opening sentences from T.S. Eliot's, *Four Quartets*:

> Time present and time past
> Are both perhaps present in time future
> And time future contained in time past.
> If all time is eternally present.
> All time is unredeemable.
> What might have been is an abstraction
> Remaining a perpetual possibility
> Only in a world of speculation.
> What might have been and what has been
> Point to one end, which is always present.
> Footfalls echo in the memory
> Down the passage which we did not take
> Towards the door we never opened
> Into the rose garden...

Speech-exploration 72 – heart centre and lips

Because our feelings and emotions reveal themselves primarily in vowels, then if it is feelings and emotions we want our speech to reveal, our consonants must be permeated with a vowel quality. To achieve this 'sacrifice' of the consonant into the vowel, requires more activity, not less. It is as though we turn what we worked towards with the will-quality 'inside out'. To achieve the will-quality in speech, the vowel sacrifices its inwardness to take on something of the density and forming power of the consonant. To express the feeling-quality, the consonant sacrifices its elemental formative activity to serve the vowel's inwardness. Full-bodied work with the heart-centre integrated with speaking from the forward placement (lips) imbues the voice with qualities of warmth and inwardness.

---

* See, *The Art of Acting*, Appendix A.

1. Warm up your heart-centre as described on pages 133–5, and integrate it with *Speech exploration 41* (by miner wafer).
2. Weave in the words:

warmth of heart   in the heart weaves our feeling

3. Extend into working with text, such as *Hamlet*:

> What a piece of work is a man!
> …the beauty of the world
> the paragon of animals…

4. Explore passages that express the outpouring of passionate feeling, such as Juliet's:

> O Romeo, Romeo, wherefore art thou Romeo?

5. Experiment with words that express sympathy and warmth-of-heart in sounds formed on or around the lips, for example:

> mama, milk, music, moan, more
> bless, beauty, baby
> poem, precious, poor
> woe, woman, womb…

6. Explore what happens to these same sounds when the heart is wounded:

> Lips that would kiss form prayers to broken stone.

7. Here they strike back with destructive power:

> murder!
> bastard, beat, batter, bitch!
> betray, bash, break, bloody, bugger!
> piss off! piffle
> whip, warrior, weapon, wound, war!

As when Hamlet vents his rage at Claudius:

> Bloody, bawdy villain!

Or Lear at Cordelia:

> Here I disclaim all my paternal care
> Propinquity and property of blood...

Speech-exploration 73 — integration and weaving of the three centres and placements

Use this passage as a further opportunity to move between the three different centres and their corresponding speech qualities:

> This is the strength that your arm knows,
> the arc of flesh that is my breast,
> the precise crystals of our eyes.

Woman to Man, Judith Wright

We are now ready to explore the connection Steiner makes between the fundamental speech placements (lips, teeth and soft palate), and the fundamental tendencies of style.

Identifying the three styles

The earliest of our ancient texts are remnants of an oral culture rooted in an experience of the world and the cosmos which beheld spirit as the source and ongoing life of all things. Because we have access to the verbal expression of ancient cultures only when it has been written down, we tend to regard the forms language took that reflect this consciousness as *literary convention*. However, for people of these early times *everything* was connected to the divine and the functioning of these communities guided by initiates and priests according to the revelations they received. The inspiration of the poets was no exception. Plato writes in *Ion*:

In like manner the Muse first of all inspires men herself; and from these inspired persons a chain of other persons is suspended, who take the inspiration. For all good poets, epic as well as lyric, compose their beautiful poems not by art, but because they are inspired and possessed. And as the Corybantian revellers when they dance are not in their right mind when they are composing their beautiful strains: but when falling under the power of music and meter they are inspired and possessed; like Bacchic maidens who draw milk and honey from the rivers when they are under the influence of Dionysus but not when they are in their right mind. And the soul of the lyric poet does the same, as they themselves say; for they tell us that they bring songs from honeyed fountains, culling them out of the gardens and dells of the Muses; they like the bees, winging their way from flower to flower. And this is true. For the poet is a light and winged and holy thing, and there is no invention in him until he has been inspired and is out of his senses, and the mind is no longer in him: when he has not attained to this state, he is powerless and is unable to utter his oracles ... and when inspired one of them will make dithyrambs, another hymns of praise, another choral strains, another epic or iambic verses – and he who is good at one is not good at any other kind of verse: for not by art does the poet sing, but by power divine. Had he learned by rules of art, he would have known how to speak not of one theme only, but of all; and therefore God takes away the minds of poets, and uses them as his ministers, as he also uses diviners and holy prophets, in order that we who hear them may know them to be speaking not of themselves who utter these priceless words in a state of unconsciousness, but that God himself is the speaker, and that through them He is conversing with us...[*]

Plato makes it clear that in his reality, all arts connected to the word are ways in which the spiritual world communicated to the human world. Hesiod, considered next to Homer in regard to the inspired level of his poetry, decribes his own gift thus:

It was the [Muses] who once taught Hesiod how to sing beautifully, as he was shep-herding his lambs under most holy Helicon ... and they cut a staff and gave it to me, a branch of blooming laurel, a thing to marvel at. And they breathed into me a godly voice that I should celebrate the things to come and things of the past, and ordered me to sing of the race of the blessed gods that live for ever, always to celebrate them at the beginning and at the end ... Happy is the man whom the Muses love; a sweet voice flows out from his mouth. For even if a man has sorrow and grief in his newly saddened mind, and lives in fear because his heart is distressed, yet when a singer, a servant of the Muses, sings of the deeds of former men and of the blessed gods who dwell in Olympus, he swiftly forgets his worries, and does not remember his sorrows; the gifts of the goddesses soon take him [from those thoughts].

Theogony, Hesiod, edited by Constantine Trypanis[†]

---

[*] Translated by B. Jowett, from *Encyclopedia Brittanica* (1952).

[†] *Penguin Book of Greek Verse* (1946).

A moving portrayal of the mission of the arts connected with the word is depicted for us by Homer in Book 9 of *The Odyssey*. There is a feast. Among those gathered sits the guest of honour. No one knows his true identity. He cannot speak of it himself, for he is still disoriented, having been washed up naked on the shore of this island without his ship, all his men drowned; he who, to escape the revenge of Polyphemus, the giant with the third eye who dwelt on the island of the Cyclops, had a short time before cleverly decided to call himself: Nobody. It was as though he knew prophetically that he would lose all he had, and sit, as now, a stranger in a strange land. The blind poet is led in. He reaches for his harp and begins to sing. The stranger thanks the king.

> Lord Alcinous . . . it is indeed a lovely thing to hear a bard such as yours, with a voice like the gods. I feel myself that there is nothing more delightful than when the festive mood reigns in a whole people's hearts and the banqueters listen to a minstrel from their seats in the hall, while the tables before them are laden with bread and meat, and the steward carries around the wine he has drawn from the bowl and fills their cups. This to my way of thinking, is something like perfection . . .*

The singer tells the story of Odysseus, the hero whose superior intelligence led to the final defeat of Troy; how Odysseus had conceived the idea of a great wooden horse which the Greeks had built and filled with soldiers; how the Trojans, seduced by cleverness that could make an image of a living being look so real, opened the gates of the city to take it in . . . and as the epic unfolds, the stranger, this nobody, listening, recognizes his story and begins to weep as he remembers who he is, where he came from, what he has accomplished. He is not nobody, after all.

Homer reveals to us the archetype of what the word can do – to tell the stories and sing the songs that help us recognize ourselves as human beings with a past, an identity, with feelings needing to be felt and honoured, a noble destiny; which remind us who we are.

These examples make it clear that it is not simple to categorize the many different forms the art of language once took. The storyteller accompanied himself with music, would sometimes speak as one or other character, would sometimes sing the praise of the gods or some outstanding human deed, dwell in detail on the beauty or the terror of some natural phenomenon, or explore the feelings roused in times of grief, despair or love. Yet, as Plato has reminded us, poets had specific gifts which made some more at home in one form of expression and others in another. And so the *epic*, *lyric* and *dramatic* tendencies declared themselves, consolidating into these specific forms.

---

*Translated by E.V. Rieu, Penguin Books (1946).

We have explored the origins of drama in some detail in *The Art of Acting* and shall expand on this when we explore tragedy and comedy in *The Integrated Actor*. It's easier for us to understand that, although it needed to be written down at some point, drama was not a literary genre but something that existed in performance. In addition to the drama which originated in the temple ritual, epic and lyric poetry are the other main styles that form the basis of our Western literary canon.

Speech-exploration 74 – identifying the three styles

To distinguish each style, we shall examine a similar content expressed in the various forms. If we can sense how each different style embodies a different consciousness and can clarify what that difference is, then we can explore how to express that difference in the way we speak. Read the following excerpts aloud and experiment with what qualities of voice and speech best communicate each one.

Theme 1: Rocky Mountains

Epic

These first excerpts are in the epic or *narrative* style.

> Far in the West there lies a desert land, where the mountains
> Lift, through their perpetual snows, their lofty and luminous summits.
> Down from their jagged deep ravines, where the gorge, like a gateway,
> Opens a passage rough to the wheels of the immigrant wagon.
>
> *Evangeline*, Longfellow

> In the other direction lie two rocks, the higher of which rears its sharp peak up to the very sky, and is capped by black clouds that never stream away nor leave clear weather around the top, even in summer or at harvest time. No man on earth could climb it, up or down ... for the rock is as smooth as if it had been polished.
>
> *Odyssey*, Homer

> Dry clash'd his harness in the icy caves
> And barren chasms, and all to left and right
> The bare black cliff clang'd round him, as he based
> His feet on juts of slippery crag that rang
> Sharp smitten with the dint of armed heels.
>
> *Le More d'Arthur*, Tennyson

Lyric

The following excerpt from a sonnet by Hopkins is in the lyric style.

O the mind, mind has mountains, cliffs of fall
Frightful, sheer, no-man fathomed. Hold them cheap
May who ne'er hung there. Nor does long our small
Durance deal with that steep or deep. Here! Creep
Wretch, under a comfort serves in a whirlwind: all
Life death does end and each day dies with sleep.

Drama

The next lines are in the dramatic style, from Shakespeare's *King Lear*:

Gloucester: When shall I come to the top of that same hill?
Edgar: You do climb up it now; look how we labour.
Gloucester: Methinks the ground is even.
Edgar: Horrible steep!
Hark do you hear the sea?
Gloucester: No, truly.

...

Edgar: Come on sir, here is the place: stand still.
How fearful
And dizzy 'tis to cast one's eyes so low!
The crows and choughs that wing the midway air
Show scarce so gross as beetles.

Theme 2. The first light in the morning

Epic

The following fragments are from Homer's *Odyssey*:

As soon as the fresh Dawn had decked herself in crimson...

...

Soon after Dawn enthroned herself in the sky...

...

When Dawn had risen from the bed where she sleeps with the Lord Tithonus, to bring daylight to the immortals and to men, the gods sat down in assembly...

...

Leaving the waters of the splendid east the sun leapt up into the firmament to bring light to the immortals and to men who plough the earth and perish...

...

As soon as Dawn with her rose tinted hands had lit the east, Odysseus' son put on his clothes and got up from his bed...

This excerpt from Ray Bradbury's *Dandelion Wine*, while contemporary prose, is also in the epic or narrative style:

It was a quiet morning, the town covered over with darkness and at ease in bed. Summer gathered in the weather, the wind had the proper touch, the breathing of the world was long and warm and slow. You had only to rise, lean from your window, and know that this was indeed the first real time of freedom and living, this was the first morning of summer.

He woke before the crystal jingle of milk bottles to perform his ritual magic.
He stood at the open window in the dark, took a deep breath and exhaled.
The street lights, like candles on a black cake, went out. He exhaled again and again and the stars began to vanish. Douglas smiled. He pointed a finger. There and there. Now over here and here. Yellow squares were cut in the dim morning earth as house lights winked slowly on. A sprinkle of windows came suddenly alight miles off in dawn country... Birds leaped from trees like a net thrown by his hand, singing. Douglas conducting an orchestra, pointed to the eastern sky. The sun began to rise.[*]

Lyric

When thou risest in the morning and shinest as Aton by day thou dost put to flight the darkness and givest forth thy rays... The Two Lands rejoice, they awake and stand on their feet, for thou hast aroused them... They wash their limbs and take up their clothes, their arms do adoration to thy rising... How manifold are thy works! They are concealed from us. O sole god to whom no other is like!... Thou hast made a heaven afar to shine in it and to see all that thou hast made... Thou didst create millions of existences out of thyself alone, cities, towns, lands, paths and streams... Thou art in my heart. There is none other that knoweth thee save thy son Akhnaton...

Hymn to the Sun, Akhenaton[†]

Full many a glorious morning have I seen
Flatter the mountain tops with sovereign eye
Kissing with golden face the meadows green
Gilding pale streams with heavenly alchemy...

Sonnet, Shakespeare

Stars circled round us where we lay
And dawn came naked from the sea.

Its holy ordinary light
Welled up and blessed us and was blest.
Nothing more simple nor more strange,
than earth itself was then our rest.

...

---

[*] Bantam Books (1959).
[†] *The Tree of Life*, Viking Press (1942).

I turned and set that world alight.
Unfurling from its hidden bud
it widens round me, past my sight,
filled with my breath, fed with my blood;
the sun that rises as I stand
comes up within me gold and young;
my hand is sheltered in your hand,
the bread of silence on my tongue.

This time alone, Judith Wright[*]

Drama

This example from Shakespeare's *Romeo and Juliet* is expressed in dramatic style – in dialogue and action by two characters, yet it has lyric qualities.

Juliet: Wilt thou be gone? It is not yet near day.
        It was the nightingale and not the lark
        That pierced the fearful hollow of thine ear.
        Nightly she sings in some pomegranate tree.
        Believe me love, it was the nightingale.

Romeo: It was the lark, the herald of the morn,
        No nightingale: look love, what envious streaks
        Do lace the severing clouds in yonder east:
        Night's candles are burnt out, and jocund day
        Stands tiptoe on the misty mountain tops:
        I must be gone and live or stay and die.

Juliet: Yon light is not daylight. I know it, I.
        It is some meteor that the sun exhales,
        To be to thee this night a torchbearer
        And light thee on thy way to Mantua;
        Therefore stay yet: Thou needs't not to be gone.

Romeo: Let me be taken. Let me be put to death;
        I am content so thou wilt have it so.
        I'll say yon grey is not the morning's eye.
        Tis but the pale reflex of Cynthia's brow:
        Nor that is not the lark whose notes do beat
        The vaulty heaven so high above our heads;
        I have more care to stay than will to go.
        Come death and welcome! Juliet wills it so.

---

[*] *Collected Poems*, Angus and Robertson (1994).

The characters interact in lyric verse. This alerts us to the fact that epic, lyric and dramatic are not to be equated only with the fundamental structure of a text, but rather we can recognize them as specific ways in which the soul experiences and expresses that experience. We could call this scene, *lyric drama*. The basic structure is dramatic but the characters express their experience primarily in language that is lyrical. They pour their feelings out in words that are musical and images of nature which express how they feel.

The next example from Tennyson's *Tithonus*, we could call *dramatic lyric* since the basic form is lyric but it is expressed by the character of Tithonus, a mortal who in Greek mythology was married to the goddess of the dawn:

> Once more the old mysterious glimmer steals
> From thy pure brows, and from thy shoulders pure,
> And bosom beating with a heart renewed.
> Thy cheek begins to redden through the gloom,
> Thy sweet eyes brighten slowly close to mine
> E're yet they blind the stars, and the wild team
> Which love thee, yearning for thy yoke,
> Arise and shake the darkness from their loosened manes,
> And beat the twilight into flakes of fire.

Speech-exploration 75 – constitution of the three styles

This exploration should help you understand what lies behind each different way the soul expresses her experience.

1. To further clarify your understanding of what constitutes each style write your own examples of a lyric poem, a narrative, and a dramatic scene, all arising out of one common theme.
2. Improvise a scene in which a group of mountaineers, caught in an avalanche, struggles to survive. Let half the group perform and the other watch. (If the group already has a shared experience of some event which could provide the necessary stimulus, then use that as a basis.)
3. Reverse group roles (performers and audience).
4. Each person write their experience in a lyric poem, a narrative and a dramatic scene.
5. Share what you have written and discuss your observations.

In a work of art, as in life itself, these different perspectives in us shift and mingle. One element predominates in a specific moment, then another. The overall style of a text is determined by the form of consciousness that dominates throughout, determining the structure. The Classical Greek drama is an excellent reminder of this principle. Some of the greatest lyrics were written to be chanted and danced by the chorus in the dramas. We need only think of the famous ode from *Antigone* by Sophocles:

Wonders are many on the earth but the greatest of these is man . . .

Likewise the dramas contain many speeches in the epic style when a character, very often a messenger, relates a series of events to the other characters, the chorus and the audience.

What distinguishes each style?

Epic
When we write or speak in epic style, although thoughts and feelings are expressed, the primary goal is to recreate an actual event in words; to tell what happens.

Lyric
When we write or speak in lyric style our primary goal is to express feelings and emotions, although thoughts and action are portrayed. We use images of the world around us as metaphors for our own soul's experience. In doing so, we heal the separation between the inner and outer world.

Dramatic
When we write or perform in the dramatic style, our primary goal is to express events through the meetings and interactions of specific characters. We do not *describe* the interactions but *embody* them. The events are not narrated, but enacted. Thoughts, feelings and actions are strongly represented, but what is important is to *show* how the destiny of one character is revealed in the encounter with another.

The three styles through the lens of the Christian Trinity
We see that these three expressive modes connect to the threefold nature of our soul activity as explored in chapter 3. Because my own path led through the Western Christian tradition, I make my meanings through its language and images. Yet connecting the threefold nature of the human being and the epic, lyric and dramatic styles with the Christian imagination of the *Trinity* does not mean subjecting them to a dogmatic scheme or formula, incapable of subtlety or variation. It is a lens, one of many, through which some patterns might emerge. For me, the Trinity is an attempt to explore the cosmic level of an aspect of experience that reaches further than our rational minds alone can grasp. Like all imaginations, it allows us to contemplate the

Figure 25 – The virgin crowned with fire

complexities and contradictions inherent in existence. Viewed through a different lens, different relationships might be revealed. Those connected with a different tradition may translate these following considerations into the language and images that speak to them.

The balance of masculine and feminine qualities found in many great works of art, suggest that creation is far more complex than the simple separation into 'male' and 'female' forms. Over the last century we have witnessed a transition from the patriarchal domination of the last millennia to a world in which the role and rights of women are increasingly acknowledged. A major shift of consciousness is taking place in this regard that involves a necessary re-evaluation of the images and language which up to now have expressed male-dominant values. Because of this, I ask you to separate this consideration of Father, Son and Holy Spirit from issues of gender.

At Chartres Cathedral, for example, the sculptures of the Father imagining and then creating the Son are filled with feminine tenderness. We can imagine that the artist found a way to depict a greater truth than dogma could allow in a patriarchal age — that the Father Creator, Ground of the world, is also Mother. Consider also Leonardo's sketch for the face of Christ; who can tell whether it is Son or Daughter?

And the third member of the Holy family has, in some cultural traditions, been understood to be the Virgin, Mother, Queen of Heaven, Sophia. The Holy Spirit is the feminine soul, who, penetrated by the fire of spirit, the bridegroom, has achieved the alchemical wedding.*

> And all shall be well.
> And all manner of thing shall be well
> When the tongues of flame are enfolded
> Into the crowned knot of fire
> And the fire and the rose are one.
>
> *Four Quartets*, T.S. Eliot

The epic stream

Let us explore the consciousness involved in recreating an event as a story or narrative. Think of Homer and the events he unravels in the *Odyssey* or *Iliad*. There are moments where characters emerge and speak, but it remains fundamentally a story in

---

*Yet, in his seminal work, the *Foundation Stone Meditation*, Steiner shows how deeply this aspect of our being, this 'holy spirit', is connected to the clear light of thinking which we frequently identify as masculine. For a study of the *Foundation Stone Meditation* and further aspects of the masculine and feminine polarities as principles at work in the act of creation quite apart from the gender-related issues of male and female, see *The Integrated Actor*.

Figure 26 – The storyteller (cover of Martin Luther's bible)

the epic style. It does not become a drama because the bard depicts in words, *what happened*.

Think of the vast scope that is encompassed and all the threads he weaves from the beginning to the end. The narrator holds all of them in one huge embrace, as it were, not losing any. Storytellers, although required to briefly assume a specific role, may not identify completely with a character, for they soon may be called upon to represent a different one or to resume the story. The all-seeing vision of the storyteller must remain impartial, beholding the mystery of all that has been and is yet to come; not identifying with the passing moment except to weave its thread into the tapestry.

For this, a vast consciousness is needed which could be likened to the consciousness of the Creator Being. In the Christianity able to unfold in a patriarchal age, this Being has been called the Father who beholds all with an equal love and values all parts equally. Such consciousness requires a detachment that is not the result of withdrawal. It is the perspective Jung referred to as *objective subjectivity*.[*] This consciousness pours its love and passion, its subjectivity, into creation. Emotion and feelings do not exist outside what is created. Love becomes event. Event is *deed*. Deed is in the realm of *will*.

To create an event in words, we need our will-forces. Not only do we share our thoughts and feelings with the audience, but we must convince them an event has happened, is happening or will happen. Generally, this style is difficult for younger people because their consciousness is rightly more determined by subjective emotion. They do not yet possess the long-term perspective which enables them to value past and future equally with the demanding present and in their wise and loving sight, value every detail's place within the whole.

Without a mastery of the will placement, we may find that our speech provides information and expresses what we *feel* about what happens, but does not create in the listener *a sense of the actual event*.

Speech-exploration 76 — epic style 1

1. Warm up the will quality, full-bodily in voice and speech as described on pages 138–9 in chapter 3.
2. When your speech and movement is thoroughly imbued with will-forces, speak the words: *I want to tell you what happened*.
3. Sustain those forces as you move around the space, gathering the other members of the class (or an imaginary audience) into your 'field'. Sustaining your contact with

---

[*] See the final chapter of *The Integrated Actor*.

them, when you sense they are with you, speak *I want to tell you what happened* into the space you have prepared. Follow this with words from any epic text you are working on, or simply: *Once upon a time...*

Speech-exploration 77 – epic style 2

You can adapt the will-forces in your voice to a whole range of events from mighty cataclysms to the delicate opening of a tiny wild flower.

1. Find the epic voice appropriate for the following passage:

   In the beginning, God created the Heavens and the earth... And from the deepest valleys of the sea, mighty mountains heaved themselves, thrusting upwards, out of the molten centre of the earth, forming citadels against the sky.

2. Now adapt your will forces to an epic voice appropriate to speak:

   And He looked upon the little fish, darting in between His fingers in quick flashes of fiery gold, and He knew that it was good. Snowflakes too He fashioned and all things small and delicate to give delight.

The source of the epic stream is shrouded in mystery, but it seems that all ancient cultures valued story and the means of training the guardians and disseminators of those epics which bound communities in a common memory of their origin and purpose. In Greece, these stories were handed on in the rhythm called *dactylic hexameter*[*] and resonated in souls increasingly isolated by the evolving intellect from a sense of belonging; and, as Plato said, would comfort them for their loss until the birth of the I AM could awaken from within each 'sole self' a new sense of community; one born from the discovery within each individual of the great story to which we all belong.

It's an interesting paradox that one of the most beautiful expressions of the sacred task of the Bard in the English language, is a lyric poem by William Blake. He sings of the storyteller who understands and weaves the mysteries of time and space:

Hear the voice of the Bard
Who present, past and future sees,
Whose Ears have heard
The Holy Word,
That walked among the ancient trees,

Calling the lapsed soul
And weeping in the evening dew:
That might control

---

[*] See chapter 4.

The starry pole:
And fallen fallen light renew!

O Earth O Earth return!
Arise from out the dewy grass:
Night is worn
And the morn
Rises from the slumberous mass.

Turn away no more:
Why wilt thou turn away?
The starry floor
The watery shore
Are given thee
Till the break of day.

Hear the Voice of the Bard

Alliteration

Practising alliteration develops the will-forces in our speech. As we will see in chapter 8, alliteration entered our culture through the barbarian invasions that revitalized what had become a tired and decadent Roman Empire. Their energy gave birth to a style of poetry based on the formative power of the consonants, in rhythmic repetition. The language of alliteration embodied the strength of will needed to survive the harshness of the Northern climate and assert the invaders' claims for territory.

Speech-exploration 78 — alliteration

The following exercise utilizes the will-placement of the 'h' and the activity necessary to fuse this breath sound with the voice in changing rhythms and tempos. It's an excellent preparation for the strength and mobility of voice required to speak alliteration.

1. Imagine you are wielding a heavy double-handed, two-edged sword. Each time you swing the sword down into the lowest point of the pendulum, the alliterated consonant 'h' is born out of its own weight and density.

    Halt! habit hoarding
    Hollow hammer
    Holy hindmost here her
    Hollow hammer!

2. This passage on which to practise has been translated in the alliterative style from the Anglo-Saxon poem about Doomsday by Cynewulf. It's interesting because the speaker must convince us of things to come as real events that happen.

Mountains shall melt, and the mighty cliffs
That buttress the earth 'gainst battering waves,
Bulwarks upreared 'gainst the rolling billows,
Shall fall on a sudden. The sweep of fire
Shall leave no bird or beast alive...
In a bath of fire the fish shall be stifled;
Sundered from life, their struggles over;
Monsters of the deep no more shall swim.
Like molten wax the water shall burn,
More marvels appear than mind can conceive,
When tempest and whirlwind o'erwhelm the earth,
And rocks are riven by roaring blasts.
Men shall wail, they shall weep and lament,
Groan aghast with grovelling fear...
The shrieks of the living shall shrill aloud
Mid the crack of doom, their cry of fear,
Their howl of fear as they struggle to hide.[*]

3. Stand with your feet rooted in the centre of the earth, like a warrior. It is not spear or sword that you wield, but the word and with it you create worlds – making those who listen believe in that great happening to which all happenings belong. Draw your forces from the earth which, as Blake reminded us, will be our dwelling till with our own will we waken this 'slumberous mass'.

When Ymir[†] lived, long ago
Was no sand nor sea nor surging waves
Nowhere was there earth nor heaven above
But a grinning gap and grass nowhere.

The Sons of Bur[‡] then built up the lands
Moulded mightily Middle Earth.
Sun stared from the south on the stones of their hall
From the ground there sprouted green leeks.

The song of the Sybil, from the *Elder Edda*
translated by P.B. Taylor and W.H. Auden[§]

4. Sit, as in so many paintings the Father Creator sits upon his throne. Or, still nearer to the ground which supports you, sit upon the very earth itself, feeling its memory

---

[*] Translated by D. Spaeth, Princeton University Press (1922).
[†] The Frost Giant out of whose body the earth was made.
[‡] Odin's father.
[§] Faber and Faber (1969).

stir within you. Then with all you draw from behind and below weave a sacred circle that encloses your listeners in its reality. Speak: *I want to tell you a story*, or *Once upon a time...*

The lyric stream

Lyric poetry is the second great stream inherited from ancient cultures. Again, its origins lay shrouded in mystery. The name, however, is derived from *lyre* and signifies words, sung or spoken, accompanied by that instrument. Whereas narrators are primarily concerned with the *event*, lyric poets are concerned with the feelings and emotions called forth in their soul by that event; their meetings with others, natural, human or divine. Lyric poetry invites us to enter a consciousness where all created things are ensouled and share that soul with us. Ancient consciousness knew this and its natural state was metaphor. But as we became 'clever' and judged such states as primitive animism, metaphor came to be regarded as a literary convention that has metamorphosed even further into *simile*. The ancient Indian consciousness expressed in the Vedic hymn as... *Mine eye is sun... My breath is wind* ... would transform and be expressed in a later age as... *Mine eye is like the sun... My breath is like the wind.*

Great lyric poems celebrate the unity of inner and outer, macro and microcosm, singing the pain of separation and the bliss of reunion. The psalmist sings:

> As the hart panteth after the water brooks so panteth my soul after thee O God.
> My soul thirsts for God, for the living God. When shall I come and behold the face of God?
> My tears have been my food both day and night while men say to me continually, Where is your God?

> *Psalm 42*

How could Keats sing of the nightingale and its song if he had not heard it in his own soul and for those few moments felt transported beyond his 'sole self' to oneness with the being of nature?

> Forlorn! the very word is like a bell
> To toll me back from thee to my sole self!

> *Ode to a Nightingale*, Keats

Or when Judith Wright sings of *The Wattle Tree*, who can tell whether it is she or the tree who 'buds' and:

> breaks into the truth I had no voice to speak,
> Into a million images of the sun, My God!

In lyric consciousness, I offer up my separate feeling life to unite with the cosmos:

not to have feelings 'about' things but to feel those things are me. We are one and separation is an illusion. It is the natural consciousness of every newborn child who comes 'trailing clouds of glory'. But it has been 'lost', dismembered in the 'shades of the prison-house' but now, through the poet's sensibilities, is found again. Perhaps that is why so much lyric poetry has been inspired by falling in love. What most human beings experience when they are in love is that extraordinary state of at-oneness with the world.

The lyric poet seeks a conscious path beyond the narrow romantic response to a special individual, to something universal; a cultivation of the heart to be an organ of perception.

> Thanks to the human heart by which we live,
> Thanks to its tenderness, its joys and fears,
> To me, the meanest flower that blows can give
> Thoughts that do often lie too deep for tears.
>
> *Ode on the Intimations of Immortality*, Wordsworth

If I perceive that water laughs on its path over pebbles it is because my soul shares the world soul and knows the water as itself. If autumn wakens a sense of contracting and dying earthly forms, a noble melancholy mingled with the glory of what vanishes from earthly perception, it is because my soul is not separate from the earth's.

Rudolf Steiner's *Calendar of the Soul* is an attempt to consciously observe the correspondence between the earth and human soul in their journey through the year.[33] This sequence of 52 lyric verses records Steiner's thorough penetration of his own soul's journey through the cycle of the seasons. For example, as the earth and human soul move into autumn in one hemisphere:

> Autumnal haze now dampens down
> The senses' animating zest.
> In radiant glory of the light
> Dull veils of mist are woven.
> My Self, in widths of space beholds
> The autumn's winter sleep.
> The summer has on me,
> Its very self bestowed.

...so they move towards spring in the other:

> 'I feel the strength of universal being;'
> Thus speaks clarity of thought,
> Remembering my own Spirit's growth

In the darkness of world nights,
And to the new World-day to come
Inclines the inner rays of hope.

translated by William and Liselotte Mann

The calendar reveals the archetype of the lyric experience cultivated as a conscious path of spiritual awakening. Used as a basis for meditation and observation, it serves to heal the split between our 'sole self' and the universal self.

The lyric journey undertaken as a conscious path leads to an awareness of the Holy Spirit, the divine Sophia, the presence of the cosmic wisdom in every detail of creation. Our soul, on its path to become the virgin, the bride who is ready for that marriage at the end of time, is purified of egoism and personal wishes. Only then, when she is without attachment, can she behold the reality behind the maya perceived as this world by our earthly senses. Plato described the act of making poetry as a trance-like possession by the gods. This was the experience in his time and culture. In our time, we can undertake to cultivate the lyric path in full, awakened consciousness.[*]

The responsibility of this path was glimpsed on some level by the English Romantic poets. Shelley sensed its relationship to the Holy Spirit when he addressed his great invocation to the West Wind:

Be, through my lips, to unawakened earth
The trumpet of a prophecy! O wind,
If winter comes, can spring be far behind?

Can it be purely a coincidence that the being with whom Shelley 'strives in prayer' to renew our humanity is none other than the One who first appeared to the disciples at Pentecost as 'a rushing mighty wind'?[†] And could this same energy belong to the being Grünewald depicted in *Concert of Angels*, the Muse who inspired the unknown mediaeval poet's words?

I sing of a maiden
That is makeless.
King of all kings
To her son she chez [For her son she chose.]

In our present culture, we scarcely have a basis for understanding what speaking lyric poetry might be. We know that much poetry of the sixteenth and seventeenth centuries was written not for publication, but to be spoken aloud amongst friends. We

---

[*] See *The Integrated Actor*, chapter 5, for Steiner's description of our own time as the era of the consciousness- or spiritual-soul.

[†] Acts of the Apostles, 2:2.

Figure 27 – Concert of Angels, *Grünewald*

hear stories of Wordsworth reciting his own poetry in his thick Northumbrian accent. We do not know if these poets brought their poetry to life, but today, when poets read their poetry, with some exceptions, they cannot do justice to their own intentions.

Can we imagine a culture where lyric poetry is spoken so that it reconnects us to the mystery of our oneness with the world and enables us to glimpse our connection to, and heal, the wound of our alienation from the being of Nature? How could that come about unless the ones who speak have striven to purify their total instrument; to make their body/voice/soul a clearer vessel? Today that cannot be done by bathing in the waters of Castalia, as once the lyric poets purified themselves at Delphi – but by bathing instead in the pure beings of the sounds; vowels so purified that they speak to us not of the personal soul alone but of that soul that belongs to the whole earth and the heavens.

Speech-exploration 79 — lyric

1. Warm up full-bodily with the explorations that connect our heart-centre with our lips, pages 134–5, chapter 3. Progress from *Speech-exploration 41 (by miner wafer, etc.)*, to *Be, through my lips, the trumpet of a prophecy . . .* and then to the words: *I want to tell you how I feel. I want to tell you how I feel and in doing so reveal to you the world-soul in my own.*
2. Move around the space radiating warmth from your heart.
3. Take it in turns to gather the others in the group (or your imaginary audience) into your embrace.
4. Pour out your soul to them in these words: *I want to tell you how I feel. I want to tell you how the world feels in me, in my soul.*
5. Follow with the words from any lyric text you know.

When I speak a lyric poem I strive to represent not just 'my sole self' but the soul of humanity. I become a chalice into which the purified vowels can pour and assuage through me a thirsty earth. They caress the souls of those who listen and bathe them in their love. In return, I offer back to the heavens my treasure; the fruits of my soul's sojourn here.

> Praise the world to the angel, not the unutterable world;
> you cannot astonish him with your glorious feelings;
> in the universe, where he feels more sensitively,
> you're just a beginner. Therefore show him the simple
> thing that is shaped in passing from father to son,
> that lives near our hands and eyes as our very own.
> Tell him about the things . . .
> And these things that live,
> slipping away, understand that you praise them;
> transitory themselves, they trust us for rescue,
> us, the most transitory of all. They wish us to transmute them
> in our invisible heart — oh, infinitely into us!
> Whoever we are.
>
> from the *Duino Elegies* by Rilke translated by C.F. MacIntyre[*]

What Rilke so passionately sings of here, Steiner has crystalized into his own unique lyric utterance; human feeling permeated utterly with cosmic love and wisdom; cosmic love and wisdom incarnating utterly into a human soul, giving rise to a new form which Marie Steiner called a 'cosmic lyric'.

---

[*] University of California Press (1961).

Stars once spoke to us.
It is world destiny they are silent now.
To be aware of that silence
brings pain
to souls on earth.

But, in the deepening silence,
grows and ripens what we may speak to stars.
To be aware of our speaking
strengthens
human spirits.

Rudolf Steiner adapted by Dawn Langman

Still today, lyrics are written to be sung or set to music, reminding us that language longs to be freed from the prison of the intellect, from the obligation to provide information only, and instead, to soar directly from heart to heart on wings of tone. Instinctively, when we speak lyric poetry our speech unashamedly moves closer towards song. Speech Formation shows us how to play the octave of the vowels no less certainly than a musician touches us with tones and intervals.

The dramatic stream

When priests from the Mystery Centre of Eleusis donned their masks and stepped for the first time out of the temple rituals and on to the stage of the world, they depicted the gods interacting with the human being, reminding us of our connection. Over the years, human destinies replaced the actions of the gods, human meetings replaced our interactions with the gods; the tragedies that result when we forget our relationship to the gods and to each other; the comedies which repair the separation, reminding us that we are never really harmed, however frightful the appearances and that, in spite of all our faults and imperfections, even perhaps because of them, we are essentially loveable.[*]

The earliest dramas were composed predominantly of both epic and lyric elements — hymns to the gods chanted and danced in chorus alternated with stories of their immortal deeds and interactions with the mortal realm. As the new form developed, interactions between the characters began to take a central place. That is why an essential aspect of dramatic form is *dialogue* arising from the interaction of two or more parts of the whole who can only find themselves through each other. Yet in all meetings the great archetype is always present; that the One I truly meet in another is myself. This was expressed in the culmination of the Egyptian mysteries, when the purified soul, brought face to face with the resurrected god Osiris, recognized, 'it is I'.

---

[*] See *The Integrated Actor*, chapter 6.

Figure 28 – The soul of the dead pharaoh meets the resurrected Osiris

What sort of person is an actor?

To create and inhabit a specific character, to step into the shoes of another, actors sacrifice their own identities. Only by doing so can they reveal the glory of God's creation in the particular, and celebrate the sacred mystery of the individual self. The actor of the future may use a different terminology, but will understand, on some level, that every self, however lost it may be on its pathway of becoming, always:

> Acts, in God's eyes, what in God's eyes he is, Christ.
> For Christ plays in ten thousand places,
> Lovely in limbs and lovely in eyes not his
> To the Father through the features of men's faces.
>
> *As Kingfishers Catch Fire*, Hopkins

This expression by Hopkins demonstrates in a lyric form the difference between the lyric and dramatic modes of consciousness. For even though a lyric poem springs out of the unique biography of the poet, in its form it seeks expression of the universal human soul — not Hamlet's or Ophelia's, for example. Even though when witnessing great drama, we recognize through Hamlet or Ophelia's experience something that sheds light on our own, it is the nature of the form to reveal it through *specific* characters. The greater the actor, the more the audience recognizes aspects of themselves in that character. The actor's art lies in creating that character's uniqueness in such a way that it reveals the universal.

In this context, the actor's work connects with the aspect of the Trinity we call the Son. The mystery of incarnation, after all these centuries, still perplexes us. Is the human being mortal or divine? If not a god, how could he endure — but if divine, how could he suffer?

A new kind of actor will awaken such questions in the audience. For more than anything, the individual character stands on the stage of the world and says: *I want to understand my destiny*. No matter the actions, emotions, relationships, what makes us human is to ask 'Why?' And we can only try to answer this question by thinking; not with the 'cool reason' that detaches us from life, but a living fire that pierces the darkness with its ray of light and probes, as it did with Oedipus, until it finds the truth: *I will know who I am! I want to understand my destiny.*

Such ideas help us to understand the initially surprising connection Steiner makes between the dramatic style and thinking. If you take any speech from Shakespeare, or any of the great plays, and try to express the content in your own words, you will soon discover how much of what is said requires you to think the character's thoughts.

For no matter how powerful the actions, how deep the characters' emotions, how lost they might be in their own pain, we, the audience, need to understand what they are saying; to grasp their thoughts through the language that they speak.

Neither actors, nor audience, must lose themselves in the emotion as perhaps the character is doing. Only if actors can clearly articulate a thought can they penetrate the intense emotion and help the audience to understand, even as they are deeply moved, what a character's specific journey and relationships reveal to them of human destiny.

Was this not, after all, the quest of Brecht, who used the terms 'epic' and 'alienation'; to find a style for his dramas that would enable the audience to understand as well as feel?

We might picture a word with its source in the star of each individual destiny. Sharpened to clarity as it passes through the region of the actor's teeth, it speeds towards the appointed meeting with the other. And in the ensuing dialogue their destinies engage. It is the style of speech we call 'direct'; the nearest of the three to our every-day experience of speech.

Figure 29 – The head-centre and the dramatic style

Speech-exploration 80 – dramatic

1. Warm up full-bodily with the explorations for the head-centre and the speech placement in the region of the teeth, *see fee shielding*, etc., described in pages 136–7.
2. Move around the space sustaining these sensations and experiment with speaking *I want to understand my destiny.*

3. Try speaking any speeches that you know from this perspective.
4. As you move around, make contact with a partner and speak your words to each other.

In the epic style, the *formative* activity of the consonants transforms the *inward* quality embodied in the vowels so that they, too, can reveal in varying degrees of density, the substances that compose our material universe. In the lyric style the consonants are transformed through vowel activity into bearers of inwardness. The dramatic style achieves a balance of inner and outer through equal tension between consonant and vowel.

Weaving the three centres, placements and styles

The cultivation of the speech placements in relation to the archetypal centres gives us the technical basis we need to experience and then communicate the three different modes of consciousness that underlie the basic styles: epic, lyric and dramatic.

Speech-exploration 81 – centres, placements and styles

To lay the foundation for the quality of each style, we stay within the archetypal nature of the placements and the centres – the purest expression of the I AM as it feels, as it thinks, and as it wills.[*] If we connect the phrases used earlier to explore and express the intention that underlies the epic, lyric and dramatic styles and the speech quality appropriate to each, we arrive at the text Steiner gave that enables us to first master each quality in turn and then develop the capacity to weave between them:

> In the heart weaves our feeling
> In the head lights up thinking
> In the limbs works strength of will
> Weaving of radiant light
> Strength of the weaving
> Light of the surging strength
> Behold the human being!

1. Warm up each centre full-bodily, refrain from speaking until your instrument is prepared.
2. Weave the text with the archetypal centres/placement exercises from pages 133–41, chapter 3, for example:

---

[*] The potential for artistic development of the archetypes is explored in *The Integrated Actor*.

Stage 1

By miner wafer
By boom
By vie
In the heart weaves our feeling
I want to tell you how I feel

Stage 2

See fee shielding
Reeled far
Full reeled needy
In the head lights up thinking
I want to understand my destiny

Stage 3

Noon air lark anger ink
Ink ringer growl
Ink ringer grows shaft
In the limbs works strength of will
I want to tell you what happened

3. Play until you are confident that you can make all the transitions between the centres in your body and the speech placements with ease.

Breath and the archetypal styles

Layering the breath styles of recitation and declamation with the styles of epic, lyric and dramatic allows us to achieve an even richer palate of expressive possibilities.

Speech-exploration 82 – Lyric, declamation and recitation

Lyric and declamation

The last stanza of Shelley's *Ode to the West Wind* is in the lyric style. As his soul plunges and soars between the heights and depths we recognize the need for a declamatory use of breath.

> Make me thy lyre, even as the forest is:
> What if my leaves are falling like its own!
> The tumult of thy mighty harmonies
>
> Will take from both, a deep autumnal tone,
> Sweet though in sadness. Be thou, Spirit fierce,
> My spirit! Be thou me, impetuous one!
>
> Drive my dead thoughts over the universe
> Like withered leaves to quicken a new birth!
> And, by the incantation of this verse,
>
> Scatter, as from an unextinguished hearth
> Ashes and sparks, my words among mankind!
> Be through my lips, to unawakened earth,
>
> The trumpet of a prophecy! O, wind,
> If winter comes, can spring be far behind?

1. Warm-up with steps 1 and 2 in *Speech-exploration 81*.
2. Layer stage 1 with the breath exercise *reforging gales* on pages 102–8.
3. Experiment with Shelley's words.

Lyric and recitation

Keats's *Ode to Autumn* is a lyric poem that requires a recitative use of breath:

> Season of mists and mellow fruitfulness,
> Close bosom friend of the maturing sun;
> Conspiring with him how to load and bless
> With fruit, the vines that round the thatch eaves run;
> To bend with apples the mossed cottage trees
> And fill all fruit with ripeness to the core...

1. Warm-up with steps 1 and 2 in *Speech-exploration 81*.
2. Layer stage 1 with the breath exercise *in the vast unmeasured world wide spaces* on page 109.
3. Experiment with Keats's words.

Speech-exploration 83 — Dramatic, declamation and recitation

Dramatic and declamation

1. Warm up with steps 1 and 2 of *Speech-exploration 81*.
2. Layer stage 2 with *reforging gales*.
3. Experiment with:

> *Hamlet*: Bloody, bawdy villain!
> Remorseless, treacherous, lecherous, kindless villain!
> O vengeance!

> *Romeo*: It is my lady, O it is my love!
> O that she knew she were.

> *Juliet*: O Romeo, Romeo! wherefore art thou Romeo?
> Deny thy father, and refuse thy name;
> Or, if thou wilt not, be but sworn my love,
> And I'll no longer be a Capulet...

Dramatic and recitation

1. Warm-up with steps 1 and 2 in *Speech-exploration 81*.
2. Layer stage 2 with *In the vast...*
3. Experiment with Hamlet's soliloquy:

> I have heard,
> That guilty creatures sitting at a play
> Have by the very cunning of the scene
> Been struck so to the soul that presently
> They have proclaimed their malefaction.
> For murder, though it hath no tongue, will speak
> With most miraculous organ.

This soliloquy from Act 2, scene 5 of Shakespeare's *Henry VI*, part 3, offers another opportunity to practise the extended thought and image-making line in the dramatic style.

Henry reflects on his life in the midst of the battle he is helpless to influence:

> This battle fares like to the morning's war
> When dying clouds contend with growing light,
> What time the shepherd, blowing of his nails,
> Can neither call it perfect day nor night...

4. Compare the declamatory style required by the previous example from *Romeo and Juliet* with the use of breath required in the stately measured sonnet form in which they first express their meeting:

> *Romeo*: If I profane with my unworthiest hand
> This holy shrine, the gentle sin is this;
> My lips, two blushing pilgrims, ready stand
> To smooth that rough touch with a tender kiss.
>
> *Juliet*: Good pilgrim, you do wrong your hand too much
> Which mannerly devotion shows in this;
> For saints have hands that pilgrim's hands do touch,
> And palm to palm is holy palmer's kiss.

Speech-exploration 84 – Epic, declamation and recitation

Epic and declamation
Refer to the alliterative text quoted on page 244.

1. Warm up with steps 1 and 2 of *Speech-exploration 81*.
2. Layer stage 3 with *reforging gales* ... from pages 102–8.
3. Experiment with the text, *Mountains shall melt* ... on page 244.

Epic and recitation

1. Warm up with steps 1 and 2 of *Speech-exploration 81*.
2. Layer stage 3 with *In the vast*...
3. Experiment with the text from page 232 ... *Dry clash'd his harness in the icy caves*, etc.
4. Here is a passage from Milton's *Paradise Lost* which describes the confrontation between Satan and the Archangel Michael. It is interesting to compare it with the alliterative passage used earlier to demonstrate the declamatory style of epic.

> ...now storming fury rose,
> And clamour such as heard in Heaven till now
> Was never, Arms on Armour clashing bray'd

Horrible discord, and the madding Wheels
Of brazen chariots rag'd; dire was the noise
Of conflict; over head the dismal hiss
Of fiery Darts in flaming vollies flew,
And flying vaulted either Host with fire.

A note on flexibility

It's important not to treat categories of style in a dogmatic way. Whether it's our use of epic, lyric or dramatic or the way we use our breath, what matters is that we expand the range of our expressiveness when we develop flexibility to differentiate in the suggested ways; through centres, placement and now as they interweave with the two ways of using breath.[*] Then, with instrument attuned, we allow our artistic instinct to declare whether an overall text, or any moment in a text, requires me:

a) To use my breath to plunge and soar between the heights and depths of my intensity, directly striking with my will into the sounds.

Or . . .

b) To hold back the direct outpouring of intensity, guided by the meter's firm resistance, and channel the breath to form the sounds in such a way that they reveal the contours of my mental images and concepts.

We cannot help but notice how even Shelley's impassioned prayer to the wind unfolds in massive sentence structures into which his thoughts and mental images are woven. And to speak these words of Juliet, we require the capacity to move seamlessly from one way of using breath to another and at times to fuse them in a perfect marriage of passion and extended thought and image-making:

Gallop apace, you fiery-footed steeds,
Towards Phoebus' lodging; such a waggoner
As Phaeton, would whip you to the west
And bring in cloudy night immediately.
Spread thy close curtain, love-performing night!
That runaway's eyes may wink, and Romeo
Leap to these arms untalked of and unseen!
Lovers can see to do their amorous rites
By their own beauties; or, if love be blind,
It best agrees with night . . .
Come night! Come Romeo! Come, thou day in night!

---

[*] See Appendix B, *Poetry and The Art of Speech*, for many examples of style in the English language.

For thou wilt lie upon the wings of night,
Whiter than new snow on a raven's back.
Come gentle night; come, loving, black-brow'd night,
Give me my Romeo: and, when he shall die,
Take him and cut him out in little stars,
And he will make the face of heaven so fine
That all the world will be in love with night,
And pay no worship to the garish sun.

Mastery of the recitative and declamatory uses of breath in the dramatic style does not replace the skills required to create a character.[*] Neither will those skills on their own provide us with the mastery of breath that allows us to inhabit and reveal the complex consciousness contained in Juliet's richly textured language.

As Plato observed of the poets, each performer, according to their stage of life and personality, may be gifted more in one style than another. An actor usually feels at home when playing someone else and takes delight in creating other characters. Lyric poetry expands the speaker's soul to represent the soul of humanity. Storytelling requires the capacity for an objective standpoint. Because each style enriches and clarifies the others, acknowledging what Chekhov called our 'artistic individuality' should not discourage us from striving to expand our expressiveness by cultivating the whole range of capacities.

---

[*] See *The Art of Acting* and *The Integrated Actor*.

Chapter 7

Goddess Most Rare: Approaching Grammar

What is grammar?

The grammatical structures that evolved through our Greco-Latin heritage form the basis of 'correct' English grammar. They have supported and made possible the development of the rational consciousness we associate with western civilization. Those of us who learned grammar at school inherited a museum filled with dead parts of speech and rules that governed the correctness of our sentences. They seemed at worst to have been intended for the express purpose of tormenting school children and at best, to offer a gateway to acceptance in a literate society. A comprehensive picture of the components and structures of English grammar may be found in other places. Our concern here is to explore in an artistic way those aspects most basic to the way we speak our language. Only an artistic exploration can integrate with an art of Speech.

The oral transmission of language reveals that grammar evolves as fluidly as vocabulary. The question of 'correctness' arises only when there is a threat to understanding. Our starting point is that consciousness organizes words into the pathways we call grammar in order to articulate its journey. We agree on the rules of grammar to help us structure our comprehension, so that we can understand each other.

The Goddess Grammatica

The idea that grammar could be perceived as a goddess may seem absurd to our 'cool reason'. Yet this was the case at the School of Chartres.* The structure of mediaeval education was built on the Seven Liberal Arts. At Chartres, *Grammatica*, as she was called, and her sister arts, were looked on as divine, feminine beings.[34] The style of learning cultivated there encouraged the understanding that the source of all branches of our knowledge lay not in the abstract conceptual life, but in the realm of *being*. That

---

* The Cathedral School of Chartres was founded around 1020 AD and reached its zenith as a centre of learning in the first half of the twelfth century. It declined in the latter half of the twelfth century due to the proliferation of universities which saw the gradual triumph of Aristotelian thinking over the more Platonic experience of reality. During its years of greatest influence, Chartres embodied the last flowering of neo-Platonist consciousness in Europe.

original perception of the supersensible which was still honoured in the school of Chartres faded until these beings could no longer be perceived.

How can we understand a consciousness that experienced grammar as a goddess? Let us imagine the sense of wonder with which people closer to the origins of language experienced that it was possible to *name* phenomena. Then, the wonder of discovering pathways to connect those names! For our capacity to make relationships between experiences cannot be separated from our patterns of connecting words. It is these complex pathways that we call *grammar*.

We know that inability to articulate our experience can lead to frustration, rage and even violence. The growing edge of consciousness defines itself and evolves as our ability to name, and to connect those names through grammar, also evolves. Grammar is like the thread Ariadne gave to Theseus, enabling him to return through the labyrinth and find his way home. Grammar is like the deed of Isis, searching for the fragments of her Lord's broken body and connecting them again. Both mythologies portray these actions as gifts of what we call 'the feminine'.

A story told by Helen Keller in her autobiography, *The Story of My Life*, confirms this at a human level.[35] She describes the gift of love that language brings to someone locked inside a mind that has no power to name its own experience. Helen recalls the moment when her teacher, Anne Sullivan, released her from the prison of being deaf and blind. For many months Anne had tried in many different ways to find the key to connect experience and language in Helen's mind. Repeated failure was frustrating for them both. Then came the moment Anne found the way for Helen to connect her experience of water with its name. In the weeks and months that followed, that single word released a flood of language and with it, Helen's consciousness, so long dammed up, began to flow.

Over her long life, words were keys that opened up Helen's inner world, nourishing one of the profoundest sensibilities of the twentieth century. In turn, her ability to use those words enabled her, in language of inspiring eloquence, to shift the world's perception of people with disabilities. Yet, how far could her mind have unfolded if expression were confined to single, unrelated words?

It is not difficult to recognize in this profoundly moving story of two human beings that language was a gift, given by one who served with faithful love. The teacher waited, watched and searched unceasingly to find a bridge between experience and understanding. When we think how language is imparted, we recognize that through the generations there has always first been 'someone' who loves. That someone, most often mother, waits and watches, observing each most delicate glimmer of consciousness awakening and matches it with sounds and structures of the mother tongue. Could we not imagine then a greater Someone; a Being of Love who stands behind our attempts to find names for our experience and to express its pathways of unfolding? Might not this being be the feminine aspect of the one the Greeks called LOGOS; the WORD who has created all things and whose body is the body of our grammar? The grammar we have learned at school stands in relation to that Being as a skeleton to a living person. In this chapter, we shall try to find the beauty in the sculpture of those bones, put some flesh upon them and find the blood within those veins.

Aristotle's categories

The foundation of grammar in our Western culture was not laid down by Aristotle, but there can be no question of his influence on its development. His works on logic and rhetoric became the basis of Rhetorica and Dialectica. In mediaeval times these, with Grammatica, were the three arts that formed the Trivium; the first pillar of the Seven Liberal Arts and the basis of a classical education for many centuries.

We know that much of Aristotle's work has not survived. It is not unreasonable to suppose that a work of his, not extant, may have formed the basis of Grammatica. A reading of any of his extant treatises reveals extraordinary powers of observation and of reasoning. Yet we can observe how closely tied these were to the clear grammatical structures that allowed him to express himself.

This connection is significant. Aristotle provided the first detailed studies of the natural world in all its intricate variety. His capacity to observe and describe in such astonishing clarity and detail evolved along with his discovery that experience can be ordered into categories. This gave him tools with which to recognize and delineate the intricate and subtle details of phenomena. Such tools could not be separate from an equally evolving power of words to name and organize what he perceived. Are not the pathways that our minds can take, the pathways of our words? And do not these words themselves express the categories that they name?

Some experience relates to time, some to space, some is related to the finished qualities of things, some to process, some to action, and so on. Aristotle's observations help us recognize that our conceptual life is built on our capacity to separate and recognize the categories of our experience. With this awareness, we arrive in grammar's kingdom. And here, we can debate forever the question: did the capacity to order our experience give birth to grammar, or did grammar give birth to our capacity to order our experience? It is telling, in this respect, that the opening paragraphs of Aristotle's treatise on the categories begins with an analysis of words and language.

Grammar taught only as pedantic rules, can kill the life of language. Its true purpose is to serve that life by making the expression of that life transparent.[36]

Relationship of categories to breathing

To shape a spoken sentence grammatically, so that the parts are clear, depends on our ability to breathe with our experience.[*] Whether it be a poem, story, or dramatic speech, we can only express the spectrum of experience contained in any sentence if we breathe with it. The living laws of grammar teach us how to do this by bringing order to our breathing. Achieving this enables us to lead an audience through the labyrinth.

A sentence is a structure that enables us to order and reveal the meaningful connections between the categories of our experience. We uncover the categories buried in each structure that the mind has made on its eternal quest to find those meaningful connections, when we recognize that each new phrase or clause we come to in a sentence is a response to an invisible question which the mind has asked, perhaps unconsciously. Our mind learns to make its questions conscious. Let us take the beginning of the fairytale *Snow White and the Seven Dwarfs* from the Brothers Grimm:

> Once upon a time, in the middle of winter, when the flakes of snow were falling like feathers from the sky, a queen sat at her window sewing. And the frame of the window was made of black ebony. And whilst she was sewing and looking out of the window at the snow, she pricked her finger with the needle and three drops of blood fell upon the snow.

The first phrase already answers an unspoken question.

Question: When did this story happen?
Answer: *Once upon a time.*
Q: What time exactly?
A: *in the middle of winter, when . . .*
Q: How do you know it was winter?
A: because *the flakes of snow were falling . . .*
Q: What did they look like?
A: *like feathers . . .*
Q: Where did they come from?
A: *from the sky . . .*
Q: Was anyone there?
A: *a queen . . .*
Q: What was she doing?
A: she *sat . . .*

---

[*] See chapter 5, Main clause and subordinate/auxiliary clause.

Q: Where?

A: *at her window*...

Q: What else was she doing?

A: *sewing*.

Each question is breathed in by the speaker and the answer will require its own out-breath. Working in this way, a sentence is not a monologue constructed in a vacuum. It arises from a dialogue, only half of which is visible or audible. Initially this dialogue took place between the storyteller's mind and an audience, real or imagined. Or, in the case of written text, between the writer's mind and an imagined reader.

An artist who satisfies an audience recreates the text so that a performance appears to be the first and only one. The unique event created in that moment is a living dialogue with those who listen, whose unspoken questions participate in its creation. Depending on the context, the audience may or may not voice these questions outwardly. Nevertheless, their interest is stirred when the performer speaks in such a way that each word spoken answers a question which has been aroused in them.

One aspect of grammar, then, records the invisible, yet no less real or meaningful, ongoing exchange between parts of our mind; the relationship between an audience and artist simply makes this exchange tangible. Punctuation is a guide to this exchange and to the pattern of breathing it demands. A comma for example, indicates a new breath is required. Yet we cannot totally rely on punctuation for the clues that inform us that we need to release one phrase, 'hear' the unspoken question it aroused and newly grasp its answer in the next. We learn to recognize the clues in the very patterns made by words.

Speech-exploration 85 (partner work)

1. Identify the hidden questions in the remaining text from *Snow White*.
2. One of you ask the questions and the other tell the story by answering, allowing each successive word or phrase to come as a response to the question that preceded it.
3. Let the interchange grow in spontaneity and energy as you become familiar with the dialogue.
4. When the story has been brought to life, tell it once again to your partner, but this time internalize the questions. Can you achieve the same sense of a lively interplay when you generate the dialogue from within?
5. Reverse roles.
6. Apply this process to other texts you are working with (including poetry and drama).

Grammar in relation to thinking, feeling and the will

When we do so, it's clear that what drives the questions is not merely a persistent need for information. Story, storyteller, listener are gathered in a sphere that cannot be accessed by the intellect alone. The intellect wants to be satisfied along the way, yet what initiates both telling and listening is not only the mind's need to understand by gathering and ordering information but the heart's desire to feel the wonder and mystery of life. What grammatical structures offer within the ordered pathways of the information they provide, are also opportunities to *feel*. We cannot feel unless we breathe. To honour grammar allows us to receive this gift: both speaker and listener giving and being given time to breathe in what is felt, and time to feel it.

Heart-moments

I shall be forever grateful to the student who many years ago suggested the name, *heart-moment*. We had been searching for a user-friendly way to render in English, the German *losslassen*. This essential part of our technique asks us to let go what has passed, in order to breathe in or freshly grasp what follows. We discovered it is the heart's need to feel the next moment of experience that signals the necessity for letting go what went before.

> Once upon a time, (heart-moment) in the middle of winter, (heart-moment) when the flakes of snow (heart-moment) were falling, (heart-moment) like feathers (heart-moment) from the sky, (heart-moment) a queen (heart-moment) sat at her window (heart-moment) sewing.

Of course, the hare, our intellect, would say: 'Ridiculous! It would take far too long. Can you imagine someone waiting all day while you indulge in moments-of-the-heart?' Indeed! Can we imagine anyone would be willing to wait longer than it takes to 'get through' the basic information in as short a time as possible; anyone who still longs to feel the heights and depths of their experience?

What does it mean to speak from our hearts and then to integrate this with the other elements of artistry, including pace? To speak truly from the heart is not the same as pushing or injecting feeling or emotion into a text we have already organized according to quite different priorities. It means to place our hearts at the very centre of the act of language, to offer our speaking to the goddess.

We have considered the human being's capacities to think, to feel and to act. When these three work healthily together, we sense we are fully human. And so, only when language provides a vessel for all three will it serve our need to articulate and communicate all aspects of experience. Even the traditional definition of verbs as 'doing' words suggests that verbs name the aspects of experience related to our will. Likewise in being taught that nouns refer to things, we understand how they reflect our thinking, by which we form our concepts and distinguish them. Adjectives and adverbs derive from them, enabling us to further qualify those things or actions; someone is sad or happy, humble or arrogant, a thing is hot or cold, high or low, large or small, it moves quickly or slowly.

The missing part of language

Our feelings and emotions manifest through vowels and through rhythm.[*] Mysteriously, there seems no category of words which *in itself* denotes the feeling aspect of our inner life. We distinguish here between the function of a word and what it means. We can think of many nouns and the adjectives or adverbs which derive from them which 'mean' for us, our feelings. They name the concepts that we have of emotions: sadness/sadly, happiness/happily, etc. Then too, there are verbs that name the actions that express these feelings. We tear our hair, we jump for joy. But they remain verbs and do not in themselves denote the feelings.

There are exclamations, but are they really words, or primal utterances that express non or pre-verbal states of inwardness, primarily through vowels? Word-making is a function of cognition. We exclaim before, or on our way to, processing and conceptualising our experience. Of course, we often use words as exclamations, when we swear for example. But usually 'swear words' have been detached from their original conceptual contexts and recruited to express quite unrelated emotion.

The research of the last decades into the differing functions of the right and left hemispheres of the brain offers some insight here. In the majority of people cognitive functions, including word formation and language skills, take place in the left cerebral cortex. Emotions and dimensions of consciousness not immediately accessible to rational functioning tend to be processed in the right cerebral cortex.[37] The act of making words serves and indeed *is* the way we conceptualize. It is only our rational function which can try to understand our emotions so it names them with its own conceptual tools. The feelings and emotions cannot themselves strive towards conceptual forms. Although they find their own ways of expression they do not, indeed cannot, make a category of words to be a function of themselves.

However, I suggest that there *is* a part of language which exclusively fulfils this function. We cannot find it if we look for it in words because it is not in the words. It is *the space between the words* where feelings live. Without those spaces we would not have time to experience emotion, however powerful the images or words. And only when we artists give ourselves the time to feel can we imbue the words we speak with

---

[*] See chapters 1 and 4.

feeling's radiance. Nevertheless, it remains a central task for human beings to understand their feelings and emotions, and for language to express them.[*]

How does Shakespeare do it?

Let us look in detail at some text from *King Lear* which gives expression to great depth of feeling. Lear's final words enable us to follow the mysterious interweaving of our cognitive and feeling realms that language demonstrates.

> Howl! Howl! Howl! O you are men of stones!
> Had I your tongues and voices I'd use them so
> That heaven's vaults should crack! She's gone forever!
> I know when one is dead and when one lives.
> She's dead as earth! Lend me a looking glass!
> If that her breath will mist or stain the stone,
> Why then she lives...
>
> This feather stirs; she lives! If it be so
> It is a chance that doth redeem all <u>sorrows</u>
> That ever I have felt...
>
> Cordelia! Cordelia! Stay a little. Ha!
> What is it thou sayest? Her voice was ever soft,
> Gentle and low, an excellent thing in woman.
> And my poor fool is hanged! No, no, no life!
> Why should a dog, a horse, a rat have life
> And thou no breath at all? Thou'lt come no more!
> Never, never, never, never, never!
> Pray you, undo this button: thank you sir.
> Do you see this? Look on her, look, her lips,
> Look there! Look there!

Only once is a feeling named directly. Except for *sorrows*, not one word, on its own, refers in any way to what Lear feels. Yet who can doubt the depth of feeling here portrayed? It is a clear example that we cannot find the feelings *in* the words. Yet where? Where does the actor go to find them?

We are privileged, through Shakespeare's words, to witness a sacred birth; the process by which the something or someone in us, striving to raise itself out of the animal, descends into the inexpressible depths of grief, bearing the one thing that can penetrate the dark: words, faltering and stumbling on their way to sentences, making

---

[*] See *The Integrated Actor* regarding the function of the word-related arts within the evolution of consciousness.

what Eliot called their *raid on the inarticulate*.[38] How can we not behold a goddess watching over him, attending him and offering him through the gift of herself, Grammatica; the pathway through his pain?

Lear's last great utterance starts with a single word: repeated, or intensified?[*] He enters, carrying Cordelia's body in his arms. He sets her down. *Howl!* Three times he utters it. Is it a word? A cry? Something in between? The emotion is so great, so uncontainable, so unready to be words. Yet it *is* a word; the word we use to name the way an animal that has no words – that part of us that yet can find no words – dumbly expresses. Yet, finding at least a *voice*, the raw emotion is granted passage. Now, being thus allowed, it can begin the task to understand itself. It seeks for language.

And how much time is needed! Each time, the descent into the darkness, the search to find his bearings, to wrest each fragment of emotion from its clutch, returning to the surface, bearing triumphant each little word, each little phrase or sentence. This is a journey that cannot be hurried; lifting those emotions into consciousness, sifting them through the filter of his mind, articulating, conceptualizing what he feels. For, step-by-step, he brings himself to understand: he will never, never, never, never, never, behold his daughter in this earthly world again. Five times he needs to say it, so he can digest the feeling/thought.[†] From *howl* to *never!* Each is an exclamation. *Howl* is all emotion, unpenetrated by cognition. *Never* is feeling, increasingly imbued with understanding. Lear has reached the gateway from which there is no need for turning back. Grateful for everything, he is ready to pass through.

Categories of words

Nouns satisfy the intellect's need to name what we experience. In doing so, they tend to fix our understanding of what we know and turn the world into a graveyard of dead and finished things. Speech Formation shows us how we can reverse this tendency and unlock the treasure buried in each sound-sequence that we call a word. These sounds lead us back through the miracle by which we give experience a name, to the primal richness of what Barfield called 'original participation'. In this way, a noun recovers something of the verb by which the 'thing' that it describes, came into being.

There follow other categories of words; the article, conjunctions, prepositions, pronouns, participles etc. They exist to make relationships between the primary two and hence connect experience. Like good servants, they do not draw attention to themselves but wear the colours of the ones they serve. Often they will be the unstressed words in lines or sentences. Speaking that aims to be artistic will respect

---

[*] See chapter 5.

[†] See chapter 4 for further thoughts about the number five.

the humble gesture of these words, not letting them take up too much space or time of their own.[*]

Within the context of the Logos, the purpose of these words could be described as being to prepare the way for one who 'greater than (themselves), comes after'.[39] Like John the Baptist in some of the old pictures, they point away from themselves towards the one they serve.[†] Within this context, I draw attention to the conjunctions 'and' and 'but'. Seemingly insignificant, *and* has a most important task; to join what is separate. *But*, on the other hand, intercepts the stream of time, creating space for something to enter that was not foreseen. It indicates to us a leap, an intervention from the world that lies outside the logic of perceived cause and effect. It announces resurrection. The function of both words *is* their meaning.

When grammar is reduced to abstract rules, it destroys the life of our imagination. Yet she has been thought of as a goddess and can be again; her function understood to be connection, not division. The division into separate words took place so we could know what we know. For that, the body of Osiris was dismembered. But it was Isis, the feminine aspect of the Egyptian Trinity, who faithfully gathered the pieces, connected them and made them whole again. In Christian mythology the feminine aspect has been sometimes called the Holy Spirit, the Divine Sophia. She it was who visited each one present on the day of Pentecost with the flame of their individual creative spirit. The first deed of this spirit was to speak through the disciples, a language which all the people listening could understand.[‡]

Evolution of the Goddess

Many novelists and poets of the present age experiment with grammar. They demonstrate that other worlds of consciousness reveal themselves when we step outside the rules and go beyond 'correctness'. In the last chapter we considered that it is an attribute of life to evolve. A *living grammar*, then, cannot be fixed in forms that expressed the consciousness of human beings in the past. How could the living being of the goddess Grammatica not evolve as human consciousness evolves demanding new pathways to articulate itself?

In E. E. Cummings' poem, *the little horse is newly*, the poet plays with the boundaries of what we find acceptable. 'Errors' of spelling, grammar, sentence structure, even of typography, shatter our expectations and 'shock' us out of our habitual awareness. His unorthodox and 'incorrect' use of written words creates new pathways in our con-

---

[*] See speech-explorations 58–61.

[†] See *The Art of Acting*, Epilogue.

[‡] See the *Bible*, the New Testament, chapter 2 of the Acts of the Apostles.

sciousness, opening us to new possibilities. This makes us aware that adherence to the rules, grasped and obeyed only as abstractions and largely sunk down into the unconscious, can close us off from fresh ways to experience.

What our rational minds perceive to be a tangle of letters and structures on the page, can open our hearts, revealing flashes of a startling world beyond the world we normally perceive. It is the world a child beholds, who comes with a 'beginner's mind'; fresh eyes and perceptions not determined by established paths of language. It invites us too, to be a little child again.

the little horse is newlY

Born)he knows nothing,and feels
everything;all around whom is

perfectly a strange
ness Of sun
light and of fragrance and of

Singing)is ev
erywhere(a welcom
ing dream:is amazing)
a worlD.and in

this world lies:smoothbeautifuL
ly folded;a(brea
thing and a gro

Wing)silence,who;
is: somE

oNe.

ee cummings[*]

The Goddess in the Trinity

Exploring grammar thus, we sense a complex consciousness; a being who moves between masculine, feminine and little child. We sense how language lets us move between these members of the Holy Family within ourselves.

The masculine

Dissecting and distinguishing, certain of its own divisions, making nouns; confidently doing, making verbs.

---

[*] *Penguin Book of American Verse* (1977).

The feminine
Questioning those separations, needing time to feel, and from those spaces in between discerning new connections, new wholenesses; making grammar of those single words.

The child
Delighting in not knowing, finding out, inquisitively disregarding boundaries, not knowing yet what is laid down to know, free to experience, experiment and test convention, discovering what happens if it tries out this or that, what lies between the cracks, breaking rules.

These aspects of our being could also be expressed as:

Logos
Awakening intimations of His thinking in us, through our left brain.

Goddess
Awakening intimations of Her feeling in us, through our right brain.

Family
The child, holding hands between them, awakening, announcing intimations of becomingness, creating new pathways in our brain.

Only speaking that releases the life in words, the action, feeling and creative thinking that lie imprisoned in those abstract written symbols, could possibly express the multi-levelled consciousness of language. *The Art of Speech* is dedicated to this possibility.

Chapter 8

On the English Language

Reflections on the evolution of the English language

Origins

The evolution of a language is a complex thing. In the case of English, the process has required many centuries, many migrations of peoples, the lives of their communities and the work of many individuals of genius; and continues still.[40] Rudolf Steiner's spiritual research suggests that such significant developments unfolding over such large periods of time cannot possibly result from arbitrary sequences of cause and effect. If we train our spiritual cognition in the way he has suggested, we too can sense the guidance of those beings who assist humanity. In this context we can recognize them in the coming into being of every culture, folk soul and language. For each language and people has its task. The English language could be likened to a cauldron of soup. Hung over fire for 15 centuries or so, new ingredients have been and continue to be added to the basic stock.

The original inhabitants of England were tribes of Celts, who occupied much of what is now called Europe. In 55 BC, Britain was invaded by the Romans and became a part of their Empire. Over the next centuries, those Celtic tribes who survived were driven to the borders where, still today, Celtic languages are spoken. No significant mingling of the Celtic and the Latin languages occurred in England. Across the channel, in those regions now called France, the Celtic Gauls had also been conquered by the Romans, but their language absorbed the Latin of their conquerors. This Celticised Latin formed the basis of what became the French language which would later flow into the English.

During the fifth century, tribes invading from the North swept through the Roman Empire. In 449 AD, Britain was invaded once again, this time by Angles from Schleswig, Saxons from Holstein and the Jutes from Jutland. Their languages were similar and are generally identified as Saxon. Over the next centuries, the language known as *Anglo-Saxon* evolved in England from these Germanic roots and is called *Old English*.

In the ensuing centuries, Christian missionaries penetrated these, what they thought of as, barbarian kingdoms. Since the language of the Roman Catholic Church was Latin and monks almost the only people who could read or write, Latin became the vehicle for scholarship and learning. Latin expressed the spiritual consciousness of the time in the form that pervaded the culture through the influence and power of the Roman Catholic Church. It lent itself, particularly, to intellectual tasks.

During the eighth century, Vikings (from what we now call Denmark) began a series of invasions, imposing their rule and language (Danish with its roots in Old Norse) on much of England. Now Old English faced the threat of dying out. Only through the efforts of Alfred the Great in 878 AD, were the Danes forced to sign a treaty. Initially this divided England but led, in time, to a fruitful interchange. Alfred decreed that Anglo-Saxon be the language of communication. He ensured it would be written down by introducing the *Anglo-Saxon Chronicle*. This required that records of significant events in each community were kept in the vernacular. During this time, hundreds of Danish words were absorbed into Anglo-Saxon.

In 1066, England was invaded once again, this time by the Normans. These were descended from the Vikings or Northmen, who at the time of those fifth century invasions, had taken back from Rome that part of Celtic Gaul we now call Normandy. They adopted as their language, the form of French that had evolved from the Celticised Latin spoken there. To this they contributed many of their own words from Old Norse. Many French words entered England now, particularly in contexts of law and administration. The three languages, existing side by side, retained their separate identities and functions:

Latin
The language of learning – it expressed the spiritual consciousness of the time, pervading the culture through the domination of the Roman Catholic Church.

Norman French
The language of the ruling class, of law-making and administration.

Anglo-Saxon
Its roots in the Germanic languages of the 'barbarian' invaders, Anglo-Saxon became the language of the peasant population – the labourers and serving class. It thus expressed a strong connection to the earth, the elements and human will.

The histories of England and the lands we now call France remained closely connected over the next centuries. But when Eleanor, Queen of Aquitaine, married Henry II, King of England and moved her court there, the languages themselves began to merge, evolving into what we now call *Middle English*.

Eleanor of Aquitaine brought this 'second wave' of French with her from the South of France. Known as the most cultured woman in Europe, under her patronage and influence a whole new sensibility began to flower. It manifested in the birth of romance and the ideal of romantic love. Celebrated first within the culture of the troubadours, it was referred to as the cult of courtly love. This phenomenon was only the first shoot to emerge from what would gradually grow into a broader valuing in culture, of the feeling life. Although it first expressed itself in what was called romantic love, its purpose was slowly to transform a culture dominated until then, by masculine warrior values. The awakening of feminine sensibilities would lead to a refining of the feelings.

Men who had prided themselves on prowess, felt invaded by this strange condition with the symptoms of an illness. It could not be controlled and rendered the afflicted one powerless; it could only be endured – but within its melancholic suffering and unrequited longing, a whole new sensibility unfolded. Delicacy of feelings, noble aspirations and the wish to prove worthy of one's love, to become a better human being; these became the new goals and striving.

This profound shift in sensibility was reflected in the transformation into English of the French word, *chevalier* – 'knight'. Derived from 'cheval', the French word for horse, a knight was a warrior who could afford to ride a horse. From this root, 'chivalry' came into English; a word that suggests a different paradigm for human striving.

In the *Cuckoo Song*, still sung today, we experience the earthy qualities of words with Anglo-Saxon roots.[41] Scholars are uncertain of its date of origin, placing it around 1250 AD.

> Somer is y-comen in,
> Loude sing, cuckoo!
> Groweth seed and bloweth meed
> And springeth the woode now;
> Sing cuckoo!
>
> Ewe bleateth after lamb,
> Low'th after calfe cow;
> Bullock starteth, bucke farteth.
> Merry sing, cuckoo![*]

In the thirteenth century *Hymn in Praise of Mary*, we see Latin and Anglo-Saxon elements existing side-by-side and quite distinct.

> Of one that is so fayre and bricht
> Velut maris stella   (as the star of the sea)
> Brichter than the dayes licht
> Parens et puella   (mother and virgin)

---

[*] *New Oxford Book of English Verse* (1972).

Ic crie to thee: thou see to me!
Levedy, pray thee son for me
Tam pia   (so kindly)
That ic mote come to thee,
Maria.

Levedy, floure of alle thing,
Rosa sine spina,   (Rose without thorn)
Thu bore Jesu, heavenes king
Gratia divina.   (by divine grace)
Of alle, thou bear'st the prize,
Levedy, quene of Paradis
Electa.   (chosen)
Maide milde moder es,   (gentle maid a mother you)
Effecta.   (have been made)

The Germanic *ic*, *ich* or *itch* continued to be used as the first person pronoun alongside 'I' in parts of England until well into the fifteenth century. The once popular Tudor comedy, *Gammer Gurton's Needle*, provides many examples like the following:

Gammer: Chill say nothing ich warrant thee, but that ich can prove it well.[*]
               Thou fetched my good even fro my door, cham able this to tell![†]
Dame Chat: Did I, old witch, steal oft was thine?
               How should that thing be known?
Gammer: Ich can no tell...

Meditation on the first person pronoun: 'I'

The evolution of the English first person pronoun from the Germanic 'ich' to the diphthong /aɪ/: 'I', is the subject of this meditation. I use my psycho-physical instrument to sense the journey consciousness has made on the path from *Ich* to 'I'.

I begin by articulating Ic, Ich, Itch, attune myself to what they ask of me and do to me; allow them to arrange my body and my soul. Ic! demands I land directly in the centre of myself – no gradual process – hesitation – no time to consider or to weigh things up. I am a sword blade – direct and firm to meet the enemy's blow – the challenge that resistance offers me in /k/, warrior consciousness awake. When I pronounce the German ich, *I shape it as I would the* /j/ (you) *but do not let the breath vibrate the vocal chords. By aspirating it,* ich *is the unvoiced hiss escaping as I sense extreme or sudden cold, brace against the bitter winter wind or am a hissing cat defending my territory. I feel my warrior self: survive only by my will. Itch is the rough-hewn, home-spun scratch, harsh against my skin the way that /t/ digs*

---

[*] Chill – I will.

[†] Cham – I am.

into softer fleshy /sh/; self- sensed on that ever irritated edge. For several centuries I practise this. For several centuries it satisfies. But then, love comes to soften me. For the first time, I hesitate to take the sword. The confidence to pit myself against the /k/, the certainty of meeting blow with blow has disappeared.

> Romeo: O sweet Juliet,
> Thy beauty hath made me effeminate...

Nothing is so simple anymore. I must surrender now to something complex, still unknown. My mouth searches for a new path, a way to some new aspect of myself. Scary, the loss of certainty! Yet unless I let it in, surrender fully to uncertainty, receive it into me /aː/ (star) how can I find my way to /ɪ/ (si̱p), to certainty? To find my way from /aː/ into the centre of myself; only arriving at myself in /ɪ/ through feeling forward in uncertainty, I have to make a journey. Now that I've made it, make it several times again.

I can slide tentatively from /aː/ to /ɪ/ not knowing where I go, yet arriving in the end at something I can call myself. Or I can slide deliciously, caressing as I go, dissolve myself in sympathy, allowing /aː/ to drown the /ɪ/.

Or, with practice (how many centuries does it take?) I can know my end in my beginning, experience the centre of myself in /ɪ/ and let it work back and permeate the /aː/. I can penetrate my own surrender; make the journey as self-conscious I.

Hundreds of years of opportunity to practise saying I. Hundreds of years to feel and understand this journey.

In the sixteenth century I realize I is also Aye! Yes! I need to feel myself in order to say Yes! The degrees of indecision, wavering, uncertainty ... and yet, sometimes, just by saying Aye! Yes! I feel my 'I'.

> It takes so many thousand years to wake.

A Sleep of Prisoners, Christopher Fry

Yes to myself, I AM

Steiner's research into the supersensible revealed the earth to be the fourth of seven planetary cycles. These 'aeons' are necessary to complete the evolution of the human spirit to be Self-Conscious Self within the All. Our investigation of the sequence of the vowels reveals that /aː/ (sta̱r) embodies the first state of consciousness within the octave, /ɪ/ (si̱p) and /iː/ (me̱) the fourth. Can it be coincidence that the diphthong /aɪ/, encompassing this interval, is how the I designates itself? Within a sevenfold cycle, the fourth is always at the centre. The purpose and the culmination of the three before, it seeks to penetrate with consciousness the three stages that have given birth to it. In doing so it raises each one to another level in the three that follow.

Each time I have the opportunity to utter 'I', I reflect unconsciously or consciously upon these aspects of my own becoming. Each time I surrender to my origins in /aː/, I bow to what has brought me to this point, where I can plant within myself, the upright staff of /ɪ/ or /iː/. Henceforth, I am responsible, co-creator of what is yet to come.

Middle English — the courtship of the masculine and feminine

Called the Father of the English language, Geoffrey Chaucer wrote the *Canterbury Tales* towards the end of the fourteenth century. His capacity to write in different English dialects shows his familiarity with them. His diplomatic role in government affairs overseas suggests he may also have been fluent in Italian, French and Latin.

The famous opening lines unfold in rhyming couplets of iambic pentameter. The earthy Anglo-Saxon words now effortlessly mingle with the softer music of the French. The ease with which the different elements have fused enables something new to sound through them; something we begin to recognize as English.

> Whan that Aprille with his shoures sote
> The droghte of Marche hath perced to the rote,
> And bathed every veyne in swich licour,
> Of which vertu engendred is the flour:
> Whan Zephirus eek with his swete breeth
> Inspired hath in every holt and heeth
> The tendre croppes, and the yonge sonne
> Hath in the Ram his halfe course y-ronne,
> And smale fowles maken melodye,
> That slepen al the night with open eye
> (So priketh hem nature in hir corages):
> Than longen folk to goon on pilgrimages...

As this harmonious integration of Germanic words with Frenchified Latin ones continues through the next centuries, English becomes increasingly subtle and refined; able to articulate a delicate feeling life and tenderness as in these few lines from the famous fifteenth century, *Song of the Nativity*:

> I sing of a maiden
> That is makeless;
> King of all kings
> To her son she chez. [For her son she chose.]
>
> He came all so still
> To his mother's bower
> As dew in Aprille
> That falleth on the flower.

We feel our hearts responding; not to the information the words provide but to the gentleness and reverence, the warmth of feeling with which they are suffused. We sense instinctively that to express such feeling the vowels must be warm and musical. For the consonants to support this warmth and beauty in the voice they must soften and caress the vowels, almost disappearing into them. Our instinctive artistry knows this will achieve a lyric quality. In chapter 6, we learned to use these aspects consciously to cultivate the lyric style of Speech.

Modern English — the marriage of masculine and feminine

By 1595/6, when *Romeo and Juliet* was written, French and Germanic influences weave seamlessly in Shakespeare's language. English as we know it has arrived. The language of the lovers' meeting and the balcony scene gives unparalleled expression to the intense and delicate emotions of first love, the tender music of the vowels.

> *Romeo*: See how she leans her cheek upon her hand.
> O that I were a glove upon that hand
> That I might touch that cheek...
>
> *Juliet*: Goodnight! Goodnight! As sweet repose and rest
> Come to thy heart as that within my breast...
> Goodnight! Goodnight! Parting is such sweet sorrow
> That I shall say goodnight till it be morrow.

The fights and quarrels between Montagues and Capulets equally delight us: sentences, tense and muscular, bristle with masculine assertiveness and testosterone-charged, percussive consonants.

> Do you bite your thumb at me sir?
> No sir, I do not bite my thumb at you sir. Yet I do bite my thumb!

Look again at Hamlet's famous speech from this perspective; the rich and separate ingredients have disappeared, submerging their original identities and re-emerging in the language we call English. In order to convey some sense of this, I have identified from which language each English word derives with the following key: Latin; French; Saxon; Dutch; Icelandic; German; Welsh:[42]

> To S be S, or S not S to be: that S is the D question: Fr
> Whether S 'tis nobler Fr in L the mind S to suffer L Fr
> The slings S D and arrows S of outrageous Fr fortune, L Fr
> Or to take I arms L against S a sea S D of troubles Fr
> And by S opposing Fr L end S them S. To die S, to sleep — S D
> No S more — S and by a sleep S D to say S D we end S

The heartache S G and the thousand S D natural Fr shocks Fr
That flesh S D is heir Fr L to! 'Tis a consummation FR L
Devoutly L to be wished S. To die, to sleep —
To sleep — perchance L Fr to dream: D ay there's the rub, W G
For in that sleep of death S what dreams may come S
When S D we have shuffled S off D this mortal L Fr coil, Fr
Must D give S us pause S. There's the respect Fr L
That makes S calamity L of so S D G long Fr L life. S

In Shakespeare's own words, from *The Tempest*:

Nothing of [them] that doth fade
But doth suffer a sea change
Into something rich and strange.

The wholeness of the vessel

What alchemy was needed, across what intervals of time and space, to create an instrument to express and shape the sensibility that we call English? So many sources contributed to make the English language what it is and many still contribute to what it will become. We have observed three main influences in its birth and infancy. Like the three kings, each bestowed a gift upon the baby language, enabling it to grow into a wondrous maturity. It is a vessel fashioned out of each of these, to bear the consciousness its people need. Latin brought the gold, enabling clarity of thinking. French: the frankincense, in which our finest feelings could ascend. Anglo-Saxon brought the myrrh, the bitterness and blessedness of earth and of our labour, of our will to live and to survive, and our mortality.

The ever-widening gap between spelling and pronunciation in English and the confusing number of variations in the diphthongs which proliferate round each pure vowel, raise the question whether the concept of 'correct' English spelling or pronunciation can be valid. For these uncertainties may be exactly what determines and defines the task of consciousness that English can perform within the range of human languages. Keats coined the phrase 'negative capability' to describe the sometimes curse and sometimes blessing of the artist's nature. Perhaps the genius of English is an artist. It, too, struggles to keep its boundaries intact, maintain a firm identity, but as a consequence, absorbs all that it meets. This makes of it 'an instrument so perfectly imperfect' — an infinitely flexible evolving vessel that can serve an ever-widening, evolving human family: it continues to unfold and to perform the unique task to which it is assigned.

A bridge to *The Integrated Actor*

> Speech that is not formed gesture is like something that has no ground to stand upon.[43]
>
> Rudolf Steiner

Actors whose speech does not stand upon such ground are in danger of becoming those 'monstrous talking abstractions' which caused Artaud such agony. Such 'talking heads' are the result of mouths disconnected from the experience of ourselves as integrated instrument of body, soul, spirit, voice; a microcosm woven in the macrocosm of its greater Self. Chekhov and Steiner show us how to reclaim our mouths as expressive organs in the gesturing instrument of actors who know themselves within that greater whole.

Chekhov acknowledges that the arts of Speech Formation and eurythmy:

> ... lead us thus through all the sounds of human speech, through all the combinations of sounds, teach us to realize the mutual connection and interrelation of these sounds, show us endless variations of each of the sounds, thus making our artistic speech into the finest possible membrane of endless subtleties and variations of our psychology ... the sound will become a fine transmitter of the actor's creative intentions ... Through his newly developed mastery to express in his speech the finest nuances of each sound of human language, (the actor) will be able to mould the manner of speech differently for each part he is going to act ... bad is the actor whose different roles on the stage always speak in the same unchangeable manner.[44]
>
> Michael Chekhov

In the third book of this series we will explore the further integration of Chekhov's art of acting with Steiner's art of Speech Formation.

Appendices

Appendix A

Steiner, Hopkins and the evolution of consciousness

Hopkins' life and work prequels an event that Steiner later indicated would become from the middle of the twentieth century, the central supersensible experience of humanity in this next phase of our evolution. The poetry of Hopkins bears witness to his experience of this event and his struggle to find language to express such a cataclysmic shift in perception. Steiner described how, at the end of the nineteenth century, human beings had reached the nadir of materialism; the identification of reality with matter devoid of spirit. This stage of our experience was necessary. Through it was made possible the self's ultimate reliance on itself, experienced as enclosed in a material body, separate from the All.

This came about when the evolution of the relationship between our different 'bodies', reached a certain point. It took place, initially, in those human beings who chose to incarnate within the stream of western consciousness, whose task it was to develop the 'consciousness soul'. In them, the etheric body fully incarnated into the material body. Such complete immersion, so to speak, resulted in the loss of capacity to perceive directly any connection of our own life or etheric body with the life-body of the whole.

The separate self's quest for survival in a universe perceived to be an infinitely complex mechanism, made it seek control of that mechanism. The ability to control and manipulate it could only be acquired by penetration and understanding of the laws by which it functioned. Achievement of this would, in turn, require the ultimate exercise of our capacity to think in freedom.

At the same time, the ultimate crossing of the boundary into what was now perceived to be a wholly material reality would herald the process of reversal. Steiner has described how, at this point, human beings would experience a loosening of the etheric body from the physical with which it had so completely merged. As this loosening occurred, so too perception would expand, to include that greater life in which we live and move and have our being. At this point, we would once again gain entry to those realms. We would take with us though, the very power of thinking and self-conscious judgement attained through separation from those realms. In such a way, re-access to the supersensible would not entail the loss of freedom or consciousness of self, won at such cost.

Steiner called this new capacity to perceive in the etheric realms, *etheric perception*. He described how, from the early twentieth century onwards, increasing numbers of human beings would experience the early stages of reality expanding. This would manifest initially as a Being of Love, whose appearance would begin a process of healing for the self, traumatized by its experience of separation. That Being of Love is none other than the I AM. It is our own greater Self, experienced as one approaching us from the outside in order to initiate the journey of return; reunion with our own true Self.

Steiner referred to this event as the first stage of what Christian tradition looked towards as the Second Coming. His own experience revealed to him that this Second Coming would be experienced in the etheric realm. He spoke of it as the *Second Coming of Christ in the Etheric*.

Hopkins lived from 1844–1899. Like so many great artists, he experienced this loosening of perception before it would unfold in western culture as a whole. Such lines as these, from two of Hopkins' sonnets, are testament to his experience of the One whose coming, foretold in Christian texts, would be perceived 'in' and 'with the clouds'.

> Summer ends now; now, barbarous in beauty, the stooks rise
> Around; up above, what wind-walks! what lovely behaviour
> Of silksack clouds! has wilder, wilful-wavier
> Meal-drift moulded ever and melted across skies?
>
> I walk, I lift up, I lift up heart, eyes,
> Down all that glory in the heavens to glean our Saviour;
> And eyes, heart, what looks, what lips yet gave you a
> Rapturous love's greeting of realer, of rounder replies?
>
> And the azurous hung hills are his world-wielding shoulder
> Majestic — as a stallion stalwart, very violet sweet!

Hurrahing in Harvest

> ...for Christ plays in ten thousand places,
> Lovely in limbs, and lovely in eyes not his,
> To the Father through the features of men's faces.

As kingfishers catch fire

His training as a Jesuit priest determined that he name that Being as Christ. Yet in these lines, we experience how he has fully integrated rhythm, which springs from an alliterative use of sounds, with that arising from the rhyme and meter of classical forms. The rhythms of Ancient Greece, the rhyme and meter of Latin, the fiercer dance of sounds of Northern tribes: these were his ingredients. In merging these, he has created new steps for the dance of One who may be named, yet cannot be contained within a single name. The Word who is beyond all separate words, all languages, weaving its way through spans of centuries and paths on earth, to differentiate and then unite again.

> I danced in the morning when the world was begun
> I danced in the moon and the stars and the sun
> I came down from heaven and I danced on the earth
> In Bethlehem I had my birth.
>
> Dance then, wherever you may be
> I AM the Lord of the Dance, said he.
> I'll lead you all wherever you may be
> And I'll lead you all in the dance, said he.

words by Sydney Carter, 1967

Appendix B

English translations of basic texts about Speech Formation

These are the basic texts available in English for the student of Speech Formation, and for anyone who wants to read what Rudolf Steiner and his wife Marie both said and wrote about this work. They also contain aspects of its history and development.

Steiner, Rudolf, 1981, *Poetry and the Art of Speech*: a translation of *Die Kunst der Rezitation und Declamation*, London School of Speech Formation at Rudolf Steiner House, London, in association with Rudolf Steiner Press. Shorthand reports, unrevised by Steiner, of a series of lectures he gave in 1920, it contains additional lectures given in various places between 1921 and 1923, together with an essay and explanatory notes by Marie Steiner. The translators have provided many English examples of the literary styles referred to in the German text.

Steiner, Rudolf and Marie, 1978, *Creative Speech: The Nature of Speech Formation* (originally published in the German as *Methodik und Wesen der Sprachgestaltung*), Rudolf Steiner Press, London. A collection of aphoristic notes from courses given on the cultivation of the art of Speech. It contains, as well, essays and notes from seminars and lectures given by Rudolf and Marie Steiner.

Steiner, Rudolf, 1969, *Speech and Drama*, Anthroposophical Publishing Co., London. Unrevised reports of a lecture series given by Rudolf Steiner just prior to his death in 1924.

Steiner, Rudolf, *Eurythmy as Visible Speech*. Anthroposophical Publishing Co., London. Although addressed to eurythmists, these lectures are an invaluable source of inspiration concerning the nature of speech and language.

Additional reading acknowledging Rudolf Steiner's work:

Pusch, Hans, 1998, *A New Kind of Actor*, Mercury Press, New York. Invaluable memoirs of one who trained with Marie Steiner in the early years in Dornach.

McAllen, Audrey E, 1989, *The Listening Ear: The development of speech as a creative influence in education*, Hawthorn Press, UK. The author presents the fruits of a lifetime of working with Rudolf Steiner's indications about Speech in the context of education. McAllen considers the relationship of the sounds to the planets and the zodiac, examining them also in the context of the physiological basis of our speaking and the physics of sound and hearing.

Burton, Michael Hedley, (planned 2014/15), *Working with the Word: The inspiration of the Logos, How it works as a redemptive and healing force in human culture. Working with the Word* is a book about what can be called 'the Word' or 'Logos' — a power that resides in the sounds we speak and which has become available to us in a new way since the first part of the twentieth century. The book looks at how this power that resides in language is today able to be used in the arts, therapy, education and personal development. Contact Michael at <www.wordrenewal.org>

Eichstaedt, Sibylle, (planned 2015/16), *Enlivening Speech – A Speech Practice Handbook*. Based on many years of working with Waldorf Teacher Trainees this book is a step-by-step introduction to Rudolf and Marie Steiner's approach to Speech and Speech training for anyone with a professional or personal interest in the spoken word. Sibylle Eichstaedt, creativespeech@mac.com

Bernhardt, Colin, 2001, *So to Speak: A Personal Approach to Voice*, Ekstasis Editions, Canada. Actor, director and acclaimed speech educator in Canada, Bernhardt draws inspiration from contemporary sources and includes his work with Steiner's insights within his more eclectic context.

Texts that provide a mainstream understanding of the aspects of speech and language referred to in *The Art of Speech*:

Ladefoged, Peter and Johnson, Keith, 2011, *A Course in Phonetics*, Wadsworth Cengage Learning.

Fromkin et al, 2009, *An Introduction to Language*, Cengage Learning.

Zemlin, Willard R., and Allyn & Bacon, 1998, *Speech and Hearing Science: Anatomy and Physiology*.

Appendix C – Trainings in English Speech Formation

Current trainings

The *Artemis School of The Living Word* was originally called the *London School of Speech Formation*. It is now directed by Christopher Garvey. It offers a variety of courses including full-time training leading to the Goetheanum Diploma in Speech Formation and the ACTL and LTCL offered by Trinity Guildhall. BAC accredited. Situated in Peredur Centre, West Hoathly Road, East Grinstead, West Sussex, RH19 4NF, UK. Contact: www.artemisspeechanddrama.com

The *North American Speech School* offers an itinerant training in Speech Formation for students who wish to take advantage of the different teachers who work in different parts of the United States. Students work with a primary teacher in a particular location but also have access to faculty members from other centres. Contact Craig Giddens: crrggddns@gmail.com

The Winged Word. Ongoing classes and workshops in the Byron Shire and in Sydney, NSW, encompassing all aspects of Speech Formation training. Contact Riana Vanderbyl: thewingedword@gmail.com

Sunstone Studio of Creative Speech offers training with a flexible structure based around the mastery of specific units. It was founded in Australia by Annika Andersdotter, previously a teacher in the Harkness Studio. Her training with Erna Grund, in Dornach, and with Mechthild Harkness has strongly influenced her focus on artistic speech for healing and educational purposes. Contact: annika@sunstone.com.au

Spirit of the Word School – a 3–4 year professional training course for actors and performers, beginning January 2014 and situated on the Kapiti coast, north of Wellington, New Zealand: taught in two blocks and two long weekends per year with ongoing private tuition. Teachers: Astrid Anderson. Penelope Snowden-Lait and Norbert Mulholland. Email: spiritofthewordschool@gmail.com

Former trainings

Chrysalis Theatre Acting School, London, founded by Peter and Barbara Bridgmont in 1975. For many years this provided an anthroposophically based training in acting and Speech. A documentary film, *Liberation of Acting, The Chrysalis Theatre Acting School*, directed by Alvaro Ramos won The Best Documentary Award (2009) at the High Desert International Film Festival in the US.[45]

The Harkness Studio, established 1973, Sydney, Australia, offered a four-year training in Speech and acting. www.mechthildharkness.net

The School of the Living Word, Victoria, Australia; directed by the author, Dawn Langman, between 1998 and 2006 offered a four year training in the art of Speech Formation integrated with the acting techniques of Michael Chekhov.

Taurus Voice — School of Science and Art, offered courses, workshops and training. Lansdown GL5 1BB Stroud, Gloucestershire, UK.

Colleagues working with Chekhov's Acting Techniques in the context of Anthroposophy and the Art of Speech Formation in English, within established training contexts
Since 2012, Dawn Langman has been teaching Speech Formation with her integrated Chekhov/Speech methodology to first, second and third year acting students at the Drama centre, Flinders University, South Australia.

At the time of publication, I am aware of the following colleagues also working at the training level, whose work is also centrally inspired by both streams, Chekhov's acting techniques and Steiner's Speech Formation:

Joerg Andrees: *Gaity School of Acting*, Dublin (GSA). *Michael Chekhov Technique Advanced Training Programme* — Chekhov/Speech Formation stream www.gaietyschool.com Contact: Joerg Andrees: Coordinator@gaietyschool.com or joerg.andrees@t-online.de

Dr Diane Caracciolo: Associate Professor of Curriculum Instruction, Adelphi University, Garden City, NY. Dr Caracciolo holds a Goetheanum Diploma in Speech Formation from the London School of Speech Formation (currently *Artemis School of the Living Word*) and a doctorate in Art and Art Education from Teachers College, Columbia. She currently co-ordinates a series of interdisciplinary arts education courses and several graduate programmes in Educational Theatre. Her course, *Creative Speech and Storytelling,* is the result of her continuing exploration of the Chekhov method and creative Speech Formation as lively means to animate the imaginative lives and expressive capacities of teachers. Dr Caracciolo also serves on the faculty of the *Winkler Centre for Adult Education* where she teaches Speech Formation informed by Chekhov methodology to Foundation Year students. Contact Diane: caraccio@adelphi.edu

Dr Jane Gilmer: Assistant Professor, Department of Visual and Performing Arts/Drama at the National Institute of Education, Singapore. See her recent article, *Michael Chekhov's Imagination of the Creative Word and the Question of its Integration into his Future Theatre* published in the journal, *Theatre, Dance and Performance Training*, Vol 4, Issue 2, 2013. Contact Jane: jane.gilmer@gmail.com or jane.gilmer@nie.edu.sg

Sarah Kane: teaches speech and acting at various centres in UK and Europe, including the Michael Chekhov Studio UK and Berlin. Contact Sarah: www.michaelchekhov.org.uk or sarah@michaelchekhov.org.uk

John McManus: teaches voice, speech, acting and Shakespeare at the Conservatory of the Performing Arts at Point Park University of Pittsburg. Contact John: shakespearealive@gmail.com or jmcmanus@pointpark.edu

Joanna Panagiotopoulos: teaches Chekhov and Speech Formation within the Steiner teacher-training at Sydney Rudolf Steiner College, Sydney, Australia and runs workshops and courses at The Harmony Centre, Mittagong, NSW. The Harmony Centre is a community space integrating artistic, therapeutic and spiritual research and practice. Contact Joanna: ioanna@harmonyfoundation.com.au or theartofspeech@harmonyfoundation.com.au

PerformInternational is a new, spirit-inspired training and research initiative in theatre and the performing arts in the UK that is launching a full-time professional training as well as part-time trainings and short courses from the autumn of 2014. *PerformInternational*'s trainings and courses have been set up by Sarah Kane, Gregers Brinch and Geoffrey Norris. The four-year, full-time professional training starting in September 2014 has two main aims:

- To renew for the twenty-first century and integrate the work begun by Rudolf and Marie Steiner in the field of artistic speech and drama with what was further developed by Russian theatre practitioner Michael Chekhov in theatre and acting.
- To create a rigorous training in theatre and the performing arts that enables graduates to both begin an independent professional artistic life in performance and teaching and qualifies them to take up further training in education and therapy at postgraduate level.

For further information please contact initiativeperformingarts@gmail.com, www.performinternatinal.org and www.facebook.com/performinterational

In languages other than English

Michael Chekhov Studio, Berlin, (MTSB) www.mtsb.de. Offers one- and three-year full-time trainings in Chekhov's methodology from an anthroposophical perspective and including Speech Formation. A number of teachers work there with Speech Formation, including Sarah Kane. Contact Jobst Langhans: jobst.langhans@mtsb.de and Joerg Andrees: Chekhov.training@gmail.com

Appendix D

Therapeutic applications of Speech Formation

Speech Formation emerges out of an holistic understanding of the human being. There is a sense, therefore, in which all this book has spoken of can be regarded as therapeutic work for those engaged in it. There are practitioners, however, whose life task has been to explore specifically the therapeutic application of Speech Formation in a more clinical context.

An excellent introduction to the scope of therapeutic Speech Formation can be found in *Anthroposophical Therapeutic Speech* by Barbara Denjean-von Stryk and Dietrich von Bonin, translated by Marianne Krampe and first published in English by Floris Books in 2003.

Information about the therapeutic work of Speech Formation in the English language can be obtained from:

Sibylle Eichstaedt
creativespeech@mac.com
37 Farriers Croft, Bussage, Stroud Glos GL6 8JW, UK.

Donald Phillips
speech@camphillmedical.org.uk
Camphill Medical
Murtle House, Bieldside, Aberdeen, AB15 9EP Scotland

Dietrich von Bonin.
Institute for Complementary Medicine KIKOM,
University of Berne,
Imhoof-Pavilion, Inselspital, CH-3010 Bern.
dbonin@svakt.ch

Appendix E

Steiner's Speech-exercises rendered by Mechthild Harkness
Although Mechthild had her own very definite sequence for these exercises, they appear here in the order explored in *The Art of Speech*:

Speech-exploration 5

Hush finish rush
These shots so sharp
Rouse spruce fighters

Speech-exploration 6

radiant rollick
rooted rumours
reason wrestle
rueing rollers
royalty russet

Speech-exploration 7

lovely lady leaping
lipping light laughter
lumbering laggardly loiterer lurch

Speech-exploration 8

prosperous prime
building bowers

princely peacock
budding blossoms

proudful prancing
beauty basket

Speech-exploration 10

droop dim dingles
dim by dense margins sparkled
dark too dark

Speech-exploration 13

the father partners armchair
rather martially crafty card
the basket nasty asks mail
starting martially hearten Carl

Speech-exploration 14

lengthening weightiness straightens wavering daintiness
wavering daintiness straightens lengthening weightiness
thrilling finish hits inch if
it irritates laymen's vainness
it irritates layman's vainness
if thrilling finish hits inch

rude storms blew forth
through rolling rooms
bold wolves bored
through rolling rooms
who drove wolves bold
through rolling rooms

eye is whiteness
whiteness is eye
fly no noise destroy
noise destroy and fly
the bride is broidered
broidered bridal

Mixed:

Brightly wisely wielding over this land

These leafless trees awaken in the spring.

Speech-exploration 28

Reforging gales
through foghorns
hails through surges
through whirlpools
whirlpool wails
in wavering
wails in quavering
waves gaping
gaping wheezing
in freezing
freezing breathing
cleaving

Speech-exploration 30

In the vast immeasurable spaces
in unending tides of time
in the depth of human soul-life
in the world's great revelation
seek the unfolding of life's great mystery.

Mechthild also used this alternative version by Christy Barnes-Mackaye:

In the wide wave's lonely reaches
in the wind's high starlit wastes
in the earth's still slumbering darkness
in the fire's unfurling fury
search and find man's world-born being

Speech-exploration 33

Hitching statistical starily
stitch strengthen stipulate
stretch nostril niche and coils
stringent tartness stirrup false

Is stridingly stern
master mustiness stiffenings
still stayed earnest statesman
stern stresses stammering
still strong staying
for stiffness stepping statesman
in standing stolidity

Speech-exploration 36

judicious genial jar
giant gentian jacket
joyous jumble gender

Speech-exploration 37

catching patchy acts clattering
lately light sceptical
catching scratching patchy acts clattering
lately plotting light sceptical

Speech-exploration 38

these sagacious crazes
sickle suitor smiting
dark shafts ending sharply
sheepish sheltering
smuggler snarling

Speech-exploration 39

moisten menace mine essence
lambent lightly lying loiter
by breathing boded blind bard
come crooked craftiest cur

Speech-exploration 40

near wren
never wreathing
grizzly grinning
notion nipping
slander nuisance

Speech-exploration 41

by my biffin
sea fee sheeting
noon air lag linger ink.

ink ringer growl
lint
far from boom.

ink ringer grows sharp
full lint needeth
prime vie.

Speech-exploration 42

Ah, but she will need these alms engaged
then.
O ship to shore wee folk
me mid myth
new to moose

hearty starkly	/aː/ – –
swing a flint	/iː/ – –
by fracturing	/aː/ – –
lustre shown	/aː/ – –
light	/iː/ – –
through sea wind	/uː/ – –

Speech-exploration 43

nimbly knitted nonsense
in nimbus mutely musing

Speech-exploration 45

clip plop plick glick
clinked clapper quickly
knocking the trappings
rapidly tripled

Speech-exploration 46

Dart saves dear loan through darkening
loading

Speech-exploration 47

march smarten ten clodhopper rockets
crackle cackle linking
fling from forward forth

Speech-exploration 48

slinging sliding a-sleeping
a-tinkling finding vacant vex
a-tinkling finding vacant a-sleeping
slinging sliding vex

Speech-exploration 66

The man – convinced that he was right – left
the town
Speak the speech – I pray you, as I
pronounced it to you – trippingly on the
tongue.

Hamlet, Shakespeare

Mechthild's renderings of exercises not dealt
with in *The Art of Speech*, are acknowledged in
The Integrated Actor.

Steiner's Speech-exercises rendered by Sophia Walsh have been published in her booklet:
Formative Speech and Stage Art. This is currently out of print. Enquiries can be made directly to:
Sophia Walsh,
Grenzweg 4, CH-4143,
Dornach, Switzerland.

Original artworks that serve as a basis for Raphaela Mazzone's illustrations

Nike of Samothrace: based on the sculpture called 'Winged Victory' or the 'Nike of Samothrace', the original of which is in the Louvre Museum, Paris.

The discus thrower: based on Myron's sculpture of the Discus Thrower. The original sculpture is in the British Museum.

The spear thrower: based on the sculpture thought to represent Zeus or Poseidon. The original sculpture is in the National Archaeological Museum of Athens.

Heart-centre based on the sculpture of Apollo: the original sculpture is in the National Archaeological Museum of Athens.

Will-centre based on a warrior 1: based on the depiction of a Trojan warrior from a Grecian frieze.

Will-centre based on a warrior 2: based on the depiction of a Trojan warrior from a Grecian frieze.

Head-centre based on the charioteer: based on the sculpture of the Charioteer. The original sculpture is in the Delphi Archaeological Museum.

The charioteer: based on the sculpture of the Charioteer. The original sculpture is in the Delphi Archaeological Museum.

The human form divine: based on the sketch by Leonardo da Vinci depicting the 'Human Being Standing in a Circle'.

The soul of the dead pharaoh meets the resurrected Osiris: based on an ancient Egyptian bas-relief currently housed in the Neues Museum, Berlin.

Martin Luther's bible cover: based on the original cover of Martin Luther's bible, circa 1500s. The original is in Lutherhaus, Wittenberg.

Other artworks

Van Gogh, *detail from Starry Night*
Rodin, *The Thinker*
Grünewald, *Concert of angels* from the *Isenheim Altarpiece*, Colmar Museum, France.

Notes

Introduction

1. Adapted by Dawn Langman from various translations.
2. Hayman, Ronald, (1977 originally published 1947) *Artaud and After, 'Van Gogh le suicidé de la société'*, Oxford University Press, 1977.
3. Steiner, Rudolf (1960, 2007 – lectures given 1924) *Speech and Drama*, lecture 3 translated by Mary Adams, Steinerbooks, USA.
4. Antonin Artaud (2010, originally published 1938), *The Theatre and its Double: The Theatre of Cruelty, the First Manifesto*, translated by Victor Corti, Alma Classics, UK.
5. Artaud, Antonin, (1977), *An Affective Athleticism* in *The Theatre and its Double* by Antonin Artaud, an essay translated by Victor Corti, John Calder (Publishers) Ltd, London.
6. Horner, Musgrave (1970) *Movement, Voice and Speech*, Methuen & Co. Ltd, UK.
7. Information regarding Sophia Walsh's *Formative Speech and Stage Art*, and versions of the relevant exercises made by Mechthild can be found in Appendix E; others will appear in *The Integrated Actor*.
8. *The Foundation Stone Meditation*; translation by John Davy, commentary by Willem Zeylmans van Emmichoven, published by Anthroposopical Press, UK. Steiner gave this meditation after the burning of the first Goetheanum and at the laying of the foundation for the second. If worked with in its totality, he intended it to be a Foundation Stone laid in the hearts of human beings – which could not be destroyed. There have been many attempts to render it in English and explore its significance, including *The Foundation Stone Meditation, a new commentary*, by Adrian Anderson, Threshold Publishing, Australia, 2002.

Chapter 1

9. Steiner, Rudolf, (1924), *Speech and Drama*, from the preface by Marie Steiner translated by Mary Adams, Steinerbooks, USA.
10. Martin Buber (1878–1965), Austrian born Jewish philosopher and professor at Hebrew University in Jerusalem, is most well-known for his book *Ich und Du*, published in 1923. He develops the idea of dialogue as a level of encounter that takes place when two beings recognize each other at the level of their beingness. In English, this has been most commonly translated as an I–Thou relationship as opposed to *Ich–Es* or I–It, in which each experiences the other as an object. Any meeting can be raised to the level of an I–Thou encounter or remain at the level of I–It; human to human, human to nature, human to the divine.
11. An alternative to Before Christ (BC), is the abbreviation Before the Common/Current/ Christian Era, (BCE) . Common/Current/Christian Era (CE) is an alternative naming of the traditional calendar era, Anno Domini (AD).
12. See Rudolf Steiner's *Occult Science*.

13. See Musgrave's book: Horner, Musgrave (1970) *Movement, Voice and Speech*, Methuen, UK.

14. Genesis, chapter 11.

15. There is much to learn from what Stanislavski called the 'personal emotional memory'. What Chekhov evolved out of Stanislavski's work invites us to expand our ideas of what constitutes 'experience'. *The Art of Speech* invites us to expand yet further.

16. Steiner, Rudolf, (lectures given 1924), *Eurythmy as Visible Speech*, Anthroposophical Publishing Company, 1957.

17. I have chosen to express this thought in words and phrases taken from *A Midsummer Night's Dream*. Shakespeare shows us the world of 'cool reason' championed by Theseus who represents the new, intellectual consciousness evolving at that time. He contrasts this with the vanishing perception of the world of 'being' revealed in Bottom's sojourn in Titania's fairy world. The view which 'cool reason' takes of such experience is expressed most fully in the words of Theseus at the beginning of Act 5:

> The lunatic, the lover and the poet
> Are of imagination all compact...

Since the Renaissance until quite recently, cool reason triumphed in our culture. Original participatory experience, accessible through primitive clairvoyant powers, was dismissed and labelled as 'mere animism'. During the last 100 years we have seen such dismissals transcended in many quarters as human beings recover supersensible perception.

18. Coleridge, Samuel Taylor, (1817 republished 1907), *Biographia Literaria*, The Clarendon Press, Oxford, UK.

Chapter 2

19. Steiner, Rudolf, (1924), *Speech and Drama*, from the preface by Marie Steiner translated by Mary Adams, Steinerbooks, USA.

20. The root of the English *word* lies in the Germanic *wort* and the root of *vortex* lies in the Latin. The connection I make here is my own.

21. Grotowski, Jerzy, (1968), *Towards A Poor Theatre*, from the article 'He wasn't entirely himself', Odin Teatrets Forlag, Denmark.

22. Steiner, Rudolf, (1993 first published 1894) *The Philosophy of Spiritual Activity*, Rudolf Steiner Press, London.

Chapter 4

23. Husemann, Friedrich and Wolff, Otto, (1989 first published 1920), *The Anthroposophical Approach to Medicine Volume 3*, Steiner Books Inc.

24. This, according to the perspective given by Steiner, is one task of the I AM. The possibility of the I AM to work within each human soul did not become available until it was first fully

realized through its incarnation in the human being, Jesus of Nazareth. Until that time and those events referred to by Steiner as the Deed of Golgotha, the governing of what unfolds within the human soul was the responsibility of those who led each culture. It was their task to guide the human beings in their care according to the temple wisdom received from the spiritual helpers of humanity.

25. Vasari, Giorgio, (1965), *Lives of the Artists*, translated by George Bull, Penguin Classics, UK.

26. From *Pippa Passes* by Browning.

27. This version of the Old English is by J. Duncan Spaeth, who has tried not only to convey content but also some sense of the alliterative nature of the lines. See *Old English Poetry*, Princeton University Press (1922).

Chapter 5

28. Goethe, Johann Wolfgang von (1749–1832), (1957), 'The Metamorphosis of Plants', *The Penguin Book of German Verse*, Penguin Books.

29. Schwenk, Theodor, (1996 first published 1962), *Sensitive Chaos*, Rudolf Steiner Press, London. Contains a comprehensive investigation of the world of etheric forces. In particular his chapter, 'The Creative Word Of the Universe' develops the ideas I have expressed in a more scientific way.

30. The information to be found in textbooks which describe the physics of sound waves is not in question here. The connection of measurable frequencies to pitch and amplitudes to volume cannot be disputed. Experiments undertaken in the eighteenth century by Ernst Chladni also demonstrated the power of sounds at different frequencies to order matter and create different forms.

But there is, still, an unbridgeable gap between the knowledge gained in this way and the artistic process of the actor/speaker. The relationship between phenomena identified as sound waves in the field of physics to the formative powers of speech implied in *Sprachgestaltung* might be compared to that which footprints have to the one who treads.

31. On numerous occasions, Steiner speaks about the future evolution of the human larynx and the creative power of speech. The thickening of vocal chords which marks the sexual maturation of the male of our species and which leads to the 'breaking of the voice' at puberty indicates this intimate connection. It is outside the scope of this book to consider these thoughts further. The following lectures are suggested:

Jeshu ben Pandira. Two lectures given 4 and 5 November 1911 in Leipzig. Lecture 1 explores successive stages in the evolution of our human speech.

The World of the Senses and the World of the Spirit. This series of 6 lectures was given by Steiner, in Hanover, between 27 December 1911 and 1 January 1912. In Lecture 6, he offers insights into the creative power of the future larynx.

32. Prospero's final speech from *The Tempest*, William Shakespeare.

Chapter 6

33. Steiner, Rudolf, *Calendar of the Soul* translated by William and Liselotte Mann, Hawthorn Press, UK. 1990. (first published in German 1912)

Chapter 7

34. Steiner Rudolf, (2002, lectures given in 1924), *Karmic Relationships*, volume 3, lecture 6, Rudolf Steiner Press, New York.
35. Keller, Helen, (1990 first published 1902), *The Story of My Life*, Bantam Classics.
36. Matthews, Paul, (1994), *Sing Me The Creation*, Hawthorn Press, UK. This book explores, in an inspiring way, the art of grammar as a basis for the creative act of language.
37. There is now extensive research which points to the flexibility or plasticity of brain structure and functioning. At this frontier, science moves away from the assumption that our consciousness is determined by a brain which is a fixed entity, that once having been 'hard wired', is incapable of change. Instead, it is possible, now, to consider that consciousness determines brain structure and functioning and that these are, indeed, capable of evolution. The increasing evidence of neuro-plasticity in the brain is recorded in such books as *The Brain that Changes Itself* by Norman Doidge, (published by Scribe, 2008).

    Variation in individuals, in relation to right and left brain functioning, has been noted for many years, as in the phenomenon of right and left-handedness. Nevertheless, there has been an overall tendency, in individuals tested for cognitive and language skills, for these to manifest in activity in the left hemisphere. Likewise, for feeling and intuitive functioning to manifest in activity in the right hemisphere.

    It is interesting to consider this question. Does this splitting of the two types of functioning, demonstrable in measurable activity in the different hemispheres of the brain, express the particular condition of consciousness which has characterized Western humanity in the last centuries? According to Steiner's research, this condition has required the split between the functions of our soul, our thinking, feeling and willing. He called this condition; the *consciousness soul*. Further consideration will be given to it in *The Integrated Actor*.

    If there is validity in current findings of the research into neurological function, and in Steiner's insights and observations, then we may well consider that human consciousness is indeed evolving. Our conscious efforts, even now, can be shown to change the neurological structures in our brains. There is evidence that the exclusivity of right and left brain functioning is not so fixed as had been thought. Does this point towards a future integration of this threefold functioning within our souls? An integration already indicated in such current terms as 'emotional intelligence'? How do or will such changes be affected by and, in turn, affect, the ways in which we use our language?
38. *East Coker* from the *Four Quartets* by T.S. Eliot.
39. *Gospel of John* 14:15.

Chapter 8

40. Bragg, Melvyn, (2003), *The Adventure of English*. DVD series produced by Granada Television for *Time Life* which takes us from the earliest beginnings of the language through to our present time, and Barfield, Owen, (1954 first published 1926), *A History in English Words*, Faber & Faber Ltd.

41. Other examples arising from the Anglo-Saxon sources in our language can be found in the earlier chapter on Rhythm and in the section 'Epic style' in chapter 6. There, I discuss them in relation to alliteration which characterized the languages of Northern and Germanic tribes and what became Old English. It is not difficult to imagine the part played by the elements and human will in language spoken by those who battled for survival in the harsh conditions of the Northern climate.

42. These derivations are listed in most comprehensive dictionaries, including the one compiled by Dr Johnson in the eighteenth century.

A bridge to *The Integrated Actor*

43. The last sentence of lecture 3 of Steiner's *Speech and Drama* lectures.

44. Chekhov, Michael, (1991), *On the Technique of Acting*, from the section called Eurythmy from The Psychological Gesture, chapter 5, Harper Perennial.

Appendix C

45. Bridgmont, Peter, (1983), *The Spear Thrower*, An Grianan Press, Ireland, and (1992) *Liberation of the Actor*, Temple Lodge, London. These excellent books explore the approach to the relationship of Speech Formation and the actor based on ideas of Rudolf Steiner and developed at the Chrysalis Theatre and Acting School. (See Appendix C).